Describing Inner Experience?

Life and Mind: Philosophical Issues in Biology and Psychology

Kim Sterelny and Robert A. Wilson, editors

Describing Inner Experience?
Proponent Meets Skeptic

Russell T. Hurlburt
Eric Schwitzgebel

A Bradford Book
The MIT Press
Cambridge, Massachusetts
London, England

For information on quantity discounts, email special_sales@mitpress.mit.edu.

Set in Syntax and Times Roman by SNP Best-set Typesetter Ltd., Hong Kong.
Printed and bound in the United States of America.

Library of Congress Cataloging-in-Publication Data

Hurlburt, Russell T.
Describing inner experience? : proponent meets skeptic / Russell T. Hurlburt, Eric Schwitzgebel.
    p. cm.—(Life and mind)
"A Bradford book."
Includes bibliographical references.
ISBN 978-0-262-08366-9 (hardcover : alk. paper)
1. Consciousness. 2. Introspection. I. Schwitzgebel, Eric. II. Title.
BF311.H87   2007
153—dc22
                                                                    2007002122

10 9 8 7 6 5 4 3 2 1

Contents

Preface

Can inner experience ("phenomenal consciousness," in contemporary philosophical lingo) be accurately apprehended and faithfully described? The question is crucially important, both for a humanistic understanding of who we are and what we know about ourselves and for the newly burgeoning scientific field of "consciousness studies." One of us, Russ, is an optimist, believing that adequate methods make faithful descriptions of experience possible. The other, Eric, is a pessimist, believing that people are prone to considerable introspective error even under the best of conditions. In 2002, at a conference in Tucson, we presented opposing papers on the matter and instantly became friends, arguing over dinner, then over margaritas, then again the next day, then in the airport waiting for our respective flights home.

This book is the product of our best attempt to make concrete progress in our dispute. We felt a need to do something more than simply continue with the usual methods of abstract argument, historical reference, and citation of favorite experiments. Thus, we recruited someone not party to the dispute (we'll call her Melanie), asked her to describe her experience in a way Russ found suitable—by random sampling and interview—and debated the extent to which the resulting descriptions could be believed. The bulk of this book is a lightly edited transcript of these interviews, in which Melanie makes her best effort to describe individual moments of her experience in careful detail, and Russ and Eric question her, argue with each other, and further pursue their disagreements (and connect with the relevant psychological and philosophical literature) in side boxes. Although Melanie's experiences are in certain respects quite ordinary, we think the reader will find at least some of her descriptions surprising and suggestive. The book begins and concludes with chapters expressing our different points of view and our different takes on what we accomplished and failed to accomplish.

Russ thanks Chris Heavey and the psychology graduate students at the University of Nevada, Las Vegas who have been involved with inner experience research. They read earlier drafts of this manuscript and provided illuminating comments and discussion. Special thanks to Sharon Jones-Forrester (who transcribed the interviews), Todd Seibert and Aadee Mizrachi (who checked the transcripts for accuracy), and Sarah Akhter (who consulted on many phases of the project).

Eric thanks the University of California, Riverside graduate students, from both philosophy and psychology, who read early drafts of the transcripts in a spring 2004 seminar; the many colleagues and students—far too many to track—with whom he has had illuminating conversations on the topics of this book; and especially his wife Pauline and son Davy. Pauline gave detailed comments on the entire manuscript, and neither sees why a tenured professor should need to go in to work every weekday from 8 to 5:30 all summer when he could be on the beach or throwing paper airplanes from their treehouse. Eric is not sure he fully understands his behavior either; but then, of course, he is a pessimist about introspection and self-knowledge.

Russ and Eric both express substantial gratitude to Melanie for her willingness to expose both her private experiences and her ability to access them to our pointed, and now public, examinations. She received nothing in return other than the opportunity to help out two people struggling to figure out important things and whatever personal insight might occur along the way. We hope the reader will respect Melanie's privacy; we trust that any reader who by chance discovers her real name will decline to make it public.

Describing Inner Experience?

Proponent Meets Skeptic

1 Introduction

On a remarkably thin base of evidence—largely the spectral analysis of points of light—astronomers possess, or appear to possess, an abundance of knowledge about the structure and history of the universe. We likewise know more than might even have been imagined a few centuries ago about the nature of physical matter, about the mechanisms of life, about the ancient past. Enormous theoretical and methodological ingenuity has been required to obtain such knowledge; it does not invite easy discovery by the untutored.

It may seem odd, then, that we have so little scientific knowledge of what lies closest at hand, apparently ripe for easy discovery, and of greatest importance for our quality of life: our own conscious experience—our sensory experiences and pains, for example, our inner speech and imagery, our felt emotion. Scientists know quite a bit about human visual capacities and the brain processes involved in vision, much less about the subjective experience of seeing; a fair bit about the physiology of emotion, almost nothing about its phenomenology.

Philosophers began in earnest in the seventeenth and eighteenth centuries to describe and classify our patterns of conscious experience. John Locke (1690/1975), for instance, divided experienced "ideas" into those that arise from sensation and those that arise from reflection, and he began to classify them into types. David Hume (1739/1978) distinguished what we would now call images from perceptual experiences in terms of their "force" or "liveliness." James Mill (1829/1967) attempted a definitive classification of sensations into the traditional five senses (sight, hearing, touch, taste, and smell) plus muscular sensations and sensations in the alimentary canal. However, despite such efforts, not even the most basic taxonomy of experience was agreed upon, and it is still not agreed upon.

The study of conscious experience acquired a more scientific look with the introspective psychologists of the late nineteenth and early twentieth centuries. Researchers such as Gustav Fechner (1860/1966), Wilhelm Wundt (e.g., 1896/1897), and E. B. Titchener (1910/1915) presented carefully measured stimuli to subjects who had been trained to "introspect"—to take careful note of their immediately occurring (or just passed) experiences. These psychologists aimed to understand how these introspected experiences covaried with changes in stimulation. However, as is well known, after a few decades, behaviorism (which stressed measuring relationships between stimulus and behavioral response rather than stimulus and introspected experience) won the day in mainstream experimental psychology, driving out or marginalizing the study of consciousness. Subsequent elaborations of behaviorism, and later "cognitivism," allowed more room for the postulation of internal states and mechanisms mediating behavioral responses, yet these internal states and mechanisms were generally assumed to be nonconscious.

Central to the behaviorists' complaint about the introspective study of consciousness was the unreliability of the introspective method. Several decades' work had yielded little consensus on even the most fundamental issues. John B. Watson, the early standard-bearer for behaviorism, criticized the lack of consensus in introspective psychology:

One psychologist will state with readiness that the attributions of a visual sensation are *quality, extension, duration*, and *intensity*. Another will add *clearness*. Still another that of *order*. I doubt if any one psychologist can draw up a set of statements describing what he means by sensation which will be agreed to by three other psychologists of different training. . . . I firmly believe that two hundred years from now, unless the introspective method is discarded, psychology will still be divided on the question of whether auditory sensations have the quality of 'extension', whether intensity is an attribute that can be applied to color, whether there is a difference in 'texture' between image and sensation and upon many hundreds of others of like character. . . . The condition in regard to other mental processes is just as chaotic. (1913, pp. 164–165)

The considerable truth in this complaint partially explains the success of the behaviorists' overthrow of introspective methodology. The fact that introspective psychologists had failed to reach consensus about such issues revealed a serious weakness in their methodologies. Furthermore, much of the consensus they did manage to reach was undermined by an early-twentieth-century shift, among those still interested in consciousness, away from the early introspectionists' focus on the basic "elements" of experience and toward a more holistic conception of a sensory "Gestalt" that could not be divided into individual elements. Thus, despite the obvious importance of conscious experience to our lives, and its apparent ready availability for research, conscious experience had largely resisted systematic attempts at scientific description, and its study fell into disrepute.

Although research on consciousness has enjoyed a considerable resurgence since the 1990s, the most basic structural and methodological questions remain unanswered. With little examination, introspection has re-entered psychology and philosophy. Even hard-nosed cognitive neuroscientists ask their subjects about their subjectively felt experience while in the fMRI magnet. However, it should be clear from the history just described that such casual and haphazard introspection cannot be trusted to yield robustly replicable results and accurate generalizations. Furthermore, it seems to us that the introspective methods employed by most current researchers in consciousness studies are less careful than the methods used by introspective psychologists a century ago. Unless better methods can be found, we fear, the scientific study of consciousness may again stall. And if there simply are no better methods, the scientific study of consciousness may prove wholly impossible in principle: vacuous without introspective report, intractably conflictual with it. Scientists could perhaps elude this difficulty if they could find a way to study consciousness without the help of introspective report. We doubt that such an enterprise makes sense, but we will not argue the point here. We will assume that any science of consciousness must take, as a fundamental source of data, people's observations and descriptions of their own experience. Thus, a re-examination of the adequacy of introspective reports is of central importance to consciousness studies.

That leads us to the question that stands at the heart of this book: To what extent is it possible accurately to report conscious experience? Russ Hurlburt has argued that we can profit from the demise of classical introspection and create methods for reporting conscious experience that largely avoid the old pitfalls. He has developed one such method, Descriptive Experience Sampling (DES), that, he has claimed (Hurlburt 1990, 1993; Hurlburt and Heavey 2006), provides largely accurate descriptions of experience. Eric Schwitzgebel, without addressing DES in particular, has argued that introspective reports in general are greatly prone to error, even in what would seem the most favorable of cases (Schwitzgebel and Gordon 2000; Schwitzgebel 2002a,b, 2004, 2006, in preparation).

In this book, Russ and Eric confront each other directly and concretely on the adequacy and accuracy of introspective reports, using the particular reports of an actual subject as the starting point. Throughout the book, we use the term "introspection" to refer only to the observation of particular instants of experience as they occur, or immediately thereafter. Sometimes, but not in this book, introspection refers to chewing over, musing, reflecting—to a certain type of self-oriented, retrospective or prospective contemplation. Our usage is quite specific: we wish to discuss whether, or to what extent, it is possible for people to report what is ongoing in their experience as it is happening.

1.1 The Origins of This Book

In April 2002, at an interdisciplinary conference in Tucson called Toward a Science of Consciousness, Russ presented a paper titled "Describing inner experience: Not impossible but also not trivially easy." This paper, co-authored with Chris Heavey, criticized earlier attempts at introspection but argued that if one employed a proper method it was possible to describe the features of inner experience (thoughts, images, feelings) with considerable accuracy. Russ had been working for decades to develop just such a method.

At the same meeting, Eric presented a paper titled "Some reasons to distrust people's judgments about their own conscious experiences." In this paper, Eric argued that the introspection of emotion, sensory experience, imagery, and thought—which together constitute much if not all of our experiential life—is unreliable, and that even in favorable circumstances of extended reflection on these aspects of our mental lives as they transpire, we often make gross mistakes regarding their basic features. Thus, he advocated a skeptical position that seemed to be considerably at odds with Russ's cautious optimism. Eric was in the midst of publishing a series of papers defending this view. (See the citations above.)

We had not met before the 2002 Tucson convention, but the papers and our conversations showed that we shared a substantial intellectual history, despite Russ's training in psychology and Eric's in philosophy. We had both independently encountered the introspective literature on conscious experience and concluded that there was good reason for skepticism. We had both examined the methodology of the early introspectionist school and had written criticisms of those practices (Hurlburt 1990; Schwitzgebel 2002a). We had both written criticisms of the armchair introspections that underlie philosophical and psychological thought about consciousness (Hurlburt 1990; Schwitzgebel and Gordon 2000; Schwitzgebel 2002a,b, 2003a,b).

Despite these similarities, by 2002 we had reached opposing positions. Russ had responded to the methodological inadequacies of introspection by creating, in the late 1970s, a method of exploring inner, conscious experience that sought to avoid the pitfalls that had doomed earlier introspective attempts. This method came to be known as Descriptive Experience Sampling (DES), and the project had culminated in two books (Hurlburt 1990, 1993). Russ argued in those two books, as well as in the paper he presented at the Toward a Science of Consciousness meeting, that his method solved enough of the methodological problems that DES could be taken as providing largely correct descriptions of inner experience (and perhaps other methods could as well). Russ will describe DES more completely in chapter 2, but for now it is enough to know that DES uses a beeper to signal the subject to pay attention to the "inner experience" that was ongoing at the moment of the beep. Subsequently, the subject and the investigator meet to discuss the details of such beeped moments.

Eric was not won over. Over the centuries, many people had made enthusiastic claims about the accuracy of their introspections, and most if not all of them had not proven credible. Why should Eric regard Russ's claim about DES any differently? He agreed that the DES beeper did seem likely to overcome some of the difficulties of introspective report, but it appeared to aggravate other difficulties, and he thought it likely that, all things considered, substantial doubt would still be warranted. Yet he had never examined the DES methodology closely.

We both recognized that it was crucial to determine whether it was possible to provide trustworthy accounts of conscious experience. Both in psychology and in philosophy, pressure to explore inner experience, consciousness, and the phenomenology of thought and emotion was increasing. If Russ was right, then we should redouble our efforts to explain to psychologists and philosophers how it is possible accurately to observe conscious experience. If Eric was right, even the most apparently credible reports of inner experience should not be accepted at face value without substantial independent support from non-introspective data.

We agreed that Eric would serve as a DES subject for a few days, right there at the Toward a Science of Consciousness conference. This would give Eric the opportunity to explore Russ's approach from the inside, to gain a more direct and intimate knowledge of it. Furthermore, it would provide a series of concrete occasions on which to discuss introspective methodology. We would thus move from the realm of general statements to the realm of concrete particulars. Eric's being a subject would turn Russ's method inside out, would let the fox explore the chicken coop from the inside. It would also test Eric's commitment to skepticism when his own experiential report was the one on the table.

We recognized that Eric was by no means a typical subject. He was open to participating in DES, but he had already thought extensively about the difficulties of introspection, and he was on the public record as a harsh critic of it. Thus, whereas most of Russ's subjects are simply trying to report the features of their experiences, Eric was trying both to report and to examine the limits of that reporting.

These interviews initiated a conversation that was continued by email over the next 6 months. We wrote each other at length, discussing the history of introspection, examining Eric's experience as a subject, and considering and reconsidering both of our skepticisms and Russ's explanations of how DES attempts to limit the risks inherent in earlier methods. That correspondence could be simplified as follows: We agreed that the history of introspection showed that most introspective reports were not to be trusted. But we disagreed about the extent to which the failure of earlier methods reflected *general, ineliminable* difficulties in introspection. Russ was optimistic. He argued that an interviewer like him, carefully avoiding bias and focusing the interview on individual moments of experience, could often generate largely accurate reports. Eric remained relatively pessimistic, even when he was the subject.

1.2   Sampling with Melanie

To continue the conversation usefully, we felt that Eric needed more experience with interview techniques in which his roles as skeptic and investigator wouldn't be complicated by his simultaneously serving as the subject. So Russ proposed a new endeavor. We would jointly take the role of investigator and interview a naive subject, someone who had not previously been interviewed by Russ. In these interviews, Eric would be free to cross-examine the subject in whatever way he found useful, probing the subject's opinions about her sampled experiences without being confined to DES interviewing principles. For the role of subject, Russ found Melanie, a friend of a friend. Melanie had just graduated from college with a joint degree in philosophy and psychology and was new in town, looking for a connection to the local psychology scene. Before coming to town, she had had no prior direct contact with either Russ or Eric or their views.

Until then, our conversations had been either about introspection in general ("Should we trust introspective reports?") or about Eric's atypical DES experience. The first topic was too broad. The second topic was confounded by Eric's dual role and by his earlier investigations. Now, however, the questions would be specific, concrete, and relatively straightforward: Should we believe Melanie's report about her experience at 11:34:21? We could explore the question in any way we wished. To what extent would we agree with one another when faced with specific, individual reports? Would we disagree broadly about all the reports, or would the disagreement be concentrated on just a few reports, or a few aspects of them? We would be faced throughout with a concrete person, Melanie. It would not be adequate to say the impersonal "I don't believe introspective reports." We would have to be concretely personal: "I don't believe Melanie's report."

Our aims were also personal. Russ wanted candidly to expose his views to Eric, who seemed an open-minded but unsympathetic audience, to gain a skeptic's perspective on his methodology, to refine his own skepticism, to reconsider how much skepticism about Melanie's reports might indeed be warranted. Eric was exploring the limits of his skepticism, wavering between the radical pessimism about introspection with which he was flirting in his papers and a more nuanced caution that admitted the possibility of progress and discovery. Our collaboration was intended to be a private conversation between the two of us, facilitated by Melanie's willingness to be questioned. We did not begin with the intention of making our conversations public.

After half a dozen sampling interviews with Melanie, spread over a month or so, we felt we had sufficient material to drive our discussion to the next phase, so we thanked Melanie for her participation and had the interviews transcribed by Sharon Jones-Forrester, one of Russ's students. The transcription was intended to serve as the basis for our continuing personal conversation about the trustworthiness of Melanie's reports in particular, and about DES reports and introspective reports in general. We independently read the transcripts and emailed comments about specific details to each other. We then replied to each other's comments and replied to those replies and so on, back and forth until we judged we had reached a point of diminishing returns. Over the course of the interviews and subsequent discussions, we gradually came to think that our concretely based considerations of the limits of skepticism, designed originally to be a private and candid conversation, might have value to others facing some of the same issues. Thus this book was born.

1.3   The Format of This Book

The sampling interviews that are the heart of this book were thus intended to be a personal confrontation between Russ and Eric. Because these interviews were real-time exchanges, we occasionally meandered, repeated ourselves, misunderstood each other, assumed shared knowledge unavailable to an outsider, phrased things poorly. In making these interviews available to the reader, therefore, we cut such portions of the transcripts; these cuts were never made unless we both agreed the remaining interview material stayed faithful to the original whole. We also slightly eased the remainder, removing some of the vocalized pauses and false starts, for example—again only where we jointly agreed to the fidelity of the alterations. Our aim was to remove unnecessary distractions, thus focusing the remainder more sharply on what we took to be the issues of greatest general interest. We will make the complete, unaltered interview sound files and their transcripts available on the World Wide Web (http://mitpress.mit.edu/inner_experience) for those who wish to compare.

This book presents the transcripts of our interviews with Melanie and 88 boxed discussions of issues raised in those interviews. To a large extent, those boxes are streamlined versions of the personal e-mail exchanges between Russ and Eric as we tried to hammer out our similar or differing evaluations of the adequacy of some particular aspect of our interviews with Melanie. We could have presented our views in the more traditional format for a co-authored pro-and-con book, each writing a discursive essay and a reply. However, we felt that the presentation of a verbatim transcript, with inserted comments and replies, would have substantial advantages over the more standard format. The transcript format forces the reader to begin with, and constantly confront, the particular. Most other discussions of introspective method begin with abstractions and general considerations, invoking particular instances, if at all, only selectively for the advancement of the author's more general thesis. While there is nothing inherently wrong with such an approach, we feel that there is something salutary in presenting the reader with randomly obtained particular reports, one at a time, before reaching general conclusions, confronting each report on its own terms before proceeding to the next. Russ's and Eric's reactions and comments, both in the course of the original dialogue and in their later amplifications, may help the reader get some bearing on the kinds of doubts that may reasonably be raised and the resources available for responding to them.

Although this book focuses on the reports of one particular subject (Melanie), the reader will swiftly discover that the issues it raises are quite general. If the reader finds some of Melanie's claims about her experience to be believable and others to warrant doubt, as we think most readers will, this book invites consideration of what might drive these evaluations, and it offers different and sometimes conflicting suggestions on that topic. Temporarily replacing the factious and general debate about the trustworthiness of introspective reports with a personal and particular look at the details of Melanie's reports will, we think, take us a long way toward honing or refining, trimming or amplifying, shifting or otherwise altering the skepticism that is desirable when encountering reports about conscious experience.

Thus, this book is not a debate between opposing partisans, each trying to convince the other. Instead, it is a forthright *collaboration* between opposing partisans, each genuinely seeking to refine his own level of skepticism and to replace partisanship with balanced critical judgment. The result, we hope, is an illumination of some of the major issues from two sides at once.

Our confrontation and dispute has also produced one potentially very useful by-product: an examination, in unprecedented detail, of random moments of one person's experience. To the extent that they accept Melanie's reports, readers will find a wealth of information about imagery, emotion, self-awareness, inner speech, and sensory experience as experienced by a particular individual at particular moments in time. We comment frequently on general issues pertaining to such experiences, such as the bearing of Melanie's reports on various psychological or philosophical theories and the apparent similarities and differences between Melanie and other subjects we have read about or studied, including ourselves.

A Note to the Reader

Chapter 2 presents the general rationale behind Russ's belief that satisfactory introspective methods may exist, and chapter 3 presents Eric's general rationale for doubting such claims. We are ambivalent about including these chapters here rather than near the end of the book. On the one hand, this background seems worth presenting at the outset. On the other hand, we have just argued for the value of starting with concrete instances instead of theoretical generalities, and on that logic it would be better for you to dive right into our interviews with Melanie beginning with chapter 4. The interview transcripts don't assume knowledge of chapters 2 and 3, though you may have a fuller sense of what is at stake if you read these chapters first. We encourage you to follow your inclinations in this matter.

2   Can There Be a Satisfactory Introspective Method?

Russ Hurlburt

Eric's and my interest in introspection stem from the same source: we agree that most attempts at the observation of inner experience have not been successful. But we have diverged in our response to that source. I have tried to capitalize on earlier introspective failures and build a better method than was used in the previous attempts; so far, the best method I have discovered is Descriptive Experience Sampling (DES) (Hurlburt 1990, 1993; Hurlburt and Heavey 2006). Eric has publicized the skeptic's position, criticizing all attempts at introspection without excluding new and perhaps better ones. In a nutshell, I want Eric to examine DES (or any other method that avoids earlier pitfalls) on its own merits without damning it by association with other not-so-sophisticated attempts; he wants me to recognize that history includes many enthusiastic supporters of introspective methods that have ultimately proven to be problematic. What makes this conversation engaging is the fact that we both recognize the legitimacy of the other's point of view, and are both sincerely trying to figure out the appropriate balance of these necessarily confrontational positions. Neither of us is trying to win the argument; both of us are as happy to hone the other's position as our own in the service of more adequately answering the question "Can we believe people's reports about their inner experience?"

This chapter makes the case that there may well be introspective methods that deserve the scrutiny of even the most skeptical observer of introspection. I use DES as an example of such a method, not because it is the best method, but because it is the best method I know of. I will show why it is reasonable to suppose that it is different enough from previous attempts to escape from the broad criticisms that have been leveled against introspection repeatedly over the last hundred years. My attempt in this chapter is not to argue that DES provides accurate descriptions.

Here I simply wish to demonstrate why I think it possible that introspective methods can be devised that avoid the earlier pitfalls.

This chapter is in many ways a reconstruction for the reader of the extended conversations that Eric and I had before we decided to sample with Melanie. Recall from chapter 1 that these conversations led Eric to recognize that introspective methods might be improved upon, and that he came to see DES as potentially interesting, sufficiently worthy of his skeptical attention to justify devoting a substantial chunk of his professional time. In this chapter I have the same aim for the reader. For a note about the term "inner experience," see box 2.1.

2.1   Toward a Better Introspective Method: Fifteen Guidelines from a Century of Science

The question we are exploring in this book is whether it is possible (or the extent to which it is possible) to obtain accurate descriptions of inner experience. Chris Heavey, Todd Seibert, and I (Hurlburt, Heavey, and Seibert 2006) surveyed the last century or so of psychological research literature to ascertain what that literature (most of it not introspective) has to say about the characteristics of a good introspective method. That paper extracted fifteen guidelines for any good introspective method; this section paraphrases those guidelines; the reader is referred to the original chapter for amplification.

Guideline 1: The stakes are high.   Bluntly stated, introspective methods failed and non-introspective methods came to dominate psychology largely because introspection failed. Should psychological science reawaken an interest in introspection without adequate discussion and improvement of introspective method, there may be an even more severe reaction (if that is possible).

Guideline 2: Skepticism is appropriate.   Except perhaps for think-aloud procedures, all introspective procedures require memory to some extent. [For a brief description of think-aloud procedures, see box 2.2.] Psychological science robustly shows that human memory is susceptible to a variety of errors.

Guideline 3: Introspect with little delay.   It is well known that if something is not encoded, it will likely not be recalled (Klatzky 1975); that meaningful chunks, not random details, are likely to be encoded (Bower 1970); and that this encoding must take place within a few seconds of the event. Because the features of inner experience that might be requested

---

Box 2.1
A note about terminology: "inner experience" or "conscious experience"?

Eric: Russ, you've called the subject matter of your work "inner experience." I don't like that term, because I think it favors experiences like thoughts and feelings (which are generally thought of as inner) over things like sensations (which are more outwardly directed). I prefer to call it "conscious experience" or even just "experience." I'm also concerned about how the phrase seems to build in the idea of the mind as interior and the world as external. I'm sympathetic with recent trends in cognitive science that reject a strict inner/outer division (sometimes called "embodied" views of the mind, or "externalism" or "contextualism").

Russ: I agree that the "inner" in "inner experience" has the disadvantage that you point out—it does seem to favor thoughts over sensations. But DES subjects don't seem to be affected by that; and it avoids the psychological and philosophical traditions in ways that I find highly desirable.

"Experience" (unmodified) can refer not only to inner experience, but also to "external" or "environmental" or "surrounding" experience, as in "I was affected by the space-shuttle-disaster experience" or "I took the job to get management experience." Thus, I think we need some kind of an adjective to indicate that "experience" refers to thoughts, feelings, sensations, and the like.

"Conscious experience" seems to awaken either (a) the contrast to the "unconscious" in Freud and many others' sense or (b) the contrast to sleeping, dreaming, or drug-altered experience.

"Attention" and "awareness" have an implication of a meta-awareness that I do not intend.

There is, thus, no non-problematic term for what might be called inner experience, conscious experience, experience, awareness, or attention. I have preferred "inner experience" as the least misleading, but it is far from perfect.

The good news is that in DES it simply doesn't seem to matter what you call it, and therefore I alternate quasi-randomly between all those terms in an attempt to distance myself from any one particular connotation. For example, in the set of interviews that we display in chapters 4–9, we use "inner experience" 5 times, "experience" about 250 times, "awareness" about 100 times, and "attention" about 70 times.

Eric: I'm not entirely convinced that it doesn't matter what you call it, but I do agree that every terminology has shortcomings. "Conscious experience" also suggests a possible contrast to "unconscious experience"—a phrase that sounds incoherent to me. And does the phrase "conscious experience" invite the idea that we're normally conscious *of* our experiences, in some self-observational way? Though some philosophers appear to endorse such a view (e.g., Rosenthal 1986; Lycan 1996), I'd prefer not to be committed to that view simply by the terminology. So maybe the phrase "inner experience" isn't worse than any other. The reader will notice that I've reconciled myself to having it in the title of this book.

Thread: Loose language. Next: box 4.1.

Box 2.2
Summary of sampling methods

Russ: For purposes of comparison, here is a brief description of some current methods that attempt to explore inner experience.

Descriptive Experience Sampling (DES) (Hurlburt 1990) uses random beepers to trigger the qualitative description of experience. DES differs from all other sampling methods in that it is descriptive, not quantitative.

Thought sampling (sometimes called cognition sampling) (Hurlburt 1979) uses beepers to trigger subjects to fill out questionnaires. These questionnaires examine a variety of features of thought and mood.

The Experience Sampling Method (ESM) (Larson and Csikszentmihalyi 1983) is predominantly a quantitative methodology that collects standardized data about internal and external aspects of experience and situational and contextual variables. ESM differs from thought sampling primarily in its interest in situational variables and in the standardization of the questionnaires.

Ecological Momentary Assessment (EMA) (Stone and Shiffman 1994) is also a quantitative time-sampling method that differs from ESM in that it is not exclusively a random method; instead EMA sampling may occur at regular intervals (every hour, for example) or may be triggered by specific events (while jogging, for example).

Think-aloud procedures (sometimes called verbal protocol analyses) (Ericsson and Simon 1980) ask subjects to verbalize their ongoing inner processes while performing some particular tasks (solving an anagram, for example).

The Articulated Thoughts in Simulated Situations (ATSS) paradigm (Davison, Robbins, and Johnson 1983) is a kind of verbal protocol analysis in which subjects listen to audiotapes describing "stimulus scenarios" designed to elicit particular responses (social anxiety, for example). Subjects are to imagine actually being involved in the scenarios; immediately after hearing each scenario, they verbalize what they were thinking and feeling during the simulated situation.

---

by introspection are not necessarily the meaningful portions of an event, those features are not likely to be encoded and therefore are not likely to be reported accurately unless the introspection takes place within a few seconds of the event.

Guideline 4: Target specific, concrete episodes.   People often engage in theory-guided recall when retrospectively characterizing their experiences (Pearson, Ross, and Dawes 1992). Characterizations of experiences over time are also likely to be distorted by features of the experiences. For example, Kahneman and colleagues (see, e.g., Kahneman 1999;

Redelmeier and Kahneman 1996) have found that people asked to characterize pain over time do not perform some sort of average across actual events, but rather are unduly influenced by the peak level of pain and the current level of pain. Targeting specific moments of experience will minimize these biases.

Guideline 5: Keep the target experience brief.   There are "severe limitations on the amount of information that we are able to receive, process, and remember" (Miller 1956, p. 56). The introspectionists recognized such limitations a century ago. For example, Watt (1905) "fractionated" problem-solving events into four parts—the preparation, the period before the presentation of the problem, the presentation of the problem, and the search for the solution—each of which was no longer than a second or so. The implication is that the shorter the experience to be introspected, the better.

Guideline 6: Disturb the experience as little as possible.   James famously suggested that it would be impossible to capture ongoing inner experience because the attempt to capture it would destroy the experience:

As a snow-flake crystal caught in the warm hand is no longer a crystal but a drop, so, instead of catching the feeling of relation moving to its term, we find we have caught some substantive thing, usually the last word we were producing, statically taken, and with its function, tendency, and particular meaning in the sentence quite evaporated. The attempt at introspective analysis in these cases is in fact like ... trying to turn up the gas quickly enough to see how the darkness looks. (1890/1981, p. 158)

John Stuart Mill suggested that it might be possible to capture ongoing experience through the medium of memory just after the experience has passed: "A fact may be studied through the medium of memory, not at the very moment of our perceiving it, but the moment after: and this is really the mode in which our best knowledge of our intellectual acts is generally acquired. We reflect on what we have been doing when the act is past, but when its impression in the memory is still fresh." (1882/1961, p. 64) James and Mill were correct in pointing out that we should try to disturb the targeted experience as little as possible.

Guideline 7: Explore natural situations.   External validity (Campbell and Stanley 1963), "mundane realism" (Aronson and Carlsmith 1968), and "ecological validity" (Brunswik 1949) concerns about generalizability indicate that explorations should take place in the subject's own natural environments.

Guideline 8: Minimize demands. Explorations of private phenomena should seek to minimize "demand characteristics" (Orne 1962) or the "Pygmalion Effect" (Rosenthal and Jacobson 1968), employing double-blind testing when possible (Rosenthal 1976) and scrupulously bracketing presuppositions when double-blind testing is not possible (as is often the case in DES).

Guideline 9: Terminology is problematic. B. F. Skinner observed that verbal behavior about private events may be impoverished because it is difficult for the verbal community to shape a person's speech about inner experience:

> The verbal response "red" is established as a discriminative operant by a community which reinforces the response when it is made in the presence of red stimuli and not otherwise. This can easily be done if the community and the individual both have access to red stimuli. It cannot be done if either the individual *or the community* is color-blind. The latter case resembles that in which a verbal response is based upon a private event, where, by definition, common access by both parties is impossible. How does the community present or withhold reinforcement appropriately in order to bring such a response as "My tooth aches" under the control of appropriate stimulation? (1953, pp. 258–259)

Thus Skinner established that talk about inner experience, such as "I was thinking . . . ," "I am feeling . . . ," and "I am depressed" are not likely to have the same precision as talk about external events.

My DES colleagues and I have made a similar observation frequently in our sampling studies. For example, people often use the word "thinking" to mean something entirely non-cognitive; others use the word "feeling" to refer to cognitive events. [For more detail, see box 4.1.] However, we have also observed that these people can substantially improve or clarify their meanings if given repeated DES opportunities to try to speak accurately about their experience. Thus, we should recognize that some speakings cannot be adequately differentially reinforced, and we should therefore be very cautious in those arenas. However, where we can improve the differential reinforcement of speakings, we should do so. The implication is that methods must clarify to the extent possible precisely what is being described.

Guideline 10: Don't ask participants to infer causation. Nisbett and Wilson (1977) reviewed research examining the attribution of causality and concluded that people often cannot describe why they behave or think the way they do. The moral seems clear: Avoid asking "why" questions.

Guideline 11: Abandon armchair observation. It follows from all that has gone before that casual observation about inner experience is not likely to yield scientifically valid results. Merely asking subjects about their inner experiences is simply not good enough. Furthermore, asking subjects to perform armchair observations about their own experiences is problematic, even if that observation is done with careful instruction or by sophisticated observers:

> I have conducted this brief examination of our introspective knowledge of visual imagery to promote the more general thesis that we can be, and often are, grossly mistaken about our own current conscious experiences even in favourable circumstances of quiet attention. . . . We must abandon not only research paradigms in psychology and consciousness studies that depend too trustingly on introspection . . . but also some of our ordinary assumptions about our knowledge of our own mental lives and what it's like to be ourselves. Human judgment about anything as fluid, changeable, skittish and chaotic as conscious experience is bound to error and confusion. (Schwitzgebel 2002, p. 50)

Guideline 12: Separate reports from interpretations. Neuroscience has effectively used introspective reports of experience by those suffering from brain damage and disease to obtain an ever greater understanding of brain processing. Neuroscience has been successful because it has appropriately separated the introspective report from the interpretation of that report. It is the patient's job to provide the introspective reports, and the neurologist's job to provide the interpretation.

Guideline 13: Don't require too much. Classical introspection observed many or most of the above guidelines and still Titchener's group disagreed vehemently with the Würzburg school about the existence of imageless thought. The Würzburgers thought they had discovered a new "imageless" element of thinking, whereas Titchener thought that images were present but very faint. Many observers see this lack of agreement as a primary cause of the fall of classical introspection a century ago (Misiak and Sexton 1966; but see Danziger 1980). However, Monson and Hurlburt (1993; see also Hurlburt and Heavey 2001) reviewed the introspectionist reports and found that Titchener and the Würzburgers substantially agreed about the phenomena in question, even though they disagreed about the interpretation of those observations. Had the introspectionists limited themselves to the careful description of phenomena, rather than trying to resolve an issue in their theory of mind, they would not have disagreed and introspection might not have been so thoroughly discredited.

Guideline 14: Value prospective research. Prospective designs offer the possibility of tapping a wide range of information relatively irrespective of theoretical perspective, collecting evidence that may or may not be related to some later question. At this early stage of the science of inner experience, this ability to allow the emergence of perhaps unexpected relationships or characteristics is especially important.

Guideline 15: Situate introspective observations in a nomological net. Those who would use introspective observations should explore the relationships of those observations to other kinds of research results.

These fifteen guidelines highlight desirable features of any introspective method. No doubt other ways of slicing the century-of-psychological-research pie would yield a somewhat different set of guidelines. That is, I am not claiming that this is the only set or the best. Yet it does seem to me that this set is a reasonable summary of the desirable characteristics of introspective methods.

2.2   Descriptive Experience Sampling

In 1974, I began developing a method shaped by the thinking that is embodied in the guidelines we have just reviewed. That method, which I call Descriptive Experience Sampling (DES), is my best attempt at an accurate method for describing inner experience.

I do not think that DES is the ultimate method, only that it is the best method that I know of at this time. Should a method come along that I judge to be better than DES, I would be happy to abandon DES in its favor. That is, I am personally, and this book is specifically, much more committed to the high-quality study of inner experience than to the DES method.

I have described DES in a variety of places (Hurlburt 1990, 1993, 1997; Hurlburt and Heavey 2001, 2002, 2004, 2006; Hurlburt and Akhter 2006). I will discuss its basics and its rationale only fairly briefly here. Readers interested in more detail are referred to the works cited above.

DES uses a random beeper in the subject's natural environments to signal the subject to pay attention to the experience that was ongoing at the moment of the beep. The subject then jots down notes about that now-immediately-past experience. The subject collects a half-dozen such beeped experiences and then meets with the investigator within 24 hours for an expositional interview, the aim of which is to describe the experiences that were ongoing at each of the six beeped moments.

The beep/interview procedure is repeated over a number of sampling days, usually between three and ten. The "iterative" nature of the procedure allows the subject's observational and reporting skills to improve over the course of the several sampling days: Each day's interview informs, refines, and differentiates the next day's observations, and in turn those newly refined observations inform, refine, and differentiate the subsequent interviews (Hurlburt and Akhter 2006).

Occasionally critics of DES have disparagingly referred to the "magic beeper," but whereas there is nothing magic about it, its characteristics are important (Hurlburt and Heavey 2004, 2006):

• The beep is random. This makes it clear that I and my subject are on equal footing with respect to the beep (that there is no manipulation involved) and that I have no presuppositional expectations about what occasions or events are important or unimportant.

• The beep has a rapid onset or "rise time." This makes it clear that I am interested in a precise moment, perhaps measured to a fraction of a second. A vibrator of the type used in pagers is not adequate.

• The beep should be easily detectable. A beep that is too loud will startle the subject, and the startle response will destroy the contents of experience. A beep that is too soft will trigger the subject's asking "Is that the beep? Is that the beep? Yes! That's the beep!" but by now the experience that was occurring at the moment of onset of the beep may be lost.

• The beep is unambiguous. It means "Sample now!" and nothing else. Some critics have attempted to simulate the DES procedure by using, for example, a telephone ring as the signaling device. That doesn't work, because the subject's response must be "That's a telephone ring, but I'm not supposed to answer the telephone, I'm supposed to pay attention to my experience." However, that response is likely to destroy the experience that was ongoing at the moment of the beep.

• The beep should be private. DES subjects generally use an earphone. If the beep is delivered through an external speaker, the subject must think about what she will say to anyone who might also have heard the beep, or must hasten to stop the beep so as not to annoy others. Either way, the ongoing experience has been lost.

• The beeper must be easily portable, so it can be easily used in the subject's natural environments.

The expositional interview asks essentially one and only one question: "What were you experiencing at the moment of the beep?" The object is to get as complete and detailed an answer to that question as possible, while at the same time avoiding confabulation. We want "the whole truth and nothing but the truth," and the interview (in fact, the entire

---

Box 2.3
The truth, the whole truth, and nothing but the truth

Russ: Society often takes the statement "the truth, the whole truth, and nothing but the truth" to mean substantially less than its literal meaning. In the courtroom, "nothing but the truth" sometimes cynically means "anything that is not technically a lie." Witnesses are routinely admonished *not* to provide the "whole truth" in the sense that they are instructed to answer only the question being asked and not to volunteer additional information, even if that additional information seems necessary to the understanding of the whole truth.

However, in DES we mean "the truth, the whole truth, and nothing but the truth" to be taken as completely literally as possible. We give subjects an explicit choice: It's okay not to tell us anything. But if you decide to tell us something about a beeped experience, we would like you to tell the truth, the whole truth, and nothing but the truth as straightforwardly as you can. Our intention is the opposite of an attorney's. We want to discover the complete truth, not to hide behind a technical truth or show only one side of the truth. We want you to help us get to the heart of your experience, not to lead us away from it. We want you to help us discover as accurately as possible the details of your experience, not to blur them in the service of hiddenness. If we overlook something in what you have said, bring that to our attention. If we distort some feature of your experience, bring that to our attention. If our questions don't help you describe accurately your phenomena, help us to ask better questions. If you are unwilling to expose as accurately as possible the details of a beeped experience, then we would prefer not to talk about that experience at all.

Thread: Interview techniques. Next: box 2.4.

DES project) is aimed at that result. The interview is not structured, but instead asks that question over and over, in as many different forms as necessary, to focus the subject on the precise moment of the beep and nothing else. [For Russ's comment about "the truth, the whole truth, and nothing but the truth," see box 2.3.]

By "the moment of the beep" we mean the last undisturbed moment before the beep begins—a millisecond before the beep. That is, we are not interested in the subject's reaction to the beep; we are not interested in what led up to the beep; we are not interested in what caused the experience; we are not interested in whether the experience is typical or rare. We are interested in the experience that was naturally ongoing at the millisecond before the beep began. We often use the metaphor of a flash snapshot: we are interested in whatever the flash (beep onset) happens to catch.

Of course it would be naive to think that we actually get to a perfectly undisturbed moment; the beep has to have been processed by the subject to identify the "last undisturbed moment." One of the aims of this book is to get a sense of how undisturbed that moment is likely to be. Most subjects report that something like a "sensory store" for experience seems to exist, giving them time to "freeze" the experience and then to report it. But the believability of those reports is at issue in this book.

The DES interviewer tries to grasp the subject's experience as it is experienced by the subject. That requires suspending preconceptions about what the characteristics of the subject's experience are, listening carefully to what the subject says, and trying to help the subject describe her own experience accurately. [For a discussion of the DES questioning technique, see box 2.4.]

We accept that Skinner was correct in observing that people, including our DES subjects, are not differentiated observers or reporters of their inner experience. (See guideline 9 above.) That is, subjects say many things about their experiences that are false or misleading, not because they wish to deceive, but because in their life encounters until now they have not learned a vocabulary that is adequate to describe their experiences accurately; they have not learned to discriminate adequately between their actually occurring experience and their self-theories about their experiences; they have not learned to focus on one moment. The series of DES expositional interviews must therefore provide training in those important observational and reporting skills at the same time as it is acquiring reports of inner experience. Therefore, the first sampling day or two (or more in some cases) is generally considered entirely training, not data gathering, and training continues past that time when necessary.

Thus, the expositional interview consists of the subject's saying some things that are faithful and some that are misleading about her inner experience. The interviewer's task is to help the subject, over the course of sampling, say more and more faithful things and fewer and fewer misleading things. A metaphor that appeals to me is that I am standing under the chute of a thresher with wheat and chaff pouring down. I try to grab the wheat and just ignore the chaff. (I actually don't know whether threshers work like that.) As the subject finds out that I'm very interested in the characteristics of particular moments and I'm not interested in the extra-sampling general statements, almost always there eventually becomes more wheat and less chaff—that is, more talk about moments and less about general characterizations.

All this assumes that the subject is truly motivated to provide faithful descriptions of her inner experience. There may be some subjects who

Box 2.4
Open-beginninged questions

Russ: DES questions are sometimes called "open-ended," but I think it makes as much sense to call my questions "open-beginninged." An open-beginninged question is one that does not presume the content about which it asks.

"Tell me about your image" is an open-ended question, because it allows the respondent to elaborate about images as much or as little as desired. But its beginning is fixed: the question is about images, nothing else.

By contrast, "Tell me about your experience, if any, whatever it happened to be" is an open-beginninged (as well as an open-ended) question, because it allows the respondent to discuss images, speech, emotions, sensations—whatever was occurring at the moment of the beep, including none of the above or no experience at all.

The failure to appreciate the importance of open-beginninged questions has been, in my opinion, one of the major problems in the development of the science of inner experience, including most of the approaches described in box 2.2. One researcher assumes that visual experience always exists, and asks about the characteristics of visual experience. Another researcher assumes that emotional experience always exists, and asks about the characteristics of emotional experience. Another researcher assumes that verbal experience always exists, and asks about the characteristics of verbal experience. Our DES research shows that there is *no* form of inner experience that comes anywhere close to always existing; if that's true, the assumptions of all those researchers are incorrect, and therefore their results are problematic.

It is possible to have a particular interest (say, in images) and still ask open-beginninged questions. You ask, in an open-beginninged way, what was going on at this moment. If the experience happens to include an image, then you include that in your study. If the experience happens not to include an image, then you discard it. Such a study is, it seems to me, the only way to ascertain how images are actually experienced. To argue that that is too inefficient actually proves my point. If it is inefficient, that must be because many moments do not include images, and to ask about images at those times must have been misguided.

Thread: Interview techniques. Previous: box 2.3. Next: box 4.3.
Thread: Richness. Next: box 3.4.

are motivated to lie, and probably nothing can be done about that. But DES does take seriously the attempt to enlist the subject's interest in faithful descriptions.

First, we present ourselves as co-investigators: the subject has something (her experience) and we have something (the DES method), and together we can discover something that probably neither of us separately can do.

Second, we are, and present ourselves as being, genuinely interested in the faithful apprehension of the subject's experience, as it occurred, with a minimum of embellishments. We demonstrate that genuine interest in a variety of ways: We question carefully to make sure we understand precisely what is being said; we encourage the careful focus on the precise moment of the beep by discouraging wandering away from that moment; we encourage the careful focus on the precise moment of the beep by discouraging speculation about what might have caused the currently experienced phenomenon; we consistently try to keep our own presuppositions out of the picture, maintaining a focus on the subject's experience as the subject experiences it; we let a random beeper choose the moment, rather than presume to know what moments are important.

Third, we protect the subject's privacy, telling her that we will not divulge her experiences until she explicitly agrees that we may do so; that she should feel free to discontinue sampling at any time without prejudice; that she should feel free to decline to discuss any experience for any reason (we have things that are none of her business and presume that she has things that are none of ours). We do ask that that if she wishes to decline to discuss an experience, she should tell us at the outset, and we will simply skip that entire beep. Then, if we do discuss a sample, we can delve as thoroughly as we desire. (Certainly the subject knows that she can change her mind and discontinue reporting or sampling at any time.)

The result of all this is that the subject typically comes to realize that our aim is actually to apprehend the reality of her experience, one moment at a time. Most subjects, I think, find that a very powerful and quite rare event: Someone really cares about my experience! Most subjects, I think, find it an unusual opportunity to be as honest as possible about personal experiences. Most subjects, I think, find it an opportunity to discover something about themselves, and the more accurate the better. [For a comment on Nisbett and Wilson's criticism of introspection, see box 2.5.]

Box 2.5
Nisbett and Wilson's critique exempted DES, and indeed (contrary to myth) exempted consciousness generally.

Russ: Nisbett and Wilson's 1977 criticism of introspection is so widely quoted as to require comment. The criticism is that "the accuracy of subjective reports is so poor as to suggest than any introspective access that may exist is not sufficient to produce generally correct or reliable reports" (Nisbett and Wilson 1977, p. 233).

Critics of introspective-like methods have often taken Nisbett and Wilson's paper to be an unconditional refutation of introspection in general. However, it is not widely known that Nisbett and Wilson, later in that same paper, recognized the possibility of accurate reports about inner experience: "We also wish to acknowledge that the studies do not suffice to show that people *could never* be accurate about the processes involved. To do so would require ecologically meaningless but theoretically interesting procedures such as interrupting a process at the very moment it was occurring, alerting subjects to pay careful attention to their cognitive processes, coaching them in introspective procedures, and so on." (p. 246)

DES, as we have just seen, involves precisely "interrupting a process at the very moment it was occurring, alerting subjects to pay careful attention to their cognitive processes, coaching them in introspective procedures, and so on." It is thus fair to say that Nisbett and Wilson, among the staunchest critics of introspection, agreed that methods like DES were at least "theoretically interesting" and might "be accurate about the processes involved." (I think Nisbett and Wilson were mistaken about their further claim of ecological meaninglessness, but readers may judge for themselves by the end of this book.)

Eric: Let me go further, Russ, and point out that—despite the myth that Nisbett and Wilson repudiated introspection generally (and the many citations of them to that effect)—they very explicitly emphasize that they mean only to challenge our introspective access to our own "cognitive processes" and not our "mental content." In fact, they devote an entire section of their famous paper to making this point ("Confusion between Content and Process," pp. 255–256). They grant, with what they take to be "almost all psychologists and philosophers," that individuals have "a great storehouse of private knowledge . . . that can be known with near certainty" (p. 255), including knowledge of our current sensations and emotions. They aim only to show that we have poor introspective knowledge of the processes leading up to—*the causes of and influences on*—our judgments, decisions, feelings, and other conscious events. They do not claim that we can be mistaken about what those judgments, decisions, feelings, and other conscious events are. They challenge, for example, self-reports about why we prefer a particular pair of socks, not self-reports *that* we prefer them or self-reports of one's current sensory experience (if any) in

---

Box 2.5

(continued)

seeing the socks. Wilson continues to be quite explicit about this distinction in his more recent work (e.g., 2002, pp. 17–18), emphasizing our ignorance of "the adaptive unconscious" as distinguished from consciousness.

In general, psychologists have done a poor job of separating skepticism about the self-reports of nonconscious processes, traits, behavioral dispositions, etc. from skepticism about self-reports of inner experience or consciousness; and when they do distinguish the two, it often turns out—as with Nisbett and Wilson—that they are only skeptical about the former.

Russ: I agree with all that.

2.3   Does DES-Apprehended Inner Experience Faithfully Mirror Inner Experience?

I acknowledge that DES reports about inner experience mirror inner experience absolutely accurately only rarely. So the issue is not whether the mirror is perfect, only whether it is scientifically adequate.

There are, it seems to me, two kinds of evidence that DES reports might faithfully reflect inner experience. First, there are what I will call *plausibility arguments*—characteristics of the world and the method that lead me to think that accurate characterizations is the most plausible state of affairs. Second, and by far more important to me, are what I will call *compelling idiographic observations*—one-case-at-a-time observations of single individuals.

2.3.1   Ten Plausibility Arguments

Here are ten plausible reasons to believe that DES reports faithfully mirror inner experience. No single reason, by itself, carries the day—one can argue against any of them. But all of them together are, to me, pretty persuasive. However, I do not think that arguments based on plausibility are ever an adequate foundation for science. They are important in that they clarify features of the method, but one person's plausibility is another's doubt. Science must be built on direct observation, not plausibility; that is why I believe that the compelling idiographic observations I discuss in the next section are far more important than the plausibility arguments I discuss here. I see these plausibility arguments only as setting the stage for what I find to be the convincing idiographic observations.

1. The DES method is sophisticated.   There are, historically, many good reasons to doubt introspective reports. However, those introspective reports have been gathered in ways that I find seriously methodologically flawed. By following the guidelines and employing the characteristics described earlier in this chapter, DES may, in a sophisticated way, avoid those flaws.

2. Prospective DES subjects are skeptical too.   Nearly all prospective DES subjects think DES will be difficult or impossible, but they find it easy once they actually engage in the DES procedure. It seems reasonable to suppose that the subjects' initial skepticism is somewhat similar to others' (perhaps the reader's) skepticism: it is based on armchair attempts at observing inner experience. But, as I observed in 1997 (p. 947), "critics [should] not dismiss the descriptive experience sampling method on the basis of informal attempts at replicating the procedure. Informal sampling attempts such as asking oneself on occasion, 'What am I thinking right now?' are nearly always discouraging, leading the typical critic to believe that he or she would be unable to perform the sampling task. However, I reported (1990, p. 269) that most subjects find the actual task of responding to the random beep to be quite easy and unambiguous, stating that 'unsuccessful [informal] attempts at thought sampling should not lead you to conclude that [descriptive experience] sampling . . . is impossible; but rather should lead you to an appreciation of the relative delicacy of the method.'" The fact is that most subjects, at the outset, believe they will have a hard or impossible time capturing their inner experience, but over the first day or so of DES they become convinced that they can in fact capture their inner experience. This often-repeated trajectory from skepticism to acceptance based on their own directly observed experience seems an argument against unrelenting skepticism.

3. DES subjects say they give accurate and complete reports.   Despite the fact that I, in a skillfully repetitive way, give DES subjects the opportunity to say that there is more in their experience that they can't quite describe, they say the opposite—that they are giving pretty complete reports. They are convinced of that, and I am confident that that is not the result of my asking leading questions.

4. Variability in within-subject reports implies their openness to a variety of experience.   People often give quite different reports at different beeps—for example, inner speech at one beep, an image at another, unsymbolized thinking (the experience of thinking without words, images, or any other symbols; Hurlburt 1990, 1993, 1997; Hurlburt and Heavey 2006) at another, a combination of inner speech and feelings at another, and so on. This seems to indicate that people have a willingness and ability to report a variety of kinds of inner experience. It is therefore *not* the case that these subjects have a "favorite" kind of inner experience, or are "blind" to all other kinds of inner experience. (Certainly they might be blind to things they never report.)

Said another way: If one believed that reports of putative inner experience were purely artifactual, one would expect the reports to be always the same. They are not.

There are other possible explanations for variability within subjects' reports—for example, that a subject views himself as highly variable and therefore gives variable reports. However, in my experience most people think of variability in content, not variability in form. A person would have to be quite sophisticated about inner experience (would have to recognize the existence of unsymbolized thinking, for example) for such a self-view to influence the form in this way.

5. *Variability in between-subject reports implies my openness to a variety of experience.* Different people have quite different patterns of responding. For example, one person reports nearly all inner speech; another reports nearly all images; another reports a mix of forms of inner experience. This seems to indicate that I, as one particular DES investigator, am open to a variety of experience. It is therefore *not* the case that I have a "favorite" kind of inner experience, or that I am "blind" to all other kinds of inner experience.

6. *The analogy from visual perception.* The phenomenology of figure-ground perception has been well known at least since the Gestalt psychologists. Their work was largely in the visual realm; they showed that people spontaneously, seemingly immediately, create strongly felt patterns out of visual arrays, and they proposed laws that govern such perception: proximity, similarity, closure, good continuation, and so on. Their main point was that people do *not* see everything that is available to be seen; they create, as part of the active perceptual process, a well-defined object to "see."

It seems likely (and this is the way it is reported by DES subjects) that a similar process occurs across modalities. Thus, much as the faces disappear when I pay attention to the vase way of seeing the ambiguous face/vase figure, it seems reasonable to conclude that the sounds around me disappear when I pay attention to the visual, and that the visual disappears when I pay attention to the tactile, and so on. Certainly there are cases where I can pay attention to two or several aspects of the environment; however, for most people, most of the time, the number of such things appears to be small. There are exceptions to that, but it is the exceptions that prove the rule. Some subjects do not "filter out" alternative modalities or alternative perceptions in the same modality. That indicates, it seems to me, that I am prepared to hear complex reports if they are given (i.e., that I am not biased against complexity). However, most people don't make such complex reports, even when given the opportunity in the expositional interviews.

7. *Compare the alternatives.*   An alternative that is sometimes advanced is that people always have ongoing visual experience. If the DES subject doesn't report it, it must therefore be neglected. I am not persuaded by that as a possibility, because the same argument can be made for other sensory modalities. Auditory experience must also always be ongoing, because, if someone says my name, I'm likely to hear it even if I'm paying attention to something else. Therefore, the argument goes, a piece of my awareness must have been auditory. Kinesthetic experience must also always be ongoing, because, if I'm walking down the street and the pavement suddenly becomes spongy, I spontaneously adjust my gait. Therefore, the argument goes, a piece of my awareness must have involved the feel of the pavement and my body's reaction to it. And I see no reason to stop there: taste, smell, and other senses are equally arguably always ongoing. So, on this model, I am always simultaneously experiencing many simultaneous multimodal things. I just don't think that's true. We certainly *process input* from multiple modalities at once, but most of that input does not become a recognizable part of our stream of experience, as the response of our immune system to invading bacteria or the expansion and contraction of our pupils as lighting conditions change do not become recognizable parts of the stream of experience. [See also box 4.8 and the discussions of Eric's rich-versus-thin study in section 10.3 and subsection 11.2.1.]

8. *Subjects are not reluctant to report everything.*   As we saw in section 2.2, the DES method tries to impress on subjects that if a feature of their experience is none of my business then we shouldn't discuss that sample. I tell them that it is far easier if they just say "This sample is none of your business," rather than try to disguise or hedge. I say "I will try to get a complete account, and if you are hiding something we'll just go around and around; I won't feel a sense of completion."

Subjects occasionally do say "None of your business," which indicates that the message is heard. But they don't say it often, primarily (I think) because the beeped moments are usually pretty mundane.

I conclude that subjects are usually not reluctant to report as completely as they can; if they were, they would say "None of your business" more often. In fact, subjects often report things that are embarrassing or that run counter to their self-concept, as is indicated by verbal ("You're sure this is confidential?") and non-verbal (blushing, stammering) evidence.

9. I myself am pretty good at bracketing presuppositions. I don't mean to be arrogant, or to single myself out, but the ability to bracket presuppositions probably has to be evaluated one person at a time. The evidence for the adequacy of my own bracketing efficacy is as follows: (1) My reports vary dramatically from subject to subject, indicating that I am not "out looking for" my favorite characteristic. (2) I have reported many phenomena that were surprising to me (unsymbolized thinking, the absence of figure-ground phenomena, the absence of inner experience altogether). (3) I have worked at it and written about it. (4) I have been observed by at least one skeptic (Eric) who acknowledges that I seem to be pretty good at it. [See chapter 10.]

10. Leading the witness is less problematic with reports about actually occurring events than with general statements. Descriptive psychology is plagued by the demand characteristics of the communications. I believe that the likelihood that demands are effective in altering a subject's perceptions diminishes as the situation becomes more concretely immediate. "See that stop sign there? It's blue with white polka-dots" is unlikely to be effective in the face of a red stop sign, because your own immediate perception can refute it. DES tries to limit reports to immediately occurring events, thus diminishing demand influences.

2.3.2 Compelling Idiographic Observations

The plausibility arguments that I have just discussed suggest to me, in a weight-of-the-evidence way, that the general answer to the question "Does DES-apprehended inner experience mirror inner experience?" is Yes. But I recognize that someone else might advance ten plausible reasons to the contrary and then conclude that the answer is therefore No. There is, I believe, no clear-cut way out of this scenario of dueling plausible generalities. However, I believe that the general attempt to answer the question "Does DES-apprehended inner experience faithfully mirror inner experience?" is somewhat misguided. While I believe that the ten factors I just listed support the plausibility of the Yes answer, I am not persuaded by those arguments. In subsection 2.3.1, I tried to give an analytic answer to a question that may require an inductive answer. So let me recast the question: Does the DES-apprehended inner experience of Allen faithfully mirror his inner experience? Does the DES-apprehended inner experience of Beatrice faithfully mirror her inner experience? Does the DES-apprehended inner experience of Chuck faithfully mirror his inner experience? Does the DES-apprehended inner experience of Dolores faithfully mirror her inner experience? And so on. If the answer to many of those sub-questions is Yes, then we can perform the true inductive generalization and conclude that the DES-apprehended inner experiences of many subjects mirror their inner experiences.

I have performed many DES investigations, and my answer to most of those inductive questions about them are "Yes, yes, yes, yes . . . and therefore Yes." Furthermore, that inductive series is capable of compelling me to believe the final Yes in a way that the analytically plausible arguments of subsection 2.3.1 simply cannot. I, as an individual, am quite sure that DES-elicited reports of inner experience often or usually mirror actual inner experience, and I believe that I have been compelled to that belief by observing a series of single individuals for whom a contrary position seems bizarre. I will cite two such cases here, both of which I have written about elsewhere.

2.3.2.1   The Case of Fran

In 1993 I reported the case of Fran, a woman who had been diagnosed as having a borderline personality disorder. In 1997 I discussed the "idiographic validity" of that case, arguing that my DES characterization of Fran's inner experience reflected her actual inner experience. The following is from pp. 946–947 of my 1997 discussion:

"Fran" [was] a woman diagnosed as having a borderline personality (Hurlburt 1993). Hurlburt described many salient characteristics of Fran's inner experiences, of which I discuss three. First, Hurlburt reported that Fran's inner experience was frequently populated by multiple (as many as five or ten) visual images, all occurring simultaneously and in the same "visual space" (that is, these images were not a side-by-side collage, but were instead all viewed straight ahead in a physically impossible overlaying that somehow did not provide any confusion for Fran herself). Fran's case is thus an example of the extreme complexity that inner experience can attain as reported by the descriptive experience sampling method. Such complexity cannot possibly be reported by any method other than sampling. For example, had Fran used a think-aloud technique, the most detailed non-sampling method, she simply could not have had time to report adequately one image, to say nothing of five or ten simultaneous images.

Second, Hurlburt (1993) reported that some of Fran's visual images (usually those with extremely negative content) often lasted for hours or days, nonstop, uninterrupted. (By contrast, the descriptive experience sampling method finds that images in healthy participants last for only a moment.) For example, Fran reported a visual and auditory image of her father "telling her off." In this image, Fran was seated at the dining room table. Her father was standing over her, pointing his finger at her, telling her she was "no good—a failure." Her mother was seen at the kitchen sink in the background looking over her shoulder at Fran. This image appeared in several successive samples, with the description being the same at each sample, and apparently continued uninterrupted during the time in between, for a total of at least several hours (pp. 202–205). This long-duration-image phenomenon might be considered impossible without sampling evidence.

Third, Hurlburt (1993) reported that Fran had no *figure-ground phenomenon* in either her inner image perception or her external perception—she took in an entire visual scene without focusing on any of its aspects. This conclusion was based on the fact that in repeated descriptive experience sampling interviews, Fran consistently denied the occurrence of phenomena associated with figure and ground: no part of an image appeared to be "closer" or "in better focus," and when she shifted her gaze from one image (or external object) to another, she had no experience of "zeroing in" or of the previous center of attention "losing focus."

A major question is of course whether Hurlburt's (1993) descriptive experience sampling reports about Fran accurately reflect Fran's inner experience: Fran was clearly the only person in a position to know that experience. Direct reliability studies are therefore impossible, so reliability must be indirectly inferred from validity considerations. Furthermore, one cannot apply standard validity-checking procedures (which intrinsically use across-group measures) to the idiographic observations of a single person; instead, one must infer validity idiographically, considering the unique characteristics of the particular description. I can identify five such idiographic validity considerations regarding the case of Fran:

First, the question of idiographic validity applies not to the descriptive sampling method per se but to the particular individuals who apply the method. In Fran's case, I was the investigator (Hurlburt 1993). I might be expected to be a valid applier of the method because my previous descriptions of different people differ dramatically from each other, are sometimes surprising even to me myself, and are in agreement with other observers in those cases where more than one observer have sampled jointly (Hurlburt 1993).

Second, the lack of figure-ground phenomenon in inner experience leads to an obvious but risky prediction that if Fran viewed the classical ambiguous figures such as the faces-vase or Jastrow's duck-rabbit, they would not "alternate" in her experience. I (Hurlburt 1993) performed this informal validity experiment and found that Fran did in fact see both aspects of each drawing simultaneously with no alternation. A correct risky prediction can be taken as support for an underlying proposition (Popper 1963) and therefore here as evidence of validity.

Third, I (Hurlburt 1993) ruled out miscommunication, misunderstanding, or language deficit as alternative explanations of her failure to report figure-ground experience as follows. Fran asked to borrow the ambiguous figures to show to her coworkers, believing that I was mistaken about the existence of the alternation phenomenon. She telephoned me a few hours later to report that to her surprise, her coworkers did in fact report the experience of alternation. In this conversation she gave an accurate description of her coworkers' alternating experiences but still denied that such alternation occurred for her. Thus it seemed clear that Fran understood what figure-ground phenomena are and was capable of describing them if they had existed for her.

Fourth, the descriptive experience sampling descriptions of Fran's inner experience provided plausible explanations of two characteristics of her external behavior. First, during Fran's discovery of her coworkers' figure-ground phenomenon, the coworkers came to realize, much to their surprise, that Fran could pay attention to many aspects of one thing or many different things simultaneously (such as her frequent multiple images), as had been discovered by descriptive experience sampling. The coworkers observed that this multiple-attention ability explained a trait that angered them all: They worked in a bank, and a frequent task was counting money. Each person would stand at a counter and count their own individual stacks of bills. Fran irritated her coworkers by repeatedly initiating conversations while counting, causing them to lose count. The simultaneous tasks of counting and conversing were impossible for her coworkers but simple for Fran. Thus, it seemed clear to me that the multiple-experience characteristic of Fran's inner world had real ramifications in Fran's exterior everyday world.

The second sampling-based plausible explanation of external behavior came from Fran's psychotherapist. Before Fran had become involved in the sampling study, her psychotherapist had responded to her complaints of being preoccupied with negative thoughts by training her in thought substitution—a cognitive-therapeutic technique aimed at teaching her to think about something positive, based on the rationale that increasing her frequency of positive thoughts would lower the frequency of negative thoughts. However, that therapeutic intervention had been unsuccessful; sampling provided the plausible explanation that Fran was quite capable of thinking about something positive without ceasing to think about something negative.

Fifth, changes in external behavior were reflected in changes in inner experience. Near the end of sampling Fran experienced a remarkable improvement in her borderline symptoms: her exterior disorganization and chaotic psychological fragility vanished. Samples obtained after this improvement were now much less complex and now included the experience of figure-ground phenomena.

Taken together, these observations led me (Hurlburt 1993) to conclude that the idiographic descriptions of Fran were indeed valid. If their validity is at least tentatively accepted, they are extremely provocative; for example, to my knowledge, no reports of visual perception without figure-ground phenomenon appear in the perception literature, and no mention is made of the possible connection of the lack of figure-ground to psychopathology.

For reasons of focus, my 1993 and 1997 accounts did not include the following additional anecdote. Recall the conversation between Fran and her co-workers when they discovered that Fran's multiple-attention ability was the reason she could count money and hold a simultaneous conversation. During that same conversation, Fran discovered that her co-workers had in their living rooms only one television. Fran had three (didn't everyone?) and watched them all at the same time without switching her attention back and forth. She was surprised when her co-workers reported that they could not do the same thing! Furthermore, after the improvement in her borderline symptoms, she reported that, regrettably, she had lost this simultaneous-TV-watching ability. This case compels me to believe that my DES characterizations of Fran's inner experience correspond in some important way to her actual inner experience. Sampling had putatively "discovered" a highly unusual phenomenon of Fran's inner experience (no figure-ground phenomenon in image and external perception). This was "corroborated" by three highly unusual external characteristics: no alternation of ambiguous figures, the ability to count and hold a conversation (the ability was actually stronger than that—Fran could count, participate in one conversation, and simultaneously listen without difficulty to one or more other simultaneous conversations), and the presence of three TV's in her living room and the ability to watch all of them at the same time. And as if that weren't enough, when Fran's remarkable recovery occurred, both her inner experience and her external skills dramatically (literally overnight) lost their unusual characteristics. It is therefore difficult for me to believe that the DES multiple-image characterization of Fran's experience was not substantially correct. How else can one explain these remarkable characteristics? It is of course possible that Fran was lying and inventing reports to seem "special," as those diagnosed with borderline personality sometimes do, or that she was trying to confirm what she supposed to be my hypotheses. That doesn't seem likely to me—she would have had to have been very psychologically sophisticated, I had no hypotheses to confirm, and I was quite skeptical about her reports. The most reasonable conclusion, it seems to me, is that sampling discovered and accurately reported important characteristics of Fran's experience. Substantially more sampling case studies and corroborating objective investigations will be required.

2.3.2.2 The Case of Robert

In 1994, Asperger syndrome expert Uta Frith, her student Francesca Happé, and I reported the case of Robert, a 25-year-old man diagnosed as having Asperger syndrome, a form of autism in which the level of intellectual functioning can be quite normal. Robert's IQ was 90, and he was quite able to perform the sampling task. Here are excerpts from our account:

> The characteristics of all Robert's 16 samples were strikingly uniform. All 16 involved visual images, with no other aspects of experience reliably available to be reported—no feelings, no inner speech, no bodily sensations, etc. All Robert's images were seen clearly and in accurate colour, with the centre of the image being most clear and losing focus at the periphery, apparently exactly the same as his real-world perception. . . . Robert's samples were marked by the absence of any characteristics of inner experience except images. Except for the imagined sensation of a cat scratch on the back of his hand in one sample of an image of a cat, no samples included inner speech, feelings, bodily sensations, or other features of inner experience that have been reported by other subjects. Robert clearly had adequate ability to describe such features, and on occasion we specifically enquired whether such features were present, so as to rule out the possibility that they were simply being overlooked. Our conclusion was that they simply did not occur to Robert as aspects of experience at any of the sampled moments.
>
> Because the lack of non-image forms of inner experience was so striking, we structured [informal, non-DES] exercises during the interviews to explore the ways in which Robert experienced unambiguous strong bodily sensations. For example, with Robert's consent one of the authors (R.H.) leaned him forward and sideways to very tilted body positions; his inner experience (seeing a recalled image) remained constant, and a bodily awareness did not occur to him. In another such experiment, R.H. twisted the skin of Robert's wrist in opposite directions, creating what in most people would be a moderately painful experience. The wrist sensation did not create its own image or disturb the image that was present in his real-time inner experience: the image that he had been describing to us remained constant. Robert said he could feel the skin twisting but insisted it was not painful. (Hurlburt, Happé, and Frith 1994, pp. 388–389)

On the basis of DES, Hurlburt, Happé, and Frith characterized Robert's inner experience as almost always exclusively visual. The question we are dealing with here is whether that characterization is true. The informal experiments we performed were specific attempts to induce non-visual experience (leaning Robert to one side, applying painful twists to his wrist). Those manipulations were only slightly effective. What in most individuals would immediately dominate experience became, apparently, only slightly or not at all a part of Robert's experience. That images persisted despite explicit attempts to elicit non-image experience seems to corroborate the characterization of Robert's experience as largely visual. Nonetheless, it is still possible that this visual focus is simply a characteristic of Robert's report, not of Robert's actual experience—maybe Robert felt pain but simply didn't have the vocabulary to report it.

However, other facts not reported by Hurlburt, Happé, and Frith (1994) compel me to the view that Robert's reports accurately mirrored his actual experience. During the session in which we had explored the painful wrist-twisting, Robert told the following anecdotes: When he lost his first baby tooth, his parents instructed him to put it under his pillow; the next morning, the tooth was gone, replaced by "a quid left by the tooth fairy"; later that day, Robert took a pair of pliers and pulled out four more teeth. A more recent incident occurred a few months before I met Robert. He was in his apartment kitchen, and he smelled something burning. Looking around, he discovered it was his hand, which was accidentally resting on a hotplate. Those remarkable and objectively corroboratable stories compel me to believe that pain does not figure in Robert's inner experience, just as sampling had shown. It is highly implausible that Robert's pain *experience* was similar to that of most other people, and that only his pain *reporting* differed from the norm. Certainly such accounts do not verify that Robert's experience is visual, but they do lend credence to the accuracy of his no-pain description of our arm-twisting experiment. That, in turn, lends credence to the accuracy of his ongoing-undisturbed-visual-image portion of that description, and that in turn supports, in my view, his credibility as a reporter of ongoing imagery. I simply cannot accept the notion that we should treat Robert's DES accounts as "mere reports." They are, it seems to me, substantially related to what Robert actually experienced.

By the way, neither absence of pain nor ubiquitous presence of images is known to be a frequent characteristic of Asperger individuals, although there are similar reports by others (e.g. Grandin 1995). It is therefore difficult to argue that we set out, knowingly or unwittingly, to look for those characteristics in Robert. Thus, it seems difficult to avoid the conclusion that these were actual characteristics of Robert's experience. [For Eric's comment on the case of Robert, see box 2.6.]

2.3.2.3 Discussion

The cases of Fran and Robert provide corroboration in instances where you might expect such corroboration *the least*. These were individuals with serious disorders, and yet their characterizations of their inner

---

Box 2.6
How compelling is the case of Robert?

Eric: I find the case of Fran more compelling (assuming that she was honest) than the case of Robert. Your phraseology here confuses me; and if I'm confused, I worry that Robert may have been confused too. What do you mean when you say, for example, that Robert had no "bodily awareness" as he was tilted forward and sideways? Was he completely ignorant of the fact that he was being tilted? You report no general disorder in his sense of balance. Or was Robert in some sense aware of being tilted (and able to report it?), though aware without "inner experience"? Do you mean to suggest that Robert navigated the world for the most part entirely non-consciously, no more having tactile or auditory experience than the rest of us have experience of our immune system or the growth of our fingernails? Or do you mean only something weaker?

How confident are you that Robert was alive to such distinctions as I'm asking about here and that he interpreted your questions as you intended them? Did you ask him about *sensory* visual experience, which you seem to assume he had, though you didn't report that in any of his samples? Especially without verbatim transcripts to look at, I don't feel I can give much credit to this strange material, confusingly presented, and therefore possibly born of confusion in the original interview. Pardon my frankness!

I concede that you have some anecdotal evidence that comports nicely with Robert's denial of pain. However, it should be noted that *total* incapacity to feel pain is a rare and serious disorder, typically accompanied by serious injury and deformity (Rosemberg, Marie, and Kliemann 1994; Nagasako, Oaklander, and Dworkin 2003). You don't report this in the case of Robert.

Russ: I offer the case of Robert only to open the reader to possibilities, not as proof. You, Eric, discredit the report because it seems "strange" to you and because it doesn't match your presuppositions about our experiences of balance and touch and the relation between bodily injury and the experience of pain. At first I, too, found Robert's reports rather strange. But, as I argue repeatedly throughout the book, we must set aside (or "bracket") such presuppositions when faced with DES reports [see subsection 11.1.7]. Furthermore, I think the general rarity of pain insensitivity strongly *supports* my point. We discovered Robert's pain insensitivity as a result of an exploration of inner experience *that had nothing to do with pain*. The ubiquity of Robert's images led to the risky prediction of little or no bodily or pain experience, and, as in the case of Fran, a correct risky prediction is supportive evidence.

I agree that our discussion of Robert is incomplete. One advantage of the present project, Eric, is that you can explore any similar presupposition-based doubts you have about Melanie's reports as deeply as you like.

Thread: Bracketing presuppositions. Next: box 3.3.
Thread: Human similarity and difference. Next: box 3.3.

experience seemed compellingly accurate. If seriously disturbed individuals can be faithfully accurate reporters of experience, healthy individuals should be able to be at least as accurate.

When I consider the many subjects I have examined with DES, some as dramatically compelling as Fran and Robert, I see little choice in believing that DES is about the exploration of inner experience, *not* merely about the *reports* of inner experience. To say that we are just examining *reports* of inner experience is, of course, true in a fundamental way that I can fully accept—everything has to be filtered through and understood in the context of reporting. But to say that we are *just* examining reports of inner experience seems substantially far-fetched, at the same level of far-fetchedness as to say that we are *just* examining perceptions of reality with nothing substantial implied. Just as I stop at red traffic lights because I believe in the substantial existence of the oncoming cars, I believe in the substantial existence of the inner experience that DES intends to describe. Just as I do not understand the nature of the reality of the oncoming cars, I do not understand the nature of the reality of inner experience. But just as I get out of the way of oncoming traffic, I treat inner experience as a fact.

It is possible to argue that the cases of Fran and Robert were exceptional—that's why I discussed them—or that perhaps my characterizations of Fran and Robert were somehow biased by my personal characteristics. The present book seeks to examine such reservations. We chose as a subject Melanie, who, unlike Fran or Robert, was not thought to be particularly exceptional—in fact, we knew little about her other than that she had been a successful college student. In the coming chapters we will expose the entire process, so that you can decide for yourself the extent to which the account of Melanie's experience that our interviews are believable.

3   Descartes Inverted

Eric Schwitzgebel

3.1   Some History

René Descartes argues in *Meditations on First Philosophy* (1641/1984) that the mind—including especially conscious thought and experience— is better known than the body. He supports this view with his dream doubt and demon doubt thought experiments, which are now standard fare in introduction to philosophy. You may think it certain that there's a book in front of you. But can you, really, be absolutely sure? Haven't you had the experience of dreaming that you were reading, falsely confident that you were awake? Or perhaps a demon is bent on deceiving you, and is feeding you false sensory impressions—or (in the more contemporary version) perhaps a genius neuroscientist from Alpha Centauri removed your brain last night while you slept, relocating it to a vat where it is being stimulated so as to mimic exactly the inputs it would receive from a normal waking day, including the reading of a hallucinatory book.

Of what *can* you be certain, according to this argument? Only that you exist, that you are thinking, and that you have certain conscious experiences—a visual experience of blackish figures against a whitish background, a tactile experience as if there were a book in your hands. Such facts about ongoing events in your mind, Descartes argues in his first two meditations, are known indubitably and infallibly as no external fact could be. Indeed, later thinkers, including Locke (1690/1975) and perhaps Descartes himself (on standard interpretations, like Russell's (1945)), argue that our knowledge of our own minds serves as the *basis* of our knowledge of the world outside. We apprehend our sensory experiences first; our judgments about the external world flow indirectly, derivatively, from a primary and more secure knowledge of our own consciousness.

You know that there is a book in your hands only because you know, antecedently and with greater certainty, that you are having visual and tactile experiences of a certain sort.

Mid-twentieth-century philosophers, despite the skepticism about introspection that was commonplace in research psychology, commonly accepted something like Cartesian introspective infallibility or incorrigibility (see, e.g., Lewis 1946; Ewing 1951; Ayer 1963; Shoemaker 1963; Rorty 1970), often supporting their claims by appealing to the example of pain. How could one be mistaken, or justifiably correctible by an outside observer, in the judgment that one is, or is not, in severe pain? A *Saturday Night Live* spoof (pointed out to me by Ned Block and Lex Newman) highlights the intuitive appeal of this idea through a mock commercial advertisement for a "home headache test" that requires users to draw and centrifuge blood to determine if they have a headache. The commercial ends as follows:

She: Oh, God, I'm in agony!

He [looking at her test results]:   Honey, you don't have a headache.

She: Oh, thank God!

He [looking at his test results]:   Neither do I! [They hug.]

Spokesman: The Home Headache Test. From Leland-Myers. Because what's worse—having a bad headache or not knowing if you have a bad headache?

The humor in this derives, of course, from the preposterous idea that one would need to look to outside sources to determine if one has a headache. Similarly, it seems difficult to imagine, when one is looking attentively, in good conditions, at a nearby bright red shirt—and consequently having a visual experience of red across a large swath of one's visual field—that one could be mistaken in the judgment that one is experiencing the visual phenomenology of "redness" (though one might be incorrect in using the label "red" for that experience, due to a purely linguistic mistake). Seeking outside confirmation in such matters seems absurd.

In the last few decades, infallibilism about current conscious experience has fallen out of favor among philosophers, or has at least been sharply curtailed. Philosophers such as Armstrong (1963) have argued, and others such as Shoemaker (1994) have conceded, that it is at least possible in principle to be mistaken about one's own current conscious experience, and that external sources of evidence might sometimes

Box 3.1
Putative examples of introspective error

Eric: Though I'm sympathetic with Churchland's aims, his examples seem to me to invite easy objection. Perhaps you really do feel pain for a moment, or perhaps your judgment in that case isn't genuinely introspective. Perhaps you're not wrong about the taste experience itself but only about how to relate it to previous taste experiences and the world, or perhaps the suggestion of orange in combination with the lime-sherbet flavoring is enough to generate an actual orangey experience.

In fact, those who would defend infallibilism seem always to have an array of options when faced with a putative case of introspective error: The subject is simply using words differently than the rest of us, or maybe she is mistaken only in her *classification* of an experience (an experience she knows perfectly well) as of a kind with other experiences she remembers, or maybe she really does experience what she says she experiences despite the behavioral or physiological evidence. To undermine all such potential responses generally requires more work (and more empirical work) than is possible in a typical philosopher's example, and definitive refutation may be out of reach—an infallibilist can always insist that the behavioral and physiological evidence is misleading.

justifiably override one's own introspective judgments. Churchland (1988) offers a typical thought experiment of the sort many have found convincing: You have been touched on the back nineteen times with a hot poker. On the twentieth trial, an ice cube is surreptitiously substituted, and for a fleeting moment as it touches you, you mistakenly think you feel pain. Or: You are blindfolded and told that you will be tasting orange sherbet, but it is really lime sherbet (which tastes very similar in blind tests). For a moment—perhaps until you taste the actual orange sherbet—you erroneously think you experience an orangey taste. [See box 3.1, however, for some concerns about these thought experiments.]

Although such examples are intended to undermine Cartesian infallibilism, embracing the possibility of error in *some* cases is quite compatible with holding—as the great majority of contemporary philosophical fallibilists (including Churchland 1985) do—that introspection is *generally* a reliable process for coming to know one's own current experiences. (See, e.g., Armstrong 1963; Hill 1991; Audi 1993; Shoemaker 1994; Dretske 1995; Lycan 1996; Goldman 1997; Chalmers 2003.) Fallibilists almost always confine their examples of error to marginal cases like

---

Box 3.2
Dennett on introspection of current conscious experience

Eric: Daniel Dennett's work, especially his 1991 book *Consciousness Explained*, is often read as arguing for the possibility of pervasive and radical mistakes about conscious experience. However, I find Dennett far from clear on the point. Sometimes he seemingly takes himself to be providing examples of gross introspective error about ongoing conscious experience (e.g., regarding the level of detail in visual experience, in chapter 11), but elsewhere he compares our authority in reporting our experiences to the authority an author has over his fictional creations— which seems to imply that we could no more go wrong in our reports than Arthur Conan Doyle could go wrong in reporting the color of Holmes's easy chair. (See, e.g. Dennett 1991, pp. 81, 365–366.) Dennett also asserts that we can come "close" to infallibility when charitably interpreted (Dennett 2002, pp. 13, 16), and he allies himself explicitly with Rorty (1970) and other "incorrigibilists" who argue that we can never be justified in overturning a sincere introspective report on the basis of outside evidence (Dennett 2000, 2002). I doubt that a coherent view can be made of all this (Schwitzgebel 2007b).

---

those discussed above—matters of fine discrimination, or mistakes made only for a moment, or in circumstances of stress and distraction, or in pathological or science-fiction cases, or only about the *causes* of our experiences rather than about the experiences themselves. Thus, the debate between fallibilists and infallibilists within philosophy has almost always been conducted under the shared assumption that introspection— that is, whatever process(es) drive our ordinary judgments about our currently ongoing or immediately past conscious experience—is a broadly trustworthy method, at least in favorable circumstances. No prominent philosopher has clearly and unequivocally put forward a case for thinking that we often go grossly wrong about our current conscious experiences, even in calm and ordinary circumstances of extended reflection [though see box 3.2]. Even psychologists who are suspicious of introspection have tended not to be entirely clear about whether they mean only to impugn self-reports of such things as motives, skills, and traits or whether they mean also to reject introspective reporting of current conscious experience, and some—including Nisbett and Wilson (1977) [see box 2.5]—have explicitly cordoned off the latter sort of reports from their doubts.

3.2   My Point of View

Why should philosophers—an ornery lot who rarely reach general consensus about anything—almost universally regard the introspection of one's ongoing phenomenology, or stream of experience, as trustworthy and reliable? People aren't especially trustworthy and reliable, most think, in reporting the real grounds of their judgments and decisions (e.g., why they chose a particular pair of socks; see Nisbett and Wilson 1977) or in reporting their implicit attitudes (e.g., about the characteristics of other races; see Gawronski and Bodenhausen 2006). Is it obvious that the introspection of current conscious experience deserves better epistemic credentials?

My interest in this issue was first aroused through my work in Alison Gopnik's developmental psychology laboratory in the 1990s, when I was simultaneously a philosophy Ph.D. student under Elisabeth Lloyd and John Searle. Gopnik (at Berkeley) and the Flavells (at Stanford) were exploring the extent to which children could be mistaken about their own attitudes and experiences. (See, e.g., Gopnik 1993a,b; Flavell, Green, and Flavell 1993, 1995, 1998, 2000; Flavell, Green, Flavell, and Grossman 1997; Flavell, Flavell and Green 2001; Flavell and Flavell 2004.) It seemed from their research that young children (4- and 5-year-olds) could be *vastly* mistaken, denying the presence of beliefs just expressed, holding that people could go for days without a single thought, and grossly misreporting their own ongoing or immediately past reflections and expectations. Here is a typical result from Flavell:

The experimenter showed the child a library-type bell and then hid it under the testing table. She said, "In just a few seconds, I'll ring it." After a 4-sec delay she rang the bell and said, "OK, in just a few seconds I'll ring it again." After another 4-sec delay she rang the bell and reiterated, "OK, one more time. In just a few seconds I'll ring it again." This time she failed to ring the bell and after a 10–12 sec delay instead asked . . . "Are you wondering or thinking about anything right now or not?" If the answer was "yes," the experimenter asked, "What are you wondering or thinking about?" (1995, pp. 72–73)

Only 38 percent of 5-year-olds responded that they were wondering or thinking about anything having to do with the bell or the experimenter's striking it, and 44 percent said they weren't wondering or thinking about anything at all. Flavell et al. assume that most of the children must have been thinking about the bell (and that virtually all must have been thinking about *something*), so they interpret the majority as mistaken in their replies. Flavell et al. perform a variety of similar experiments, varying

---

Box 3.3
How should we interpret Flavell's children?

Russ: An alternative explanation of Flavell's results is that many 5-year-olds simply do not have thoughts, and that therefore they are not mistaken at all, let alone "*vastly* mistaken." I fear that the Flavells and Eric reject this possibility because it is too different from their own experience. One of my recurrent themes in this book is the desirability of bracketing pre-suppositions about others' experience, in particular resisting the tempta-tion to believe that everyone's experience is like one's own. I think that bracketing presuppositions is of vital importance to the advancement of a science of inner experience, while Eric thinks my dismissal of earlier research is too cavalier. See my extended treatment of the Flavell studies in subsection 11.1.7.8.

Thread: Bracketing presuppositions. Previous: box 2.6. Next: box 4.6.
Thread: Human similarity and difference. Previous: box 2.6. Next: box 4.1.

---

their methodology and sometimes going to great lengths to explain to the children what "thinking" means. I don't view the results as decisive—surely, children may fail to understand the tasks or the language, despite the Flavells' near-heroic efforts in various versions of these experiments. Still, I am drawn to the Flavells' overall conclusion that young children know very little about the processes of thinking and are remarkably poor introspectors—and, as Gopnik suggests, if children struggle enormously with understanding the task or the language, that itself already tells you something. Unfortunately, I know of no attempts to replicate Flavell's work on this outside his laboratory. [For a concern about Flavell's inter-pretation of his results, see box 3.3.]

If Gopnik and Flavell are right, young children are far worse at intro-specting their experiences than they are at perceiving outward objects. Now, are we to suppose that this situation reverses itself by adulthood? Are ordinary adults, unlike young children, at least as accurate in their judgments about their stream of experience as they are about the phys-ical and social world around them? Do they largely avoid gross errors? I was surprised to find that little empirical work has been done on the question.

Such questions are not straightforwardly testable. We can't directly observe someone else's experience. We may be tempted to infer error or accuracy in particular cases, but with no dependable, general theory to hand about the relationship between conscious experiences and publicly observable brain states or behavior—no theory more dependable than the subjective reports themselves, anyway—we are on shaky ground in the many cases where a person's judgment about her experience diverges from what one might expect her experience to be based on other evidence. Witness my criticisms of Churchland's examples (in box 3.1) and Russ's criticism of Flavell (in box 3.3). We have too much liberty to posit whatever conscious experience best matches our theory, whether we wish to shield the subject's report or refute it. How can this be good science?

Still, I think the issue admits of exploration through a careful blend of introspection (by researchers and independent subjects), theoretical reflection, and attention to outwardly observable empirical facts. In the face of ambiguous evidence, we can at least weigh the plausibilities. The remainder of this chapter will provide a taste of the kinds of consideration I find persuasive.

Consider, for example, not the infallibilists' favorite cases of severe pain and foveal red, but rather the experience of visual imagery. Create a visual image right now, if you can—for example, an image of your breakfast table as you sat down to it this morning (following Galton (1880)), or an image of your house as seen from the street. Now consider the following questions. Can you, indeed, form and retain such an image? If so, how stable is that image? Does it fluctuate as you think about different aspects of the scene, as your attention waxes and wanes, or does it stay relatively constant? Does it have a focal center and a periphery, or is everything equally present at once? How detailed is it? Are objects to the side well articulated in your image before you specifically think about them (and "fill them in," as it were)? If you concentrate on one object in the image (assuming you can do so), how are the other objects experienced? Do they "fade" in some way? What is that fading like? Is everything present in color all at once, or does some of the image have indeterminate color? How is that indeterminate color, if there is any, experienced—as black and white, or gray, or in some other way?

Most people of whom I ask such questions—although these are questions about major features of presumably (but see box 5.1) ongoing conscious experience—eventually feel confusion or uncertainty. Certainly I do. I don't *think* this confusion is merely about words and theories, about how best to describe a patently obvious visual imagery experience. Rather, it extends, to some degree, to the experience itself. It's not absolutely certain what our visual imagery experience is like. Consequently, it shouldn't be surprising if some people, at least, occasionally go wrong about it. Furthermore, subjective reports about visual imagery experience vary widely—in apparently normal people, all the way from the complete denial of visual imagery experiences to descriptions of visual imagery as detailed as ordinary visual experience of outward objects or even more detailed. (Galton's compendium (1880, 1907) is still the most useful.) Yet psychologists have generally failed, over a long history of hundreds of experiments, to find consistent correlations between subjective reports of visual imagery experience and performance on the types of tasks commonly thought to involve visual imagery, such as mental rotation tasks, visual memory tasks, and tests of visual creativity. (See McKelvie 1995; Slee 1995; Schwitzgebel 2002a.)

Or consider emotional experience. What is your emotional experience right now? Do you even have any? Try to conjure some if you think you don't. Is it completely obvious to you what it is? Even if you are fairly confident in giving it a general label, how much do you know about its particular experiential character? Does introspection reveal its details, its somatic manifestations in experience (if any), its full phenomenological structure, as clearly and certainly as visual inspection reveals the contents of your desktop? Does this seem to you to be a topic on which you could not go wrong? I suspect that my wife reads my emotional phenomenology better in my face and posture than I do in my own introspection.

These reflections are meant only to be suggestive. Not every reader will find the same uncertainty and doubt that I do. Think of these reflections less as arguments than as invitations to a point of view too little defended by philosophers—as, similarly, infallibilists' reflections on the apparent impossibility of being mistaken about one's headaches or about vivid color experiences are really more invitations to embrace infallibilism than demonstrations of its truth. Or, if you like, for the purposes of this chapter, think of these reflections as merely an expression of my point of view as it stood before our interviews with Melanie.

3.3 Sources of Introspective Error

The introspection of conscious experience is difficult for several reasons.

First, experience is fleeting and changeable—or so it seems to me right now as I reflect, introspectively, upon it. The page before me, as I read these paragraphs, is relatively steady, but my *visual experience* as I look at the page is in constant flux. As my eyes move, what portion is clear and what portion is hazy changes constantly. I blink, I glance away, I change my focus, and my experience shifts. My eyes slowly adapt to the black and white of the page, to the contrast with the surrounding desk, to the changing light as the sun goes behind a cloud. I parse some bit of the page into familiar words as my eyes scan down it; I form a visual image, reflecting the content of the discussion; my attention wanders. All this, it seems, affects my visual experience. Consider your own experience as you read this paragraph. The text in your hands changes not a whit, but your visual phenomenology won't stay still a second, will it? (Or will it?) The same is true, I'm inclined to think, for our auditory experience, emotional experience, somatic experience, conscious thought and imagery, taste, and so on: Even when the outside environment is relatively steady, the stream of experience flies swiftly. It doesn't hold still to be examined. [For some of Russ's concerns about my claims here, see box 3.4.]

Second, we're not in the habit of attending introspectively to experience. Generally, we care more about physical objects in the world around us, and about our and others' situation and prospects, than about our conscious experience, except when that experience is acutely negative, as with the onset of severe pain. This may seem strange in view of the importance we sometimes claim for "happiness" (which we generally construe as bound up with, or even reducible to, emotional experience), but, despite the lip service, few people make a real study of their phenomenology. We spend much more time thinking about, and we have much subtler an appreciation of, our outward occupations and hobbies. And when we do "introspect," we tend to think about such things as our motives for past actions, our personality traits and character, and our desires for the future. This is not, in my view (or Russ's), introspection strictly speaking. But call it what you like, it isn't the sort of introspective attention to ongoing (or immediately past) conscious experience that is central to consciousness studies. Introspective attention to experience is hardly a habitual practice for most, perhaps any, of us (except maybe a few dedicated meditators of a certain sort). If accurate introspection requires a degree of skill, as I suspect it does, in most people the skill is uncultivated. Relatedly but perhaps to some extent independently, experience is extremely difficult to remember. Generally, what we remember are outward objects and events—or, rather, outward objects and events as interpreted, and possibly misperceived, by us—not our *stream of experience* as we witness those objects and events. We remember, usually—*usually*—that the boss said the work wasn't up to snuff, not that our visual experience as he said it was such-and-such or that we felt

Box 3.4
On experience while reading

Russ: Your description of the experience of reading and vision, Eric, is the current view held by philosophers and psychologists, but I think that view is mistaken. The experience of reading is never or at most rarely like that. Certainly the eyes move and the retinal representation of words becomes more or less distinct as it is closer or farther from the fovea. But I think that level of processing takes place always (or almost always) outside experience. The actual experience while reading, I think, has little or nothing to do with such things.

We can disagree so dramatically about such a fundamentally important issue because science has done a horrible job of exploring experience. That's why I think this book is so important. If it is possible, as I think it is, to obtain accurate observations of the experience while reading, then science should do so, and then replace the current view (and your view) with a more accurate one based on carefully obtained experiential data. On the other hand, if it isn't possible to obtain accurate observations of experience, then science (and I) should refrain from embarking on a second round of introspection.

Eric: I agree that we know very little about the experience of reading and about naturally occurring visual experience generally—an amazing lacuna, really! Perhaps because I incline toward a relatively "rich" view of experience [see box 4.8 and section 10.3], I have assumed that the reader has a visual experience as she reads the text, and that this experience changes with the position of her eyes and the overall state of her visual system. Maybe I could be talked out of this, though, by clever enough arguments and experiments. My main point, of course, is that we shouldn't simply trust our own introspective judgments about our experience—and I don't exempt my own introspective judgments from doubt.

[For more on the experience of reading, see box 5.3.]

Thread: Richness. Previous: box 2.4. Next: box 4.8.
Thread: Sensory experience. Next: box 4.8.

some particular sinking feeling in the stomach afterward. These conscious experiences fade like dreams in the morning unless, as with dreams, we fix them in mind with deliberate attention within a very short space.

Third, in part because of our disinterest in conscious experience, the concepts and categories available to characterize it are limited and derivative. Most language for sensory experience is adapted from the language we use to describe outward objects of sensation. Objects are red or square or salty or rough, and usually when we use the words "red" and "square" and "salty" and "rough," we are referring to the properties of outward objects; but derivatively we also use those words to describe the sensory experiences normally produced by such objects. That's fine as far as it goes, but it is likely to invite confusion between the properties of objects and the properties of experiences of those objects. The practitioners of certain specialties—for example, wine tasting and sound engineering—have refined language to discuss sensory experience, but even here our conceptual categories are only rough tools for describing the overall experience. And, anyway, isn't the gustatory experience of eating a burrito as complex as that of tasting a mature wine, and isn't the auditory experience of sitting in a restaurant as complex as that of hearing a well-played violin? We almost completely lack the concepts and competencies that would allow us to parse, think about, talk about, and remember this complexity. (For more on this point, see Schwitzgebel 2004.)

Fourth, the introspection of current experience requires attention to (or thought about) that experience, at least in the methodologically central case of deliberately introspecting with the aim of producing an accurate report. Problematic interference between the conscious experience and the introspective activity thus threatens. Philosophers and psychologists going back at least to Comte (1830) have objected that the act of introspection either alters or destroys the target experience, making accurate report impossible. (See also Russ's chapter 2, section 2.1, guideline 6.) Much of experience is skittish—as soon as we think about it, it flits away. Suppose you reflect on the emotional experience of simple, reactive anger, or the auditory experience of hearing someone speak. Mightn't the self-reflective versions of those experiences—those experiences as they present themselves to concurrent introspection—be quite different from those experiences as they normally occur in the unselfconscious flow of daily life? A number of psychologists have attempted to remedy this difficulty by recommending immediate

retrospection, or recall, of past experience, rather than concurrent introspection, as the primary method. (See, e.g., James 1890/1981; Farthing
1992.) However, deliberately poising oneself in advance to report something retrospectively may also interfere with the process to be reported;
and if one only reports experiences sufficiently salient and interesting to
produce immediate spontaneous retrospection, one will get a very biased
sample. Furthermore, retrospection is likely to aggravate the fifth difficulty I'll discuss here.

The fifth difficulty is that reports of experience are likely to be considerably influenced and distorted by pre-existing theories, opinions, and
biases, both cultural and personal, as well as situational demands. The
gravity of this problem is difficult to estimate, but in my opinion it is
extreme (and considerably larger than the influence of bias and preconception now generally recognized to permeate science as a whole). Given
the changeability and skittishness of experience, and our poor tools and
limited practice in conceptualizing and remembering it, we lean especially heavily on implicit assumptions and indirect evidence in reaching
our introspective and immediately retrospective judgments. One major
source of such error is what the introspective psychologist E. B. Titchener
(1901–1905, 1912) called "stimulus error" (see also Boring 1921): We
know what the world, or a particular stimulus, is like (we know for
example that we are seeing a uniformly colored red object), and we are
likely to infer that our experience has the properties one might naively
expect such a stimulus to produce (e.g., a visual experience of uniform
"redness"). Ordinarily we attend to the world, not to our stream of experience, and the difference between sensory attention to outside objects
and introspective attention to the sensory *experience* of those objects is
a subtle one; so the former is likely to substitute for the latter. (For a
related point, see Dretske 1995; Tye 2003; Siewert 2004; Schwitzgebel
2005; Stoljar 2006.) Even when experience isn't so easily traceable to an
outside object, I'm inclined to think, our theories can profoundly affect
our reports. If we think images must be like pictures, we are more likely
to instill reports of imagery with picture-like qualities than if we don't
hold that view. [See box 5.2 and Schwitzgebel 2006.] If we think
cognition takes place in the brain, we are more likely to locate our
cognitive phenomenology there than if we think it takes place in the
heart. [See box 7.12.] If we think memories must be imagistic, we are more
likely than those who don't think so to report memory images.

Thus, in my view, Descartes got things almost exactly backwards. The
outside world of stable objects, people, and events—the world we spend

most of our time thinking about—is what we know most directly and certainly. The "inner world" of conscious experience is reflected on only rarely and is known only poorly. I'm practically certain there's a tissue box here before me, and I know quite a bit about its physical details; however, I'm much less certain of my visual experience as I look at that tissue box, except at the crudest level. Furthermore, what I do know or suspect about my visual experience is grounded to a considerable extent in my knowledge of the properties of the box itself. My judgments about the box's shape, color, and other visible features in large part (though not exclusively) drive my judgments about my visual experience of shape, color, and so forth—not, as many philosophers inspired by Descartes have suggested, the other way around.

3.4 Our Difficult Situation

Going into this collaboration with Russ, I didn't feel that introspection, or ordinary naive reflection on ongoing or immediately past "inner experience," was *completely* hopeless as a method for learning about consciousness, but I did—and still do—feel it must be treated with enormous caution. We cannot blithely assume that even the most credible-seeming introspective reports are likely to be true.

Yet, despite its untrustworthiness, introspection must be given a central role in the study of consciousness. Without introspection, we might not even know that we *are* conscious in the relevant sense—that a stream of phenomenology accompanies our outwardly visible behavior. Behavioral and physiological measures alone tell us nothing about consciousness unless it is established that those measures correlate with conscious experience; and introspection is the most straightforward way to establish such correlations. *All* tools for understanding consciousness are problematic in their application. Perhaps this is why consciousness studies has been so slow to find firm scientific footing. It's not as though, in the face of the unreliability of introspection, we can substitute some simple set of behavioral or physiological measures that will consistently generate accurate and detailed answers to questions about our phenomenology.

Our situation, I think, is in some ways analogous to that of a foreign intelligence agency that must depend for its information on a network of unreliable, double-crossing spies. Just as the reports of spies can to some extent be corroborated or cast into doubt by such independent means as satellite photos and bank records (which by themselves may say little), so also can introspective reports be to some extent checked against behavioral, physiological, and cognitive measures; and just as consistency or inconsistency between the reports of independent spies provides at least prima facie reason to accept or doubt the reports, so also consistency or contrast between independent introspective reports, when there is no reason to suspect corresponding differences in conscious experience, may justify tentative acceptance or rejection of the reports. Given the unreliability of naive introspection, we need such methods of confirmation, shaky as they are—and perhaps introspective training too (Schwitzgebel 2004)—before we can be truly justified in accepting introspective data.

It seemed to me at the beginning of this project that Russ's DES methodology did not change this basic situation. Although the methodology seemed likely to alleviate my fourth concern above, regarding the division of attention and selectiveness of retrospection, it seemed simultaneously to aggravate the fifth concern: distortion by pre-existing opinions and situational demands. By 2 seconds after the beep, it seemed to me from my own sampling, and thus still at the beginning of the articulation and categorization of the experience, all but the grossest and most salient features of the experience were gone from memory. This left a large opening, it seemed to me, for biased or theory-guided reconstruction—an opening that only expanded as time progressed. (This remains my opinion after the completion of this project. See sections 10.4 and 10.5.)

How serious is this problem? Russ and I agree in general about the difficulties and potential sources of error in reporting experience, but we disagree about how to weigh them and the extent to which they can be alleviated with adequate care. All reasonable people must, I think, stand somewhere between thinking such reports, from experience sampling or other sources, are absolutely infallible in every detail and thinking that only sheer accident could ever allow a person accurately to report basic and apparently obvious features of her own experience. Russ and I hope the reader will find the following dialogues useful in assessing how much skepticism is warranted and the extent to which it may be overcome by careful questioning.

II Interviews

4   The First Sampling Day

This chapter and the next five—one for each sampling day—present annotated transcripts of our interviews with Melanie. We remind the reader of the context of the interviews. This was understood to be a private, personal exercise between Russ and Eric—the result of Russ saying to Eric "Let's you and I, who have publicly opposed positions, perform some sampling together and see what happens." Russ has long sampling experience, but perhaps he has been "captured" by his own history; opening the process to a skeptical outsider might expose aspects of the procedure that he has overlooked. Eric, on the other hand, has a public role as a skeptic, but perhaps he has overstated that skepticism; confronting the concrete reality of another's inner experience might alter his perspective.

Eric can be said to be at a triple disadvantage in this situation: First, he is "playing in Russ's court" for the first time, while Russ has been performing interviews for decades. Second, the sampling interviews took place with Russ and Melanie together in Russ's office and Eric participating by speakerphone from his office hundreds of miles away. Third, it was Russ who recruited Melanie, and therefore he had a (small) prior relationship with her.

Apart from informing Melanie of the anticipated presence of a philosopher interested in exploring the method, the setup was standard DES procedure (for details, see Hurlburt and Heavey 2006; Hurlburt 1990, 1993): She had been given a beeper, set to go off at random intervals ranging from a minute to an hour, and she had been given a notebook to jot down whatever might be helpful to her after each beep. She was to wear the beeper in her natural, everyday environments for several hours at her convenience, collecting 6–8 "samples" within the 24 hours before a scheduled interview with us. She was to respond to the beep by trying to "freeze" and remember whatever experience was ongoing at the last undisturbed moment before the beep began—whatever was "before the footlights of consciousness"—whether that was one thing or many things or nothing. She was not to worry about whether the experience was typical or about its causes. Nor was she to go beyond what she could report accurately: She was told that "I don't know" was always a respected answer. If she was not able or willing to interrupt her activity to immediately note her experience, she was asked to skip the sample entirely.

In several respects, these interviews diverged from DES procedure. Most notable, of course, was the presence of Eric, who was not trained in DES interviewing principles and was explicitly invited to question Melanie in whatever manner he saw fit. Furthermore, as the reader will see, Russ and Eric engaged in theoretical conversations about the reported experience and about Melanie's trustworthiness as a subject, right in front of Melanie, and Melanie was permitted to participate in these conversations. This would never happen in standard DES. There was, of course, a substantial risk that such conversations would have an impact on Melanie, biasing or otherwise altering her reports. (See, e.g., box 5.11 (regarding imagery) and the end of beep 2.4 (regarding the timing of the beep).) Despite this risk, we thought it best, rather than debating after the fact about a more standardly collected DES-style report, to try to hash out our differences with Melanie present and available to amplify her reports in response to our queries and disagreements and to contribute her own sense of her experience.

We interviewed Melanie six times, discussing six separate sampling days over the course of several weeks, concluding when we decided that we had reached a point of diminishing returns. The interviews were recorded and transcribed word for word. For ease of reading we have removed vocalized pauses and, in some places, eased awkward locutions, repetitions, and brief digressions. Where we've cut longer portions of the dialogue, a specific note is included in the text. Except where explicitly noted, the issues raised in the boxes were not discussed in Melanie's presence. The entire transcript and original audio files are available at http://mitpress.mit.edu/inner_experience.

Preliminary Discussion

Russ [after briefly introducing Eric and Melanie to each other]: There aren't any particular rules about this exercise except to get to the truth, the whole truth, and nothing but the truth about Melanie's inner experience.

Eric: Right.

Russ: And as long as we think that's an interesting deal, we'll do it. And as soon as we decide it's not an interesting deal, then we won't do it anymore.

Eric: That sounds good.

Russ: I don't care how we proceed in this regard. [to Eric] If you want to be the primary interviewer, that is totally all right with me. If you'd prefer me to be the primary interviewer, that's okay with me as well. And, if you want, we can just pass it back and forth as seems sort of natural. . . . I've usually found it makes sense for somebody to be the primary ball carrier just because that's easier, but . . .

Eric: Right. Why don't I let you do that, because you've had so much experience with this. I may just jump in from time to time.

Russ: I've told Melanie that we may very well get into conversations along the side that we wouldn't normally do in a typical sampling situation. She would probably be interested in those conversations. She just graduated from college with a dual major in psychology and philosophy . . .

Eric: Oh, wow! Okay, great.

Russ: . . . so she may be able to contribute to the conversations we're having. She was saying just before you called that . . .

Melanie: I was just saying how it took me quite a while at the beginning, when I first put the beeper apparatus on, to forget that I was wearing it and to forget that I should be thinking something of great importance or interest or something like that. So . . .

Eric: [laughs] Right.

Russ: So, Melanie, is there anything else we should be talking about other than that sort of mechanical difficulty?

Melanie: No, aside from that everything went pretty well.

Russ: Okay. So then I'm ready to go to beep number one. And these beeps are from yesterday. Is that right?

Melanie: Yes. They're from yesterday evening from about 6 P.M. to 9 P.M.

Eric: Okay, great.

Beep 1.1

Melanie: Number one requires a little bit of background, so this may take a couple of minutes. I had just received this huge box in the mail, about as big as I was. It was a chair from my university, one of those heritage chairs that you get. I had unwrapped it and everything, and there were protective plastic coverings over the back of the chair and the handles and all four legs. So I'm standing in the living room and I had it tipped back on its two hind legs, and it was leaning against the couch in my home. I was removing the plastic covering from the front two legs when I looked up and there was a white manila envelope taped to the bottom of the chair. There were some papers in it, so I pulled out the papers and was looking at them. It was a family tree that you can fill out that goes back to my great-grandparents and then to my great-grandchildren, so I could document who I pass this chair on to. And right at the moment of the beep I was kind of thinking in my head how funny it was that I had just received this chair fifteen minutes ago and all of a sudden here was this paper I was supposed to fill out about who was going to inherit it.

Russ: And by "right at the moment of the beep" do you mean like right at the very beginning of the beep? Or . . .

Melanie: No, right before. And then right as the beep started I was aware of the fact that I was smiling. So right before the beep I had this thought in my mind, but I didn't really know what the rest of my body was doing. But then the beep went off, and then I was aware of what I was sitting and doing.

Russ: Okay. So the moment that we're interested in is that last undisturbed moment before the beep came. So if the beep starts here and we can wind the experiential clock back a microsecond or something, *that's* the moment we are talking about. So at that moment are you thinking about how strange it is? Or . . .

Melanie: Just how amusing it is that I'd just gotten this chair, and here I needed to plan out who was going to inherit it.

Russ: Okay. And this thinking, how does it proceed?

[On different uses of the word "thinking," see box 4.1.]

Melanie: Well, it's not aloud, it's in my head, so I'm silent. And it's a voice going through my head that isn't my own voice. I'm not hearing

Box 4.1
What is "thinking"?

Russ: With striking regularity, subjects early in their sampling refer to their own most-frequent kind of inner experience as "thinking," saying things like "At the moment of the beep I was thinking that I don't want to take that exam." Carefully examining the details of those experiences reveals that people differ substantially in what they mean by "thinking." When Alice says "I was thinking . . . ," she means that she was saying something to herself in her own naturally inflected inner voice. When Betty says "I was thinking . . . ," she means that she was seeing a visual image of something. When Carol says "I was thinking . . . ," she means that she was feeling some sensation in her heart or stomach and that she had no awareness of cognition whatsoever.

"Thinking" refers to cognition in its dictionary definition, but it is decidedly *not* necessarily used that way in DES self-descriptions, even by sophisticated subjects. My sense is that this is an unsurprising result of the way children learn language. Children observe adults say "I'm thinking . . ." and gradually realize that this utterance "thinking" must refer to whatever is going on in the adult out of direct sight of the child. Children then, on this understanding, use the utterance "thinking" to refer to whatever is most frequently going on inside them, out of sight of others. Those whose principal inner experience is inner speech will come to use "thinking" to refer to inner speech; those whose principal inner experience is emotion will come to use "thinking" to refer to emotion.

This exemplifies why experience sampling or any other method that honestly seeks to understand inner experience cannot blindly rely on the words people use to describe their experiences. This was B. F. Skinner's primary criticism of attempts to describe inner experience: that words used to describe private events receive impoverished differential reinforcement. (See guideline 9 in chapter 2. See also Hurlburt and Heavey 2001.) I see this as a surmountable difficulty, albeit one that has not been taken seriously enough by most other methods.

Thread: Loose language. Previous: box 2.1. Next: box 5.16.
Thread: Human similarity and difference. Previous: box 3.3. Next: box 4.7.

Box 4.2
Doubts about Melanie's "inner thought" voice

Russ: Melanie's general claim here about having a distinctive inner thought voice, different from her external speaking voice, that she hears "all of the time whenever I'm thinking" is undermined by later samples. My research has shown over and over that people's general claims about their inner experiences are often not entirely true, and sometimes dramatically false, even in relatively normal, quite sophisticated people. So I recommend being heavily skeptical about all general claims about one's own inner experience, including Melanie's. Usually, as here, I simply ignore such claims. But I don't hold the fact that Melanie has made such a claim (even if false) against her: Our culture has encouraged people to be sloppy in their observation of and claims about inner experience. This does not impair her ultimate credibility when it comes to reporting specific moments once she has mastered the method. Eventually, as sampling progresses, most people (as did Melanie, as we shall see) stop making general claims, because (I think) they see that many of their own general claims about themselves are not true.

Eric: So I wonder: Is Melanie accurately reporting this sample and just overgeneralizing? Or is she committed to a false general theory about herself that distorts even her specific report of this sample—despite the confidence and "convincing detail" with which she answers our questions about this voice?

Thread: Melanie's trustworthiness: Influence of generalizations. Next: box 4.10.
Thread: Inner speech and hearing. Next: box 4.4.
Thread: Retrospective and armchair generalizations. Next: box 4.11.

---

my own voice. It's my inner thought voice, so it's the one I recognize and hear all of the time whenever I'm thinking. But it *is* different from the voice with which I speak. [For some doubts about this claim, see box 4.2.]

Russ: Okay.

Melanie: And at the same time as that was going on, I was aware of this kind of glow inside my head that kind of says "That was a funny aspect of the thought or a humorous aspect of the thought." So I wasn't aware of the fact that I was smiling, but I *was* aware of the fact that I found that thought humorous. If that makes sense.

Russ: Okay. Well, I think it makes sense, but I'm not exactly sure that I understand it totally yet. So you're hearing something, which is a voice that's familiar to you but is not your voice. Is that what you're saying?

Melanie: Um hm.

Russ: And does this voice have vocal characteristics, like I've got sort of a deep voice, and . . .

Melanie: It's . . . the only way I can compare it is to my own voice. It's a little smoother; I'm a little more modulated.

Russ: You're more modulated?

Melanie: No. The voice inside my head is.

Russ: And by more modulated you mean more up and down, and more . . .

Melanie: Yeah.

Russ: . . . and more dynamic?

Melanie: Yes, exactly!

Russ: Okay.

Melanie: And I'd say it also has a lower pitch than my normal voice does.

Eric: Is it a female voice?

Melanie: Yes it is.

Eric: Does it have your regional dialect? It wouldn't have a Southern accent or something?

Melanie: No, it's mine. Well, it has the same dialect that I do.

Eric: So what makes you think it's not . . . why don't you say it's just your voice but smoother and more modulated?

Melanie: I suppose it could be. But at the same time, if it were my voice but smoother and more modulated, then it's not my voice anymore. I'm not sure.

Eric: Could you speak like that if you wanted to?

Melanie: No. I know I couldn't. I've tried.

Russ: The question of whether this is your voice or not in some absolute sense is probably unanswerable because it requires definitions that go beyond our ability. But whether it seems to be your voice or not, that is something that I think is answerable. So the question is, does this voice seem to you to be your voice?

Melanie [emphatically]:   No.

Russ: So it seems like it's a voice that is quite similar to your voice but is not your voice. Experientially it's a different thing from saying [affects a Southern drawl] "Well, I'm going to try and talk with a Southern accent, and I can talk with a Southern accent if I want to" . . .

Melanie: Right. I almost feel as though if I could take a tape recorder and record that voice and record my own, you'd be able to hear the difference between them.

Russ: Okay. And the differences are enough that it doesn't seem like your voice trying to talk . . .

Melanie: . . . in a different manner. Um hm.

Russ: Okay. So this voice is like a voice that is being heard rather than a voice that is being spoken? Is that correct?

Melanie: Yes.

Russ: So this is a different experience from your talking out loud?

Melanie: Yes.

Russ: This is more like you've recorded this and now you're playing it back. Experientially I mean.

Melanie: Right. Um hm.

Russ: There's no recording part . . .

Melanie: No [laughs].

Russ: . . . but it seems like this is coming towards you like a recording would come?

Melanie: Yes.

Russ: Okay. And at the moment of the beep, what exactly was this voice saying?

Melanie: It was saying . . . it was towards the end of the thought about the chair, thinking about who was to inherit it. It was right at the end of that phrase.

Russ: And can you tell me exactly what that phrase is?

Melanie: Well, the phrase was that I was thinking how funny it was that I just received this chair and here I was thinking of who was to inherit. What was going on right at the moment of the beep was "who was to inherit."

Russ: And right now you're saying that in the past tense: "how funny it *was*." Was the thought originally in the past tense?

Melanie: No, it was originally in the present.

Russ: So at the moment of the beep this voice was saying, quote, How funny it is . . .

Box 4.3
Present tense or past tense?

Russ: Melanie reported that her voice was saying "Who *was* to inherit" when the situation that Melanie was describing called more appropriately for her voice to be saying "Who *is* to inherit." This confusion of verb tense is a sign that Melanie is quite likely not reporting the actual phenomenon that she had experienced at the moment of the beep. This is Melanie's first beep, and we shouldn't hold her inaccuracy against her—she has probably heretofore in her life had no reason to describe with accuracy the characteristics of her inner experience. My questioning here is largely for training purposes: I'm not so much interested in what she says about this particular beep as in conveying to her that, on future sampling days, we will want to know what exactly was occurring at the precise moment of the beep.

Thread: Interview techniques. Previous: box 2.4. Next: box 4.6.

[On Melanie's use of tense, see box 4.3.]

Melanie: Um hm.

Russ: "... that I just got the chair, I just received the chair ..."

Melanie: "Just received."

Russ: "... and ..."

Melanie: "... and now I have to plan who is to inherit."

Russ: And the beep comes at the end of that ...

Melanie: Um hm.

Russ: ... somewhere in the "who is to inherit" portion?

Melanie: Yes.

Russ: Okay. And does that voice ... where is that voice? Is that in your head, or outside your head, or in the front of your head?

Melanie: It's in my head. If I have to give a specific location, I'd say it's somewhere here, right between my temples.

Russ: You don't have to give a location if it doesn't make sense to give a location.

Melanie: Um hm. No, it was there.

Russ: Okay. And then you said that there was something like a glow about this.

Eric: A little more on the voice before we get to the glow, actually. It takes a certain amount of time to say something like "How funny it is that I've just received this chair and I have to plan who is to inherit it." It takes a few seconds. Would you say that the voice was roughly the pace of the speaking voice, so that it took several seconds? Or was it going faster or slower? Or was it all kind of compressed into an instant?

Melanie: It was compressed. I wouldn't say it was compressed into an instant—it was a little bit longer. But it was significantly faster than it would normally take to say a sentence like that out loud.

Eric [rapidly]:   So would it be like someone who was a fast talker getting it out really fast like that? Or was it something that seemed a little different from how speech could be paced?

Melanie: I guess I'd have to say it was something a little different because when it was in my head it didn't feel compressed. It didn't feel rushed or jammed into a really small time like it sometimes does when someone speaks quickly.

[On the rate of inner speech, see box 4.4.]

Eric: Um hm.

Russ: So the experience of it is that it's going at a normal rate. But you think that actually if we put a stopwatch on it, it would have been faster.

Melanie: Yes.

Box 4.4
Fast or normally paced speech?

Russ: Most often, my subjects report that inner speech moves apparently at the same rate as external speech. However, it's also fairly common for subjects to report that inner speech actually transpires somewhat (or much) faster than external speech, even though it is experienced as occurring at the same rate as external speech. Thus, whereas the inner and external speech *rates* may be experienced to be the same, the inner and outer *durations* required to utter the same sentence may be experienced to be much different. This may seem impossible, but inner experience does not operate under the same constraints as outward behavior. [See also beep 6.4.]

Thread: Inner speech and hearing. Previous: box 4.2. Next: box 4.5.
Thread: Rules of inner reality. Next: box 4.6.

Russ: Okay. And what makes you think it would have been faster? If the experience is that it was going at a normal rate?

Melanie: Because there was a sense of speed to it. Not of rushedness and not of compression, but . . . I don't know. The best way I can think to describe it is it felt like it was racing through my head in a way.

[On whether Melanie shows promise as a subject, see box 4.5.]

Russ: More, Eric?

Eric: No, I think that's all right. Let's go to the glow.

Russ: Okay. So there was something you said that was a "glow." I didn't quite understand what you meant by that.

Melanie: I couldn't feel myself smiling. I wasn't aware of myself smiling, but after the beep I was, you know, "Oh! I'm smiling right now." But when that thought was going through my head there was this kind of rosy yellow glow in my head just as those words were going through that kind of reflected the humor I felt in that sentence.

Russ: Now when you say "rosy," "yellow," and "glow," do you mean that there was something rosy-yellow—some experience of rosy yellow? Or do you mean that as sort of a metaphor?

Melanie: I think a bit of both. There *was* color involved. That's the best way I can describe it. It was pale color—it wasn't vibrant and rich and bright—but there was a hint of color, almost like wrapped up with the words.

Russ: And where was this color, if that question makes sense?

Melanie: All over. It was in my head, but it felt more all over as opposed to the distinct location of where the words were.

Russ: And is this color like a wash of color, or . . .

Melanie: Yes.

Russ: So it's not like there's some specific place where there's a rosy yellow color?

Melanie: No, it's all over.

Russ: And is this a uniform color, like rosy yellow all over, or is it rosy here and yellow there?

Melanie: It's uniform.

Russ: Okay. And is this rosy yellow like a light that creates rosy yellow luminance? Or is it rosy yellow like a picture has . . .

Box 4.5
Evidence that Melanie is careful. The pace of inner speech, continued.

Russ: This exchange is the kind that leads me to believe that Melanie will learn to be a good subject. First, she's clearly trying to be careful, correcting and modifying herself. Second, she's adept at keeping track of close distinctions (here between rushedness and compression, for example). Third, she's willing to stop at "I don't know" and is comfortable with qualifications such as "the best way I can think to describe it is . . . ," which indicates that she is not likely to go too far. In saying this, I don't mean to imply that Melanie is, or will be, an *unusually* good subject; in my experience, most subjects are good subjects. But Melanie is more intelligent than my average subject, and so is likely to be more nuanced.

Eric: You rightly point out that the distinction between rushedness and compression is a close one; and now I wonder whether other subjects would tend to be as careful as Melanie in making that distinction. In my own earlier sampling, in fact, I believe I reported that my inner speech was paced at roughly the same rate as my external speech, but now I find myself wondering if I was correct in that observation. Could it be that inner speech is, for most people, temporally compressed, but only a minority of your subjects notice that fact because it does not seem rushed?

   Just now, I confess, I was walking across campus deliberately producing inner speech and attempting to observe its pace as I did so. I found myself getting tangled up, feeling like I often produced the speech twice, once in forming the intention to produce a specific instance of inner speech and then again in carrying out that intention (as though I didn't realize the intention was already executed in the forming of it). I also found myself unsure of the pacing especially of the first of these two acts of inner speech—indeed, unsure even of whether the first was in fact an act of inner speech at all. I suppose, Russ, that you will say that I would do better to explore these issues with a beeper, that the deliberate self-observation and the intentional formation of inner speech hopelessly corrupts the act I'd like to observe. Maybe so, but the difficulty is still striking.

Russ: You characterize my reaction to your experiment quite precisely. I think you could in large measure become untangled if you used a proper method (such as a beeper). I applaud you for noticing the striking difficulty of informal or armchair introspection, but I hope that you don't hold that strikingness against *all* introspective attempts (including those that are designed to reduce or eliminate precisely that difficulty).

Thread: Melanie's trustworthiness: Attunement to distinctions. Next: box 6.4.
Thread: Inner speech and hearing. Previous: box 4.4. Next: box 4.11.

Melanie: I'd say it's a luminance.

Russ: So there's some kind of illumination . . .

Melanie: Yes.

Russ: . . . that seems like it's rosy yellow colored in your experience . . .

Melanie: Yes, exactly.

Russ: . . . in a visual way. And I'm gathering that you think or know or something—and I'm trying to clarify this—that this rosy yellowness is associated with the humorous aspect of it?

Melanie: It was a feeling that was very familiar to me, or I guess, the sight, you could say, of this color that is really familiar to me and is one that I commonly associate with laughing at a joke or something that involves humor.

Russ: So the experience of this rosy yellow is not unusual—it's part of Melanie being Melanie. When something funny happens she turns rosy yellow inside.

Melanie: Yes. [laughs] Exactly.

Eric: I don't know whether you can answer this or not, whether you remember well enough, but how would it interact with your visual experience? Would it seem as though this paper . . . I assume the paper you're looking at is probably white.

Melanie: It was parchment colored.

Eric: Ah. So would it have discolored the paper visually in some way, or . . .

Melanie: No. It wasn't as though I saw through my eyes at all. It felt very much in my head as opposed to something that was out in front of me.

Eric: So when you say it was all over, it's not kind of like all over your visual field, or something like that . . .

Melanie: I wasn't wrapped up in this color, no. I mean it was like it was all over my brain or thought field, if that helps.

Russ: If you'd been here when she said it was all over, she held both hands up in the vicinity of her head near her temples, rocking them back and forth as if she was trying to say "all over inside my head."

Eric: [laughs] Um hm.

Melanie: But there wasn't any outward manifestation of it.

Eric: So when you look at something, when you look out at the world, there's only a certain range of degrees of arc that you can see, right? You can see forward, say, 120 degrees of arc, maybe a bit more. You can't really see anything too high up or too low down or too much to the side or behind you. So is that where the glow is? In that kind of non-visual area, then, which would include your head, say? Or is that not the way to think about it?

Russ: Let me ask a different question if I can, here, because that's the kind of question that I wouldn't ask. I wouldn't ask that question because it has, too close to the surface for my taste, the intrusion of reality. If I were interested in that question I would ask it sort of like this: When you say this rosiness is inside your head and sort of throughout your head, do you mean you're looking sort of forward at it, or up at it, or down at it, or backwards at it, or all of the above, or . . .

[On why Russ objected to Eric's question, see box 4.6.]

Melanie: Neither. It's just mainly . . . I'm trying to think of the best way to describe it. It feels like, in my head, I guess you could say, is this other world and I'm just looking straight at it. I can see—it's a 360-degree vision. I can see above me, below me, behind me, in front of me, through the sides. It's all over.

Russ: So the 120-degree rule doesn't apply in this . . .

Box 4.6
Bracketing the known characteristics of the outside world

Russ: I agree with your account of the characteristics of real perception here, Eric. But I feel that the comparison you suggest might lead Melanie to think that her inner visual experience must be in that same 120-degree field—or, alternatively, that it must be outside it. It is crucial to be as neutral as possible on such matters during the interview, since inner processes do not necessarily abide by the same rules as outer processes— as we have seen already in the case of the pace of inner speech.

As the subsequent conversation shows, Melanie doesn't seem to have been overly influenced in this way by Eric's question.

Thread: Bracketing presuppositions. Previous: box 3.3. Next: box 4.10.
Thread: Interview techniques. Previous: box 4.3. Next: box 4.15.
Thread: Rules of inner reality. Previous: box 4.4. Next: box 4.13.

Melanie: No. It's not like the visual field. It's almost like looking from beneath, and looking up—and being able to see everything—kind of like in a planetarium.

Russ: So it seems more above you than below you, is that right, the rosy yellow?

Melanie: No, because it seems all around me. It's really like a 360-degree view—I can just see it everywhere.

Russ: So it's 360 in three dimensions. It's 360 in front and in back and 360 above and below?

Melanie: Yes.

[On color in emotional experience, see box 4.7.]

   [Here we have excised a brief discussion of the issue discussed in box 4.6; as always, the excised text can be found at http://mitpress.mit.edu/ inner_experience.]

Russ: So is there anything else going on at this particular moment? You're seeing the white parchmenty paper . . .

Melanie: Um hm.

Russ: And does that seem to be in your awareness, or is it . . .

Melanie: No it's not. I'm not aware of how my body is positioned or of what I'm holding. It's very much just in my head.

Russ: You you're paying much more attention to your thought process here, about "isn't it strange . . . ?" "isn't it funny?" You're obviously seeing the parchment, because that's what started this process, but it's not in your awareness.

Melanie: Yes, exactly.

Russ: Okay. Have you got further questions about that, Eric?

Eric: Right. Yeah. I don't know how fruitful it is to push on that, so . . .

Russ: She looks pretty confident, if you were here watching her.

Eric: Right. Well, there is a debate about whether there are things you experience that are peripheral. So some people think that when you're visually attending to something but there's, say, a jackhammer in the background, you may not be paying any attention to the jackhammer, but the jackhammer is part of your experience anyway. Or if you're sitting in a chair, in the periphery of your experience there's some kind of a feeling of the chair on your back and on your bottom. So, do you

Box 4.7
Color in emotional experience

Eric: Not many philosophers or introspective psychologists have described emotional phenomenology as literally involving color. (I do take this to be, in some broad sense, a report of an emotion.) Melanie could, of course, be unusual in this respect, as synaesthetes are unusual, who experience color when they see numbers or hear musical tones; or philosophers and introspective psychologists could have missed a common aspect of emotional experience. However, as many people seem to find emotional experience hard to describe (as Melanie does in later samples), and we consequently reach for metaphors, I think it is possible here that Melanie is being taken in by her own metaphor.

Russ: I agree that the literature has overlooked the experience of color along with emotion. I am quite confident on the basis of my own work and that of my colleagues that *some* people literally experience color along with emotion. My subjects have (I think credibly) reported "seeing red" when angry, "being blue" when depressed, and "seeing rose-colored hues" when optimistic; furthermore, my careful questioning leads me to conclude that these phrases were meant to be straightforward descriptions of robust visual phenomena (they can specify the precise color of blue, for example), not mere metaphors. I don't think we should be more skeptical of this than of any other of Melanie's claims. There are two mistakes that could be made: to be taken in by a metaphor and understand it as a claim of seeing rosy when it's not there; and to presume incorrectly that Melanie has been taken in by a metaphor and therefore fail to understand and/or credit her straightforward descriptions.

Eric: One piece of evidence that might support or undermine your view about the literalness of such phrases as "seeing red" when you're angry would be evidence from very different cultures. Do speakers of non-European languages say similar things? An informal poll of my acquaintances suggests that such stock phrases are quite different across cultures. (Cross-cultural research suggests there may be some consistency in the association of chips of color with emotion terms, but hue may be less relevant than brightness and saturation. See D'Andrade and Egan 1974; Johnson, Johnson, and Baksh 1986.)

Russ: I, too, would find such cross-cultural studies interesting, but there is no reason to be confident, I think, that the experience of anger is the same across cultures. For example, the British, known for their restraint, might have very different experience of anger than do the Italians, known for their expressivity. Thus the mere fact that their descriptions of anger might differ would not mean that their descriptions are merely metaphors. So what would be more interesting to me would be careful, moment-by-moment observations by people whose ability to bracket presuppositions I trust. The more different cultures, the better.

> **Box 4.7**
> (continued)
>
> Eric: And if under such conditions only English speakers (or English and German speakers) claimed literally to see red when they were angry, you'd willingly embrace the view that anger experiences literally differ in coloration between cultures?
> Russ: I would.
>
> Thread: Melanie's trustworthiness: Unusual claims. Next: box 4.11.
> Thread: Emotion. Next: box 5.13.
> Thread: Human similarity and difference. Previous: box 4.1. Next: box 4.18.
> Thread: Influence of metaphors. Next: box 5.2.

have a sense for this beep whether there were these sorts of peripheral, marginal experiences? Or was it pretty much the things that you were focusing on that you have reported so far, and that's it?

Melanie: I think it primarily was just that I was focusing on what I've already said.

Eric: Um hm.

Melanie: It wasn't until after the beep that I became much more aware of the fact that, Oh I am sitting with the my legs tucked underneath me, and I have this smile on my face, and I am holding this piece of paper. That didn't come until after the beep kind of compelled me to examine what I'm doing.

[Here we have excised a brief discussion of the "periphery of experience." See box 4.8.]

Russ: So, anything else in this beep other than that?

Melanie: I think that was it.

[On whether we should believe Melanie's report, see box 4.9.]

Beep 1.2

Melanie: Okay. I was walking kind of aimlessly between the kitchen and the dining room waiting for the shower to stop running and my boyfriend to get out so I could finish making dinner. The beep caught me just as I was going in from the hallway that comes from the living room

Box 4.8
The periphery of experience

Eric: John Searle (1992) and others have argued that conscious experience is rich, in the sense that although *attention* may be limited to one or a few topics at a time, conscious experience is not. On this view, the fact that Melanie's eyes were open is strong evidence that she was indeed having visual experience at the time, despite the fact that she denies it now (in a qualified, hedging way). Likewise, on this view, we all generally have, at the periphery of experience, sensations like that of the pressure of the chair against one's back, the noise of a distant jackhammer, background feelings of anxiety, slight feelings of hunger, etc., all at once.

Russ: Most of my subjects are quite clear that there is in their experience at the moment of the beep only one or a small number of things. The jackhammers and chairs are part of my skilled navigation through the world, and I pay enough attention to them as necessary not to run into the jackhammer or fall off the chair. But that doesn't mean I have them as part of my awareness or experience at all times that they are in my presence. In particular, many of my subjects quite persuasively deny visual experience despite the fact that their eyes are open, saying things like "My eyeballs were aimed at the book I was holding, but I wasn't paying attention to it. I was entirely focused on the image I was having."

Eric: Perhaps such experiences are swiftly forgotten if they are not the object of immediate attention after the beep. What would have happened if Melanie's task had been, upon hearing the beep, simply to report whether she had visual experience at that moment or not? I have been inspired by our conversations to try beeping a few subjects with that question deliberately posed to them in advance. My tentative finding is that they report visual experience in the vast majority of cases in which their eyes are open. (I describe this experiment in more detail in section 10.3.)

Russ: I fear you make more of Melanie's statement than she intended. I don't think she intended to say that she had *absolutely no* experience of the papers (and if she did mean that, I wouldn't believe her because I don't think she can know that). She meant to say that she wasn't really paying attention to the papers, she was involved in the thought process. She was at that moment indifferent to the papers. Maybe a visual experience of the papers existed in some way; maybe no visual experience of the papers existed. The theoretical question about the existence of visual experience at that moment was not what she was talking about.

I suspect that it is impossible to provide an exhaustively complete description of experience. The aim of DES is not to be exhaustive but to be accurate about as much of experience as possible. Thus I don't know whether Melanie had visual experience of the paper at the moment of beep 1.1. If we become overly concerned about the fine details at the edge of

---

Box 4.8
(continued)

experience, I think we undermine the ability to be faithful to what we can access. [For more on the consequences of pressing too hard on details, see box 5.14 and subsection 11.2.1.]

Eric: Okay, but I think what you've just said sounds much different from your first comments in this box! Here, as elsewhere, I think you waver between restraint when pushed (e.g., subsection 11.2.1) and a stronger denial of the rich view when you're not on guard (e.g., box 2.4, subsections 2.3.1.6 and 2.3.1.7).

Thread: Melanie's trustworthiness: Memory. Next: box 5.4.
Thread: Richness. Previous: box 3.4. Next: box 6.2.
Thread: Sensory Experience. Previous: box 3.4. Next: box 4.18.

Box 4.9
Should we believe Melanie's report of her first sample?

Eric: I have raised some concerns about Melanie's report in boxes 4.2, 4.7, and 4.8, but I am tentatively willing to accept that Melanie had a thought with something like the content she describes, accompanied by amusement, somewhere in the temporal vicinity of the beep. I'm also willing to accept Melanie's reports about the other samples today at roughly the same level of generality. (But see also box 4.13.) The beeping task does not strike me as so hopeless and impossible that Melanie would be forced to pure invention.

That, at least, is the level of skepticism I personally feel—which is not to say that more skepticism, or less, might also be sensible and appropriate.

Russ: I would remind us that this is Melanie's first sample on her first sampling day, and much of what she said about her experience may well be untrue or misleading. That should not be held against Melanie or the method; first-day reports often reflect the presuppositions subjects hold about inner experience and the fact that they have never before been asked to describe their experience with substantial care or instructed how to bracket their presuppositions.

Thread: Melanie's trustworthiness: General. Next: box 5.7.

into the kitchen. Right before the beep happened, I was thinking—and it was a kind of inner speech thought—of how you can think you're really busy and doing something and you can block time out of your day to do something but there's still little empty spaces of time that happen even while you think you're really busy.

Russ: And when you say that's "right before the beep," do you mean that that's actually *before* the beep or is that *at the moment of the beep* as I've defined it (the last undisturbed moment before the beep)?

[On whether we miss the dynamics of experience by focusing on a single moment, see box 4.10.]

Box 4.10
Focusing on a single moment and the dynamics of experience

Eric: While the precise focus on a single moment seems in many ways desirable, Russ, for reasons you describe in chapter 2, I wonder also if something is lost—some sense of the dynamics of experience as it evolves over time. Could experiences sometimes be integrally connected with each other over time in such a way as to require, for their accurate description, a relatively extended temporal story? If so, your resolutely narrow temporal focus may lead the distortion or minimizing of the dynamic, evolving flow of experience—don't you think?

Russ: I agree that it's desirable to capture flow or dynamics, but that desirability is trumped, I think, by the desirability of using randomly selected time slices to aid in the bracketing of presuppositions. The random beep says, in effect, "Let's discuss this particular instant, not because Melanie or Russ or Eric thinks this instant is important or significant or interesting, but merely because it was selected by a neutral, dispassionate, random trigger." If we allow Melanie to stray from the moment to describe the flow of experience, her description would necessarily involve a series of instants that *she* (not some random trigger) selected because they seem to cohere with the flow; she would exclude other nearby instants. That selection/exclusion process would be based on Melanie's presuppositional self-understanding of her own conscious flow, and I, like Nisbett and Wilson (1977), don't think people's understanding of such processes can be trusted.

Describing the single last undisturbed experience before the beep is as clean as you can get; any departure from the moment of the beep is shrouded in the murk of presuppositional self-theory.

Thread: Bracketing presuppositions. Previous: box 4.6. Next: box 5.7.
Thread: Limits of DES. Next: box 5.14.

Melanie: It's at the moment of the beep.

Russ: Okay. That again is sort of a long phrase: "you can think you're really busy" and . . .

Melanie: "You can think you're really busy but even during those busy times there are periods of empty time."

Russ: And where does the beep come?

Melanie: Again, right toward the end, about "empty time."

Russ: And is that an exact quote, do you think?

Melanie: Yes.

Russ: Okay. And this, you said, was more like *speaking*, as distinct from the last one, which was more like *hearing*. Is that right?

Melanie: Yes.

Russ: And is this more like in your voice as opposed to . . .

Melanie: Yeah. It was much more myself saying it.

Russ: And when you say it's "much more myself saying it," do you mean it *was* myself saying it?

Melanie: Not quite. It was more of a hybrid between the voice I was hearing in the last one and my own voice. It was again in that kind of accelerated manner as the last one was, where it wasn't compressed and didn't feel rushed, but I think had anybody been timing that thought going through my mind it would have gone significantly faster than had it been actually spoken.

Russ: Okay. And the speaking portion of it: Is the sensation exactly like you are speaking? Or is it somehow different from when you're speaking out loud?

Melanie: Well, it's different because my mouth's not moving. But I'd say I hear it in the same way. For instance, that thought was more located between my ears and in a way down my throat like where your vocal cords are than the earlier one was. But it was different in that I couldn't feel my throat working, and there was no vibration going around in my skull, and I couldn't feel my mouth moving.

Russ: Right. And when you're talking out loud do you generally feel those things?

Melanie: Yes.

Russ: Sort of explicitly? So when we're talking right now you're sort of aware of the vibrations . . .

Melanie: Um hm. Yes.

Russs: . . . and that is true whenever you talk out loud? That you're aware of the . . .

Melanie: Not always, but often. Quite often.

Russ: So let me make sure I understand this. So while you're talking about whatever it is that you're talking about, there is a part of your awareness that is paying attention to the kinesthetics and the vibromechanics or whatever it is.

Melanie: Yes. But not always. Usually if I get very wrapped up in what I'm saying or really excited about something or if I feel really, really comfortable with the person I'm talking to and almost let myself go a little bit and feel a little bit free in speaking with someone, then I'm not as aware of it. But the times when I'm a little bit tenser and a little more careful about what I say, then I tend to notice the way I talk as well. The way my vocal cords work and the way my voice sounds in my own ears.

Russ: And when you say you notice this, there are other things going on too, your lungs are pumping and whatever . . . are you aware of that?

Melanie: No, I'm not as aware of that. I'm not aware of that at all.

Russ: Okay. So what you're aware of is in your neck and the bottom of your chin . . .

Melanie: Down to the jaw, yes.

Russ: Okay. [For skepticism about this aspect of Melanie's report, see box 4.11.] So at the moment of this particular beep, you have an awareness that's sort of in that region, but it doesn't include the usual vibration stuff.

Melanie: Yes, exactly.

[Here we have excised a brief exchange in which Melanie asserts again that the voice was more spoken than heard.]

Russ: And is there anything else in your awareness at that moment?

Melanie: During this beep I was significantly more aware of where I was and what I was doing. I had just stopped right before coming into the kitchen, and right in front of me I could see the microwave and the stove. And I was aware that I was looking at them.

Russ: So you were seeing in your awareness the microwave and the stove.

Melanie: Yes.

Box 4.11
Melanie's awareness of the mechanical aspects of speech #1

Russ: Melanie's description of herself as typically paying attention to the mechanical/muscular/sensory aspects of her external speech is worthy of some skepticism, for three reasons. First, it is a generalization about her own typical behavior and experience, and as we saw in chapter 2, I am highly skeptical of all such general characterizations. (I asked here about her general speaking-aloud characteristics not because I would believe her general answer but to clarify what she was saying about the moment.)

Second, very few of my subjects report attending to the kinesthetic or vibromechanical characteristics of their speaking. This doesn't imply that she is mistaken, but it should alert us that she may have an unusual way of speaking, an unusual way of experiencing speaking, or an unusual way of reporting that we should bear in mind in our questioning.

Third, we need to keep in mind that this is Melanie's first sampling day, and all first-day reports should be treated with extra skepticism. Imprecision when one is learning the task is not unusual.

Eric: I wonder whether her claims here arise from her desire to draw a contrast between inner speech and external speech. She knows there is a contrast; this seems a plausible place to locate it; she leaps to the generalization and now finds herself committed to it, perhaps?

Thread: Melanie's trustworthiness: Influence of generalizations. Previous: box 4.2. Next: box 4.14.
Thread: Melanie's trustworthiness: Unusual claims. Previous: box 4.7. Next: box 4.14.
Thread: Inner speech and hearing. Previous: box 4.5. Next: box 5.7.
Thread: Retrospective and armchair generalizations. Previous: box 4.2. Next: box 5.6.
Thread: Self-awareness: Melanie's unusual. Next: box 4.14.

Russ: And so this is different from the previous beep?

Melanie: Yes.

Russ: In the previous beep your eyes were aimed at the paper but you weren't actually in your awareness seeing it.

Melanie: Right.

Russ: Here your eyes are aimed at the microwave and the stove and you were seeing them in your awareness as well?

Melanie: Yes.

Eric: I think it might be useful to draw a distinction between being aware *of* the microwave and stove visually and being aware that you're *looking* at the microwave and the stove. Does that distinction make sense? And if so, is it more one or the other of those? [For Eric's complaints about Russ's use of the word "awareness" here and elsewhere, see box 8.6.]

Russ: How about this? Awareness of the stove: the attention is aimed at the stove. Awareness of looking at the stove: the attention is aimed at yourself doing the looking?

Eric: Yeah.

Melanie: Okay. Then I'd say it's the former, not the latter.

Russ: You're seeing the stove.

Melanie: Yes.

Russ: There is a philosophical position out there that says if you have consciousness of the stove you also have to have consciousness of yourself seeing the stove.

[On philosophical theories of self-awareness in perception, see box 4.12.]

Melanie: Correct.

Eric: Right.

Russ: And you're saying as far as you know that's not in your awareness.

Melanie: No.

Russ [to Eric]: Which is the way most my subjects say it is, by the way.

Eric: Okay.

Russ: And so does that exhaust your awareness, the fact of the thinking and the seeing of the stove and the microwave?

Melanie: Yes. After the beep happened I was aware of the fact that I had my hands behind my back and I was just about to step onto a linoleum floor from a carpeted floor. But I wasn't thinking of any of that at the moment of the beep.

Beep 1.3

Melanie: My boyfriend and I were having dinner. We were having a discussion about this country house that his family has. Right at the moment of the beep I just finished saying the sentence "I remember the shed now," because we were talking about how someone was going to go and add on the second story to the shed that's on this property. I'd

> Box 4.12
> Self-awareness in perception
>
> Eric: As Russ remarks, some philosophers (including Descartes and Locke, according to many interpreters, and some advocates of "sense-data" theories in the early twentieth century) think that one cannot be directly aware of (i.e., know in some unmediated way) objects in the external world. What you know directly is always just yourself and your own consciousness; we reach judgments about the outside world on the basis of a more immediate and primary knowledge of our experiences.
>
> While I am not sympathetic with such views (see especially the conclusion of section 3.2), this issue is not what I meant to be asking Melanie about, and I don't think Melanie's report here really bears on it. If you are *always* attuned in some way to your sensory experiences, then you might, and probably should, interpret my question as a question about whether you are *especially* aware of them—that is, attentive to them in some additional or more robust way.
>
> Russ: My line of questioning was also not aimed at the philosophical position, but was designed to try to further our understanding of Melanie's earlier (unusual) self-consciousness of her facial musculature while talking. There, she had said that she was both talking and, separately, aware of the (kinesthetic) features of that talking. Here, I wanted to clarify whether she was both seeing and, separately, aware of that seeing. She said that she was not. This is groundwork for any future claims that she might make that involve a separate observer, in the sense that we are getting practice at talking about what might and might not count as a separate experience for Melanie. If, at some later beep, she maintains that she has a separate observer, we will have a few "like this" and a few "not like that" experiences to compare.
>
> Thread: Self-Awareness: General. Next: box 6.1.

forgotten what he was talking about, and then he reminded me and I said "Oh, I remember the shed now." And right as I finished speaking the beep came.

Russ: So you're saying "Oh, I remember the shed now" aloud?

Melanie: Yes.

Russ: And the beep comes near the end of that phrase?

Melanie: No, right at the end of it.

Russ: Right at the end of it.

Melanie: Yes.

Russ: "Oh, I remember the shed now" *beep*.

[On the timing of the beep, see box 4.13.]

Melanie: Yes.

Russ: And in your awareness is . . .

Melanie: In my awareness is that I can feel my mouth close. And then also I have a mental image of the structure we're talking about, of the shed.

Russ: And when you say "I can feel my mouth close," that's in your awareness?

Melanie: Um hm.

Russ: And is that part of the same kind of deal we were talking about a minute ago . . .

Melanie: Yes.

Russ: . . . with the awareness of the speaking act?

Melanie: Exactly.

[On Melanie's awareness of her speaking, see box 4.14. On the subject's notes during DES, see box 4.15.]

Russ: So you had been aware of the vocal cords and whatever, but now we're right at the end and the vibrations have stopped and the mouth is closing. That's where we are?

Melanie: Um hm.

Russ: Okay. And at the same time you also have an image of the shed.

Melanie: Right, as if you've opened the front door and you're standing just inside. I've only seen this building once, and I'm just remembering it from the view I saw that day.

Russ: And in your image, whether or not it's the same as anything that actually exists on the planet, what do you see in the image?

Melanie: It's a very bright day, so it's pretty dark inside, and there are four walls. [See box 4.16.] The wall to my right has a small window in it. The wall to my left has a couple posts on it for like hanging up jackets or something like that, and then . . .

Russ: And there are jackets on them or just . . .

Melanie: Yeah.

Russ: . . . in your image?

Box 4.13
The timing of the beep

Eric: We have three samples in a row where the beep comes right at the end of a sentence. That seems too coincidental. Why doesn't the beep sometimes catch her in the middle of a sentence? Perhaps she is not accurate in locating when, in the flow of her experience, the beep occurs.

In our conversation before the first sample, Melanie had expressed a desire to find interesting thoughts during the sampling (as did I when you sampled me). I wonder whether, without being aware of it, Melanie is doing something like fishing around for the nearest interesting thought or experience in rough temporal vicinity of the beep.

Russ: Melanie's task is to report experience at the time she *hears* the beep, not at the time of the *actual* beep, and those two times may be quite discrepant. Furthermore, that discrepancy is probably *not* due to the particular nature of the DES task, because similar discrepancies occur in simple tasks. For example, Fodor, Bever, and Garrett (1974) reviewed research where subjects listened to tape-recorded sentences that had clicks embedded; subjects were simply to report where the click was located in the sentence. These subjects made substantial errors, with a strong tendency to relocate clicks to natural breaks in the sentence.

Similarly, many DES subjects, including Melanie, experience the beeps as occurring at natural breaks in their inner or external speech. (This is more frequent on the first sampling day; some subjects, with practice, seem to become more able to locate the precise moment that the beep occurred during speaking.) I don't think this temporal inconsistency damns the method. If I'm involved in a conversation, I think it likely that my *experience* of the conversation does not track the actual conversation in perfect synchrony. Sometimes I may find a part of the conversation difficult and my auditory experience may lag behind as I parse it, then catch up in a subsequent pause. And there's no reason why I'd have to recognize that I'd lagged behind.

While the DES task is to describe, not to explain, it seems reasonable to suppose that due to the limited processing capacity of the cognitive system (whatever that is), generally one finishes one micro-task before undertaking the next. It takes several fractions of a second to recognize the beep and launch the sampling intention, and perhaps for some subjects, at least some of the time, if a beep comes during speech, the speech is completed before the beep is experienced and the sampling intention is launched.

Thread: Melanie's trustworthiness: Details. Next: box 5.14.
Thread: Rules of inner reality. Previous: box 4.6. Next: box 4.16.

Box 4.14
Melanie's awareness of the mechanical aspects of speech #2

Russ: In box 4.11, I commented that it was unusual for my subjects to say they are noticing the mechanical aspects of their speech, as when Melanie said she felt her mouth close. As I explain in chapter 2, my methodology requires viewing all reports skeptically; this is especially true the first day. Melanie's description of her speaking phenomena here deserves an additional dose of skepticism because what Melanie says about her sample accords with the just-a-moment-ago general account. [See box 4.11.] Perhaps she has been "captured" by what she herself said about her general speaking phenomena, so that now she is describing a sample just to be consistent with what she said earlier. We should suspend judgment and communicate to Melanie that saying things inconsistent with previous statements is okay. Note that skepticism means suspending judgment, not disbelief. In fact, I came to believe, on the basis of the entire sampling with Melanie, that it's likely that this report was accurate. [See box 8.9.]

Eric: In a separate conversation some time after these interviews, Melanie said that she did not record on her notepad the experience of feeling her mouth close. This, I think, should amplify our concern that the purported mouth-closing feeling is a postulation she is led to by her earlier remarks. While I share your sense, Russ, that Melanie's interview reports should generally trump her written notes, the written notes might be useful for clues on matters such as this. I might pay more attention to them than you are inclined to. [Unfortunately, Melanie's original notes are not available; see box 4.15.]

Thread: Melanie's trustworthiness: Influence of generalizations. Previous: box 4.11. Next: box 4.18.
Thread: Melanie's trustworthiness: Unusual claims. Previous: box 4.11. Next: box 8.9.
Thread: Self-Awareness: Melanie's unusual. Previous: box 4.11. Next: box 6.4.

Melanie: Yes, there's one jacket. And then there's directly in front of me—half of it is a wall and the other half is a cutout for a bathroom but the bathroom's not installed yet, and against the wall there is a bench. And it's all in light wood, like oak.

Russ: That's quite a few details. Are you seeing all those details?

Melanie: Yes.

Russ: And at the moment of the beep are you seeing all of them sort of equally or are you paying more attention to part of them?

Box 4.15
On the subject's notes during DES

Russ: In box 4.14, Eric lamented that it was unfortunate that we did not have access to Melanie's notes. I don't share that lament, because I don't generally consider what a DES participant jots down in the sampling notebook to be very important data.

I regard Melanie's jottings in her notebook merely as tools to the end of getting the most accurate possible view of her inner experience at the moment of the beep. These jottings are often accurate but occasionally are distorted or incorrect. Either way, they are merely steps in the process, much like a writer's outlines and drafts, which are used, reacted to, and eventually discarded.

And just as we wouldn't judge a finished scientific paper on the merits of its preliminary outlines and drafts, so also we shouldn't judge Melanie's reports on the basis of her notebook jottings. We should give Melanie space to amplify, reject, or otherwise correct what she has written. It is simply not possible to expect that Melanie will be able accurately to portray all the features of an experience in words that come to her shortly after the beep. Nor would we wish her to become self-conscious about her notes, to worry about our potential reactions to the particular words she might jot. The jottings are notes from Melanie to herself, and she should be free to use them in whatever way she thinks will help her most accurately convey her experience to us during the interview.

Thread: Interview techniques. Previous: box 4.6. Next: box 4.17.

Melanie: It's all equal. It's a memory just like when you take a snapshot. It's a snapshot memory of the first time that I saw the shed, or the inside of it.

Russ: And so when you say it's a snapshot do you mean it has a border around it like a snapshot has or. . . ?

[For Russ's discussion of leading the witness, see box 4.17.]

Melanie: No, but it's still. There's nothing moving. It's a snapshot in that it's one moment out of time.

Russ: Okay.

Melanie: And I only stood there for a couple of seconds and then someone came up next to me and I walked inside and everything like that. But it's just that first moment when the door was opened as I was looking inside.

Box 4.16
Imagery violating the rules of visual perspective?

Eric: If what Melanie seems to be saying here is literally true of her experience—that her image was as if she was standing just inside the shed and also that the image contains four walls—then this bit of imagery violates the ordinary rules of visual perspective. Unfortunately, we did not press on this point during the interviews. It's hard to know how Melanie would have reacted if pressed, though later she seems to contradict that interpretation of her claim here by saying of the image "It's as though it's in that 120-degree visual field."

I see no reason to suppose that the experience of visual imagery *has* to obey the laws of visual perspective, though most psychologists seem to assume it does (see, e.g., Shepard and Metzler 1971; Kosslyn 1980), and that is the most common report among people I've spoken to about such matters.

Francis Galton, in his classic (1880, 1907) survey of imagery experience, found that a small percentage of respondents claimed to be able to imagine things from multiple angles at once. Jorge Luis Borges also describes such a case in a fictional story about a man obsessed with a coin called "the Zahir": "There was a time when I could visualize the obverse, and then the reverse. Now I see them simultaneously. This is not as though the Zahir were crystal, because it is not a matter of one face being superimposed upon another; rather, it is as though my eyesight were spherical, with the Zahir in the center." (Borges 1962, p. 163)

Russ: It is not uncommon for DES subjects to report images that violate the rules of external perspective: seeing an image of the living room beyond the dining room even though in actuality there is a wall separating the two; seeing an image of a person seated in a chair where the chair is seen from the side and the person from the front; and so on.

Thread: Rules of inner reality. Previous: box 4.13. Next: box 9.8.
Thread: Visual imagery: Structure. Next: box 5.2.

Russ: And so does this seeing then seem like the same kind of seeing that happened back whenever that was, some number of days or weeks ago or . . .

Melanie: Yes.

Russ: So it's like you're looking the same as you had been looking then?

Melanie: Um hm. Exactly.

Russ: And as we're talking about it now, do you seem to be doing the same thing again?

Box 4.17
Leading the witness

Russ: In box 4.13 we discussed the possibility that Melanie gets "captured" by what she has said or by what we have said. It's difficult if not impossible to ask questions that are perfectly non-leading, so the next best strategy is to ask questions that lead mildly in many different directions, some likely and some not. Here I ask a mildly leading question in a direction where I expect that the answer is likely to be "No," because it is rare that subjects report edges or borders to images. Melanie easily denies this, raising her credibility in my view.

Thread: Melanie's trustworthiness: Interview pressures. Next: box 5.1.
Thread: Interview techniques. Previous: box 4.15. Next: box 4.19.

Melanie: Yeah. The mental image that I have is the exact same as it was last night.

Russ: And is this image clear, like . . .

Melanie: Yeah, it is.

Russ: As clear, more clear, not quite as clear as it was the first time you saw it?

Melanie: Probably not quite as clear. Just because time has passed and I probably don't remember it 100 percent accurately . . .

Russ: Okay.

Melanie: . . . although it may be actually accurate. I don't know. But . . .

Russ: And here I'm not asking you actually to speculate about whether it's actually as clear as it was back then, because that would require you to have a veridical memory of the way it was back then, which I don't think you can do. The question is, does it seem crystal clear? In the same sense . . .

Melanie: Yes.

Russ: . . . that it seems crystal clear. . . . Well, let me ask you this. When you see things in general, do they seem crystal clear?

Melanie: Yes.

Russ: Okay, then. When you were looking at this image at 6 o'clock or whenever it was last night, did it seem like you were looking at this shed in a crystal-clear way?

Melanie: Yes.

Russ: And did the looking seem to be as detailed? Was this a very visually richly detailed thing with posts and windows and benches and the like?

Melanie: Yes.

Russ: And so there are three things going on. There's the speaking aloud, there's the awareness of the end of the musculature (the mouth closing at the end of the speaking aloud), and there's the image of the shed.

Melanie: [nods Yes]

Russ: Is there anything else in your awareness?

Melanie: No, that's it.

Eric: So you're saying that there's not a kind of center and periphery of the image or anything like that.

Melanie: Nope. In a way you could say that it's all that I can see. The best way to describe it is going back to what you were saying about the first one with the glow. I'm seeing it as though it's in that 120-degree visual field. It's not in my head. I'm seeing it as though I'm looking at it through my own eyes.

Eric: Um hm. Right.

Russ: In reality, you're looking at one thing at a time. Right now you're looking at me, and no doubt this TV monitor is in your peripheral vision. And you could see it when you're actually looking at me . . .

Melanie: But not hyper-concentrating on it.

Russ: Right. And at the moment of the beep, as far as this image is concerned, are you looking at a piece of the image, like the bench, or the window, or the pole . . .

Melanie: No, I'm just seeing the whole thing.

Russ: You're seeing the whole thing?

Melanie: Yeah.

Eric: So in a sense the image might be clearer, are you saying, than when you see something and you're kind of focused on one thing that maybe is clear and something to the side is not as clear? I'm not sure if that is your visual experience but it sounded like it was when you just responded to Russ a little bit ago.

Melanie: Well, it's difficult to answer because I admit in the mental image that I had there are things in my very periphery that I probably don't see. But on the whole I'm not staring at one thing, so nothing. . . . And even when I do, in everyday life, when I'm looking directly at someone, the things around it, in okay, let's say at least 100 degrees are pretty much clear, and I can see what they are and where they are and the color and everything like that. So it's vision like that.

Eric: Um hm.

[On the experience of vision, see box 4.18.]

Russ: So when you're thinking about this image now, it looks—at least, it did a minute ago—like you're recreating the image again. Is that true?

Melanie: Yes.

Russ: So there's the post and the lights and the whatever, and when we're talking about this, does it seem or not seem that your attention is going within this image now to the window and now to the bench and now to the post . . .

Melanie: No. I'm just seeing the whole thing.

Eric: What's the level of resolution? Can you see the nails—I don't know if it has nails—or the fineness of the grain, or that kind of stuff?

Melanie: No, I can't. First of all it's dark. I can see more than just the outline of the objects in the room but beyond that I couldn't tell you the grain of the wood, or, you know, where one board stops and the next begins.

Eric: Although is that just because the image is dark, or is it because there's some kind of unspecificity in it or . . .

Russ: Let me interrupt that line of questioning and ask the kind of question that I would prefer to ask in this kind of situation. [to Melanie] You said there was a post with some hooks on it.

Melanie: There were a couple hooks on the wall.

Russ: And there was one coat hanging on the wall?

Melanie: It was a jacket.

Russ: What does that jacket look like?

Melanie: It was like a windbreaker that you just casually toss upon a hook and it's just kind of hanging there drooping a little.

Russ: And what color is it? Does it have a color?

Box 4.18
The experience of vision. The refrigerator light phenomenon.

Eric: Melanie says here that in her ordinary visual experience everything within at least 100 degrees of arc is "pretty much clear." When I casually ask people about their visual experience, I find they commonly make claims of this sort.

In my view, visual experience degrades much more rapidly away from the center. Fix your eyes on the period at the end of this sentence, and then, without moving your eyes, notice what the rest of your visual field is like. How clearly can you see the words two inches from the point of fixation? Without gazing directly at it, how clearly do you see the thumb that holds the page? I expect you'll discover a substantial decrement in clarity. This decrement does not depend on holding your eyes still. With a bit more effort, one can attend to one's peripheral visual experience while moving one's eyes around more naturally. Most of the people I've persuaded to try these experiments eventually conclude that visual experience does not consist in a broad and stable region of clarity. Rather, visual experience involves a fairly small region of clarity moving rapidly around a fairly indistinct or sketchy background. (There is, of course, a wealth of scientific data on our poor visual acuity outside a narrow, central area of focus; but it's a further leap, one distinctive of consciousness studies and far from settled, to the conclusion that visual *experience* is also indistinct outside that area.)

Perhaps what leads Melanie and others into error here (or, at least, what I think is error) is a version of what is sometimes called the *refrigerator light phenomenon*: Just as my 7-year-old son might think the refrigerator light is always on because it is always on whenever he opens the door to check it, so also someone might mistakenly think her entire visual field is clear simultaneously because, unless one uncouples one's attention from one's eye movement, the act of checking part of one's visual field for clarity will *create* clarity in that part of the visual field. Wherever in one's visual field one thinks to attend, one will *look* that direction and find clarity. One may thus erroneously conclude that the whole visual field, within a certain range of natural eye movement, is clear simultaneously. (For more on this, see Dennett 1991; Noë 2004; Schwitzgebel, in preparation.)

I don't know whether Melanie's claim here arises from a refrigerator light error of this sort—that's a lot to read into a small bit of conversation—but it does occur to me to wonder whether Melanie's general views about visual experience might be partly driving her attribution of broad clarity and detail to her visual imagery in this sample. She said earlier that her visual imagery experience at the moment of the beep was very much like her original visual experience of the shed; if she is confident of that, she might leap unwittingly from a theory about the one to a conclusion about the other.

Russ: First, most DES subjects do not make such claims—it is much more frequent for subjects to say the center of the visual field was clear and the

Box 4.18

(continued)

periphery indistinct. Second, I don't know or care whether what Melanie says here is true or false. She is not yet a good observer of her own experience. In chapter 2 I used the metaphor of a thresher—my task is to try to grab the wheat and ignore the chaff. This is Melanie's first sampling day, and much of her talk here is "chaff." Third, she indicates in five ways that I will later call subjunctifiers [see box 5.13] that she herself doesn't really believe what she is saying: "well," "it's difficult," "probably," "pretty much," and the unsignaled change of direction at "so nothing. . . ." Fourth, she is also speaking in generalities of the sort that DES seeks (usually successfully) to avoid. [See boxes 4.2 and 5.17.] However, we encouraged her to make this generalization, in violation of standard DES procedure.

For those four reasons, let's not draw too much from this remark. Melanie's talk here should be considered an inconsequential utterance of the sort typically encountered on the first sampling day. It is *not* adequately tied to Melanie's beeped experience, and therefore, regardless of whether it is true or false, I don't count it for or against Melanie or the method. We have to do better (and, I think, will do better on later sampling days) in keeping our discussions focused on the moment of the beep before it makes sense to take anything Melanie says about her experience seriously.

By the way, while I accept that many, and probably most, people who engage in your vision experiment experience what you describe, that doesn't imply that *everyone* would. I'm confident that Fran (discussed in chapter 2) would not, for example. I don't think we sampled long enough with Melanie to know about this aspect of her experience. And furthermore, visual experience in such an experiment might be unrepresentative of what it's like in the wild. Thus I think you make a large mistake here, Eric: assuming without warrant that Melanie's visual experience is like your own. [See box 7.4.]

Thread: Melanie's trustworthiness: Influence of generalizations. Previous: box 4.14. Next: box 7.1.
Thread: Human similarity and difference. Previous: box 4.7. Next: box 4.20.
Thread: Sensory Experience. Previous: box 4.8. Next: box 9.1.
Thread: Visual imagery: Detail. Next: box 4.19.

Box 4.19
Detail by detail

Russ: I started us on the detail-by-detail line of inquiry, rather than continuing to inquire about abstractions, because I think that keeps us focused on the experience itself rather than on the presumed characteristics of the image, and thus is likely to generate a truer and less theory-driven report than more general questions would.

Eric: That makes sense to me. Furthermore, going through the image detail-by-detail like this gives us a quite precise sense of how much detail Melanie is willing to impute to the image [though see boxes 4.20 and 5.4].

I was hoping that by pressing for ever-finer details, we would eventually get to the point (as we did) that Melanie would say that her image left something unspecified—thus opening the door to the possibility of indeterminate imagery. [See box 5.6.] Unfortunately, in this particular case, it remains unclear whether her image is indeterminate in a way a photo could not be indeterminate, or whether it is more like a dark or blurry photo.

Thread: Interview techniques. Previous: box 4.17. Next: box 5.10.
Thread: Visual imagery: Detail. Previous: box 4.18. Next: box 4.20.

Melanie: It doesn't have a color different than the rest of the room. It's all pretty much the same dark bluey gray.

Russ: Okay. And does this windbreaker have a hood or sleeves or what . . .

Melanie: I couldn't tell you that . . . it has sleeves because they're a little bit longer than the coat.

Russ: So you can see the sleeves.

Melanie: Yes, one longer than the other.

Russ: Which one?

Melanie: The one closest to me, the left-hand one.

[Here we have excised a brief discussion between Russ and Eric about the importance of going detail by detail rather than jumping immediately to a more general question. See box 4.19.]

Eric: So could you tell how the coat was wrinkled? Was it a little rumpled, or was it really straight . . .

Melanie: It was a little rumpled, just because it's hanging over a hook, so it's falling in a particular manner.

Eric: And could you see the particular direction of the rumples in it? Could you count them?

Melanie: Probably not . . . no. I wouldn't say it's that sharp.

Eric: Um hm.

Melanie: I could tell the difference in the sleeves because they hang below the coat, and it's something I could just see instantly. But no, I probably couldn't count them.

[For some reasons why Eric is skeptical of this imagery report, see box 4.20. On indeterminate imagery, see box 5.6.]

Box 4.20
Eric's doubts about report 1.3

Eric: I'm nervous about this report for several reasons, some of which are expressed in boxes 4.13 and 4.14. While I grant that it's possible that Melanie's image here is as detailed as she claims, I don't think *my* imagery is anywhere near that detailed. (Russ will say "don't judge others by yourself!" See box 7.4.) Surely, Melanie could just be very different from me, but as I've mentioned before (section 3.2), psychologists (not using DES) have generally failed to find differences in imagery report to correlate very well with performance on seemingly imagery-related tasks—suggesting, perhaps, that people generally aren't as different in their imagery experiences as they say. (For a fuller version of this argument, see Schwitzgebel 2002a.)

This is hardly decisive, of course—and even if we accept it, maybe it's I and not Melanie who's mistaken about his imagery. But also I wonder whether Melanie fully appreciates the possibility of indeterminacy in vision and in imagery [see boxes 4.18 and 7.8], whether Russ's invitation to compare her imagery experience to visual experience near the beginning of this discussion might have led her too quickly to assimilate the two [see box 8.1], and whether she might commit a type of refrigerator light error as she thinks about and possibly fills in different aspects of her reconstructed image [see also boxes 4.18 and 5.4].

I don't wish to be dogmatic—I don't think I *am* being dogmatic—but Melanie's confidence alone, here, and Russ's careful interviewing style, aren't enough to persuade me to relinquish these concerns, and I'm not sure further interviews of this sort could by themselves persuade me. I want something more in support of her report, some independent corroboration, if possible, something externally observable.

Thread: Human similarity and difference. Previous: box 4.18. Next: box 5.3.
Thread: Visual imagery: Detail. Previous: box 4.19. Next: box 5.1.

Beep 1.4

In lieu of the full transcript of the discussion of this sample, here is a description of this experience as Melanie conveyed it in the interview.

Melanie and her boyfriend had just put in a videotaped movie, and, as always, had started at the very beginning so they could see all of the previews. The tape had begun with a several-minute-long picture of the MGM logo with the lion frozen in mid-snarl and the words "ARS GRATIA ARTIS." At the moment of the beep, the boyfriend was saying to Melanie, "Didn't the lion used to [beep] roar?" Melanie was hearing and comprehending what he was saying, and at the same time was paying attention to the green color of the screen. The color had been gradually changing, and was now green. She was paying particular attention to the greenness because it happened to be the same shade of green as the MGM Grand Hotel in Las Vegas where she lives. She wasn't thinking about the greenness in any cognitive way, but she was paying attention to it.

After we finished discussing beep 1.4, we discussed the extent of Russ's and Eric's skepticism, the "refrigerator light phenomenon" as a source of skepticism about Melanie's claims about her visual experience and her imagery in beep 1.3 [see boxes 4.18, 4.20, and 5.4], the desirability of finding performance differences between people who report different levels of detail in their imagery experiences [see section 10.1], and doubts about whether Melanie is timing the beep accurately, given that it seems to catch her at the end of thought [see box 4.13].

Melanie seemed relatively unbothered by Eric's skepticism about her reports, saying she did not take it personally. Since Melanie participated in these discussions, they may have affected her later reports.

The full transcript is available at http://mitpress.mit.edu/inner _experience.

5 The Second Sampling Day

Beep 2.1

Melanie: I was reading. It's a book set on the island of Kefalonia in Greece. And the part where I was reading right before the beep happened was, the main character pulls aside this British soldier to ask when the British are coming to liberate the island during World War II. And right at the moment of the beep, I had an image in my head of that little scene on the island, with lots of sunlight on a dirt road, with the green olive trees and shrubs, and a woman—the main character—is speaking to this soldier.

Russ: And when you say you "had an image in your head," what exactly does that mean?

Melanie: Just a picture. I mean an imagined picture of what the scene kind of looks like.

Russ: And does it seem like you're just looking at it? Or does it seem like you've got a postcard of Greece? Or . . .

Melanie: It's not a postcard in that it seems confined to one little space and there's something else surrounding it. It's more like being in an IMAX film in your head where it's a little bit more surrounding you and it's all you can see.

Russ: And does it seem like a clear picture of Kefalonia?

Melanie: Reasonably, yes.

Russ: And by "reasonably" do you mean not so clear as if you were in Kefalonia? Or sort of the same way, or . . .

Melanie: Not as clear, because I was making it up. But reasonably clear.

Russ: Okay. And what exactly do you see?

Melanie: There's a dirt road that's kind of going diagonally across the space.

Russ: And by diagonally, judging from what your hands are doing, sort of from close left to far right?

Melanie: Exactly.

Russ: Okay.

Melanie: And there's a hedge of greenish shrubbery lining the far side of the road with a couple of olive trees sticking up out of them, that have that kind of olive green leaf. And then on the road is this woman dressed in kind of traditional Greek clothing, with a long dark skirt and kerchief around the head and a white kind of peasant blouse.

Russ: And you say "on the road," like walking on the road? Driving on the road?

Melanie: Just standing on the road.

Russ: Looking which way?

Melanie: Looking not at me but more toward my right . . .

[On the reasons for inquiring about the details of images, see box 5.1.]

Box 5.1
Asking for details of an image

Eric: I wonder whether asking for such details invites confabulation. Although Melanie could choose to say "I don't know" or "that wasn't specified," there may be some subtle pressure on her to give determinate answers.

Russ: The request for details is a necessary part of the attempt to understand what Melanie is trying to tell us. Melanie says she's seeing an image. It is simply a mistake (albeit a common mistake) to assume that that means she is experiencing inner visual phenomena. If she is experiencing some relatively clear inner visual phenomena, then she should be able to provide some visual details. Many of my subjects say they have an image but then, under questioning, cannot provide any visual details at all. Those subjects generally come to accept that they did not actually have inner visual phenomena at the moment of the beep; that is, that they had used the term "image" in a non-visual way. (This is not the sign of an ill-intentioned subject, but rather one who has, like most people, not adequately differentiated the terminology of inner experience.) So Melanie's being able to provide visual details about her image enhances the credibility of her claim that she had inner visual experience. It also conveys the important message that we are interested in the details of her experience and take what she is saying seriously but not blindly. [See box 7.3.]

Box 5.1
(continued)

I think you are quite correct to suspect confabulation in many (perhaps most) studies of imagery. Many (non-DES) studies of imagery *do in fact demand* confabulation. They instruct people to form images and then ask about the images generated (as you yourself do, Eric, in section 3.2). But many people simply do not have imagery, even when (or perhaps especially when) instructed to form an image. Those studies ask about the details of their images anyway. That is an *actual* demand, and I think such a demand *does* lead to substantial confabulation. But that is much different from asking Melanie to describe whatever characteristics happened to be naturally, unmanipulatedly occurring at the moment of the beep, and only if she happened to report an image do we ask whether visual details existed and if so what they were. The demands of such a sequence are very gentle.

I agree there is a general concern about the accuracy of memory for details. Therefore, I think it reasonable to believe that of all the details of Melanie's description of her image (sunlight, dirt, olive trees, shrubs, woman, soldier, diagonally, skirt, kerchief, etc.), some were not actually present at the moment of the beep. How many were not present? I don't know, but I would guess most were present. If we were concerned about the long-term memory issue, we could ask Melanie to write more details immediately after the beep.

Eric: I can't avoid thinking, though, that the history of psychology shows that what seem to be subtle and gentle situational pressures often ultimately have large effects on behavior. In the current line of questioning (as in beep 1.3), Melanie quickly commits herself to the image's being IMAX-like in its detail. Now, if she doesn't want to undermine herself, she has to produce details. A different line of questioning—I'm not saying a better line, since it raises its own pressures—might have begun with questions about whether particular details were specified or not, letting the answers to general questions about the clarity and structure of the image fall out at the end. The research on eyewitness testimony in particular suggests that our memory of detailed, concrete events is surprisingly inaccurate and subject to a variety of distortive pressures. [For more on interview pressures and the comparison to eyewitness testimony, see sections 10.4 and 10.5 and subsections 11.2.3 and 11.2.5.]

I confess that my line of reasoning in section 3.2 assumes that most readers can form an image on demand—or at least can realize it if they fail to do so. If I'm wrong about this and most readers only mistakenly *think* they have visual imagery, that of course only further supports my skeptical point there.

Thread: Melanie's trustworthiness: Interview pressures. Previous: box 4.17. Next: box 5.11.
Thread: Visual imagery: Detail. Previous: box 4.20. Next: box 5.

Russ: Okay.

Melanie: . . . and a British soldier standing next to her. They're stand-ing reasonably close, just a couple of feet apart.

Russ: And by "standing next to her" do you mean shoulder to shoulder? Face to face?

Melanie: Not quite face to face, but turned towards one another as though in a conversation. And the soldier is wearing fatigues, olive green and tan color. And she's kind of speaking. It's more of a frozen picture, but she's speaking, kind of gesturing a little bit with her hands. And he's just standing there listening.

Russ: And when you say a "frozen picture" and yet "gesturing with her hands" . . .

Melanie: Well, she has her hands out as though in a gesture, like when you speak and you talk with your hands a little bit, but it's frozen in one.

Russ: Okay. So like a snapshot has been taken . . .

Melanie: Yes.

Russ: . . . or a frame has been taken out of a video?

Melanie: Exactly.

Russ: And was it originally a moving video, which at the moment of the beep is frozen? Or are you just sort of creating a still picture?

Melanie: Just creating a still picture.

[On the media references in this dialogue, see box 5.2.]

Russ: Okay. And as far as you recall at this particular moment, does this picture seem like it adequately reflects what was in the story? You're reading about this kind of scene, I gather?

Melanie: Yeah. There's probably more going on in the book than just in this picture. Like I think there were a couple of additional characters, but they weren't in the mental picture that I had.

Russ: And has the book described these hedges, and a few olive trees, and the road going left to right diagonally or . . .

Melanie: No.

Russ: Those are details that you . . .

Melanie: Made up.

Russ: . . . constructed that are consonant with the book but not neces-sarily identical . . .

Box 5.2
The comparison of images and media

Eric: Notice all the comparisons to pictures and movies in this dialogue (and elsewhere, e.g., beep 4.1). I wonder to what extent such analogies might affect Melanie's impressions about her experience. Perhaps a lot. People in the 1950's (unlike now) believed their dreams were black and white. I have argued (in Schwitzgebel 2002b; Schwitzgebel, Huang, and Zhou 2006) that this is a consequence of our opinions about our dreams being inappropriately and excessively shaped by analogies to the media. 1950's reports about dreams were not, of course, based on DES, but I do think they suggest that media analogies can have a surprising grip on our impressions about our own experience. (See also Schwitzgebel 2006)

Melanie describes the woman's hands as "frozen," rather than as moving or of indeterminate posture. Is Melanie assimilating her image too much to a photograph? The description here is so much like a photographic "snapshot" that I wonder.

Russ: I agree that there is a risk that a subject will presume that images have some of the same characteristics as photographs. But the response to that risk, I think, is to question the subject carefully about that; to make clear by word and deed that images may or may not have the same characteristics as pictures. The DES results show that still or "frozen" images are common across many subjects, but that most subjects deny photograph-like characteristics such as edges, borders, and frames.

Melanie herself indicates that she is not taken in by the "snapshot" metaphor: "It's more like being in an IMAX film in your head where it's a little bit more surrounding you and it's all you can see." That indicates that she uses the snapshot metaphor to convey the frozen-ness and the IMAX metaphor to convey the surrounding-ness, which argues *against* her being captured by either metaphor.

And a theme that bears repetition: In my view there is a huge difference between a general opinion, which is greatly susceptible to influence, and a careful observation of an externally identified moment, which is not nearly so susceptible.

Thread: Trustworthiness: Influence of metaphors. Previous: box 4.7. Next: box 9.10.
Thread: Visual imagery: Structure. Previous: box 4.16. Next: box 5.5.

Melanie: Yes.

Russ: Okay. You're reading, actively reading?

Melanie: Um hm.

Russ: And is anything in your awareness other than this picture? So my question is: Does the content of the reading just seem like it's coming in and being reflected in the picture? Or are you saying the words to yourself and somehow . . .

Melanie: There's nothing else aside from the picture. It almost feels like what I'm reading is being directly translated into a movie going on inside my head.

Russ: Okay. And is there an emotional reaction or sensations or anything? Or just the picture?

Melanie: Not at this beep. There is another one when I'm reading and there is emotion [see beep 2.2], but here it's just . . .

Russ: At this moment you're reading and making a picture and paying attention to the picture, I gather.

Melanie: Yes, and just watching, yeah.

Russ: So you're not really even paying attention to the book. You're obviously looking at the book, and your eyes. . . . There's a retinal image of the words . . .

Melanie: Right.

Russ: . . . but you're not really paying attention to that. You're paying attention to the picture. Is that correct?

Melanie: Yes.

[For Russ's comment on the phenomenon of reading, see box 5.3.]

Russ: Okay. Eric, you want to . . .

Eric: Were you pausing in your reading at this time, to just reflect on the scene and create this image? Or were you just going along reading without pausing, and the image was coming on?

Melanie: No, just going along reading. No pauses. Until the beeper went off, and then I stopped and turned off the beeper. But at the moment of the beep my eyes were just going down the page.

Eric: Right. And were you recreating that image now when you were just reporting it?

Melanie: Yes.

Box 5.3
Little is known about the phenomenology of reading.

Russ: Sampling has shown that there are a number of different ways to experience reading. Some people create, apparently automatically, images as they read. Melanie's example here is quite typical. Such images are usually over-detailed, as was Melanie's, in the sense that the image includes details that were not mentioned in the text. As the reading progresses, occasionally the text will contradict such a detail. The typical person simply corrects the image without noticing. So if Melanie's reading along and the next paragraph happens to say that the soldier is wearing a beret, then she is going to include a beret. A second ago, she was seeing the soldier wearing a helmet, maybe, or perhaps it was unnoticedly unelaborated. Now she's seeing the guy wearing a beret. That would be a surprise in the real world, but not surprising in the world of imagination.

Other people (like you, Eric, as I recall from your sampling) speak the words they are reading to themselves in inner speech. Yet others apparently simply read, comprehending the meaning without images or speech. Melanie's general view of her own reading, expressed in a different discussion and not based in sampling, is that she starts a passage in inner speech and then "takes off" into images. She reports that the sensation is like the difference between an airplane's taxiing and flying: reading with images is faster and smoother. (Because of its retrospective generality, I view this report with substantially more skepticism than her reports of individual beeps.)

Very little is known about the basic inner experience of nearly any activity, primarily because very few accurate reports of inner experience exist. If we can agree that experience sampling produces (at least) modestly accurate descriptions, then we can potentially start to fill this huge gap in our knowledge.

Eric: Although I am more skeptical about the details of this report than you seem to be (for reasons similar to those expressed in box 4.20), I am willing tentatively to accept that Melanie had an image of some sort near the time of the beep. It would be very interesting to see if there were behavioral differences between people like Melanie who report mainly imagery while reading and people like me who report mainly inner speech. For example: Would imagers be more likely to remember, or falsely impute, visual details? Would inner-speakers be more likely jarred when they heard someone else "mispronounce" a character's name with ambiguous pronunciation? If generalizations of roughly this sort hold up, that would in my view boost the credibility of the reports. If not, however, I think that would reflect badly on experience sampling.

Thread: Human similarity and difference. Previous: box 4.18. Next: box 7.4.

Box 5.4
Dangers of recreating the image. Detail in imagery.

Eric: If Melanie is recreating the image as she is reporting it, it seems likely that her knowledge of the recreated image could affect her reports in ways she may not realize. She may impute details of the reconstructed image to the original image.

For example, she may unwittingly add detail to the image as she thinks about it. When she thinks about the background of the imagined scene, she may add olive trees to her present image without realizing that she has done so (if she was not previously thinking about whether there were olive trees or not) and then mistakenly attribute that detail to her original experience. (Compare the "refrigerator light phenomenon" discussed in box 4.18.)

Russ: I agree that Melanie probably is reporting on her reconstructed image, which she trusts to be similar to the original image. And I grant that the (re)created and the original image are probably not identical, and therefore some reports said to be of the original image are confabulations. What is at issue is the magnitude of those confabulations. I doubt, for example, that Melanie would have a vague, indeterminate image at the moment of the beep and "recreate" it with a clear, detailed image merely as a result of our asking for details—or, worse, use a visual image to "recreate" a non-image experience, such as inner speech or sensory awareness. If subjects simply caved in to such demands, we wouldn't find cases like those in which subjects decided they did not have a visual image at all (as described in box 5.1).

Thread: Melanie's trustworthiness: Memory. Previous: box 4.8. Next: box 7.5.
Thread: Reconstruction. Next: box 7.1
Thread: Visual imagery: Detail. Previous: box 5.1. Next: box 5.11.

[On why this might be worrisome, see box 5.4.]

Eric: So, I'm not sure . . . um . . . it's probably not standard DES methodology . . .

Russ: Feel free to be as skeptical as you like.

Eric: Well, just out of curiosity, if you can recreate that image now . . .

Melanie: Um hm.

Eric: . . . when you're focusing, say, on the soldier . . .

Melanie: Okay.

Eric: . . . are the things that you're *not* focusing on simultaneously clear? Or is it that when you move your focus around from one part of the image to the other, the thing at the focus of your attention comes in some way more clearly into your experience or something? [On whether this comment illicitly imports assumptions about imagery, see box 5.5.]

Melanie: I'm not really sure how to answer that. I think the best way to describe it is, it's almost as though I am looking at a postcard with this scene on it.

Eric: Um hm.

Melanie: And I'm just staring at it. I mean, when I think of looking at the soldier, for instance, there aren't any more details that are coming up. It's more like having that image blown up . . .

Eric: Um hm.

Melanie: . . . a little bit. But it's not like I can suddenly see whether or not he's wearing a wedding band, or how his feet are positioned, or something like that.

Eric: Um hm.

Melanie: It's not more added detail.

Eric: So you *can't* see how his feet are positioned?

Melanie: No.

Eric: Um . . . so maybe this is a totally crazy question, and you can just tell me that it's crazy if you want. [Melanie laughs] But how can you be visually imagining some legs without imagining some particular way in which they're positioned?

Melanie [apologetically]: I guess you could say that that wasn't part of the image that I was really concentrating on.

Eric: Um hm.

Melanie: I know that he's standing. I couldn't tell you what directions his feet are pointed in.

Eric: Um hm.

Melanie: It's almost like that that's below a level that I'm looking at.

Eric: So if the image were, say, like a postcard picture, you could have just looked at the feet and said "Oh, well. . . ."

Melanie: Right.

Eric: It's not like they were occluded by a bush or something?

Box 5.5
Images don't exist separately from the seeing of them.

Russ: We need carefully to avoid two unwarranted, albeit common, pre-suppositions about inner visual experience: (1) that inner visual experience follows the same rules as external visual experience in having a focus and periphery and (2) that there is an image separate from the perception of that image.

For example, do people frequently hold an image in mind and shift their "attention" from one part of it to another? I don't know the answer to this question, but my sense is that that is not the way imaginal visual perception usually works. If Melanie continued reading and started thinking more about the trees in the background, it may be tempting to say that "her attention shifted to the tree portion of her image." But that is not necessarily strictly true. Instead, it seems likely, or at least possible, that she would have a *new* inner seeing, in which the trees are more centrally interesting. Because the imagined soldier and trees don't really exist separate from the inner seeing, it may not make sense to say one's attention can shift back and forth between them, as it could between a real soldier and real trees or a photograph thereof.

When Melanie (or anyone else) has an inner visual experience, it is *not*, I think, that she creates an image and then looks at it. When she has an inner visual perception, she innerly sees what she intends to see, and what she does not intend to see may (unlike external perception) simply be not there, period. In like manner, what she *does* intend to see can (unlike external perception; see box 4.18) all be clear simultaneously.

I think it likely that at least some inner seeings do not have pieces that are somehow out of the experience of the seeing. Contrast this with a photographic image of a soldier-on-a-road scene like the one Melanie is imagining here. All sorts of things would be in the photo, unattended until you look at that particular aspect. Perhaps they are out of focus; but they are undeniable a part of the photo. That is not necessarily true in an inner seeing.

I myself sometimes use the expression "seeing an image" because it seems natural, but that is a seductively dangerous usage because of its implication that the seeing is separate from the image. Maybe that implication is really true, although I doubt it. But for sure, it is a mistake to *assume* it's true without careful examination.

Eric: I think I agree with most of what you say here (assuming we give "intend" a weak reading to account for images that come unbidden). Nonetheless, I'm inclined think there is a sense in which one can attend to part of an image. If I hold an image in mind for an extended period of time, it seems to me that I can think serially about different parts of the imagined scene. There is often some potentially shifting focus of energy in maintaining the image, some part of it that is more vividly or centrally

---

Box 5.5

(continued)

experienced. You may prefer to say that this means I've had a sequence of related but distinct "inner seeings," but maybe our disagreement on this point is only semantic.

Even if we grant that it isn't nonsense to talk about a focal center of an image, it doesn't follow that *all* images have a focal center. So I agree I should not simply have assumed that Melanie's image did.

Thread: Visual imagery: Structure. Previous: box 5.2. Next: box 5.6.

Melanie: No.

Eric: So in that respect, at least, there is an aspect of it that is sketchier than a picture. That it's somehow able to leave a detail like how the feet are positioned unspecified, despite the fact that it's visual in some way.

Melanie: Yes.

Eric: Well, it's *not* that you kind of, when you focus on something, you add specification to it?

Melanie: No, not at all. I *could*, but that's not what I'm doing.

Russ: So there is, of course, the philosophical question about whether it's possible to have an image of a triangle that is at once scalene and isosceles, or whatever, however that argument has been made. [For the quotation Russ is thinking of here, and for more on indeterminate imagery, see box 5.6.]

Eric: Right.

Russ: And there are those who say it can't be done. But this is an example of how it can be done. And I find this kind of thing in my work all the time, where people will have indeterminate images. This is not a particularly *good* example of it . . .

Eric: Right.

Russ: . . . but she could in a similar way have had a picture of a triangle as part of this, where the particular angles in the triangle were not specified even though the triangleness of the image was specified.

Eric: Right. Yeah, I'm inclined to agree with that. One of the reasons that I tend to be nervous about people reporting a huge level of detail in their images is that I wonder whether there's some kind of implicit

Box 5.6
Indeterminate images

Eric: The quote you were thinking of was from Locke (1690/1975): "For abstract *Ideas* are not so obvious or easie to Children, or the yet unexercised Mind, as particular ones. . . . For example, Does it not require some pains and skill to form the *general Idea* of a *Triangle*, . . . for it must be neither Oblique, nor Rectangle, neither Equilateral, Equicrural, nor Scalenon; but all and none of these at once." (pp. 595–596).

Berkeley famously comments on this passage: "If any man has the faculty of framing in his mind such an idea of a triangle as here described, it is in vain to pretend to dispute him out of it, nor would I go about it. All I desire is that the reader would fully and certainly inform himself whether he has such an idea or no." (1710/1965, p. 12) Berkeley goes on quite explicitly to commit himself to the impossibility of such "abstract ideas" or indeterminacies in imagery. This is a very old issue in philosophy.

I think—as you do too, Russ, I believe—that Berkeley and others who have expressed similar views are quite mistaken in this. (A famous twentieth-century example is that of a striped tiger that is not imagined to have a determinate number of stripes. See Dennett 1969 and Block 1981; see also Price 1941.)

How could people be mistaken about such a basic matter of phenomenology, apparently discoverable with the least introspection? As Berkeley says, "What more easy than for anyone to look a little into his own thoughts, and there try whether he has or can attain to have [such an] idea . . . ?" (1710/1965, pp. 12–13) One of the principal themes of my work has been that, perhaps surprisingly, people can indeed be, and often are, radically mistaken about their ongoing stream of experience.

Russ: My DES work shows that it is not uncommon for people visually to represent indeterminateness. For example, Susan, a college student, was critical of her roommate Helen's relationships with boys. Susan had an image of Helen, seen from the waist up sitting on their couch with a boy. Helen in the image was wearing only a bra. Helen and the couch and the bra were seen clearly in this image, but the boy's face was unelaborated or indistinct. Susan had images at many of her other samples, and most of them were richly detailed and clear throughout. Thus I think her indeterminate boy was not merely the result of weak imagery but was a highly skilled construction of indeterminacy precisely where she meant indeterminately to represent *lots* of boys.

This issue highlights the difficulties of armchair observation. Perhaps Berkeley himself was not a skilled imager, and therefore mistakenly assumed others to have the same low level of skill.

Eric: Or one might think, contra Locke, that a poor imager would have difficulty conjuring up a richly detailed image and be stuck instead mostly

---

Box 5.6
(continued)

with sketchy, indeterminate images. Maybe there's more than one way to be weak at imagery?

Thread: Visual imagery: Structure. Previous: box 5.5. Next: box 5.8.
Thread: Retrospective and armchair generalizations. Previous: box 4.11. Next: box 5.7.

---

commitment to a picture-like theory of what images are like. And since pictures can't be underspecified in this way, then the assumption is that images can't be either. And then they create the detail and report it as having been there all along—something like that.

Russ: Right. But it seems like Melanie is not doing that.

Eric: Or at least not doing that to an extreme degree.

Russ: And this by the way is the kind of an image report that I would credit. It's hard for me to imagine that Melanie was not having an image at the moment of the beep, and that that image was being created sort of on the fly as she was reading, making her style of reading much different from yours, Eric. She watches images while she reads, and you create inner speech while you read.

[Here we have excised a discussion of the phenomenology of reading in general. See box 5.3.]

Eric: I guess it occurred to me that one potential source of skepticism about the level of detail in Melanie's image, maybe not about whether she was having an image at all, is this: There is some research in imagery [e.g., Kosslyn 1980] that suggests that it takes a certain amount of time to construct a complicated image. And if you're reading very fast, then if that research is correct, it's unlikely that you're getting one very detailed, complicated image after another in that one second at a time, every second. Now it could be that you have a very detailed image that you build up over the course of, say, 15 seconds. Or it could be that you have a series of sketchy images that replace each other faster than that.

Russ: My impression is that most people who image as they read update the image as they go along—so they have one stable, enduring image that is being modified.

[We continued this conversation, discussing issues presented in boxes 5.3 (on the phenomenology of reading) and 5.1 (on demand). On Melanie's believability contrasted with Eric's believability as a subject, see box 5.7. On whether children construct images slowly, see box 5.8.]

Beep 2.2

Melanie: Okay, I was reading again. In this part of the book it was the arrival of the German invasion of the island. The line I was reading had to do with the arrival of a formation of Stukas—German planes. And so I had an image in my head, a really simple image, the kind that you get if you watch those World War II movies or footage from back then, of a line of military planes against a blue sky background with a couple of white clouds. It was a very close image of one of the planes, of only the top, the beginning portion of one of the planes, and then another one behind that, and another one behind that.

Russ: So this is two separate images?

Melanie: It's one image.

Russ: It's one image. So you're looking like you've got a camera mounted on the wing of one of these airplanes . . .

Melanie: Exactly.

Russ: . . . and you're looking down on the formation? Okay. And is this camera . . . this artificial camera that we're talking about, on the left wing or the right wing?

Melanie: It's more like it's on one of the planes that you can't see, because where the camera is it's looking across . . .

Russ: So looking across a space . . .

Melanie: Yes. And seeing a bunch of other planes.

Russ: . . . and seeing the left side of the plane or the right of the plane?

Melanie: Seeing the left side.

Russ: And what does the plane in your image look like? Do you know what a Stuka is?

Melanie: I have no idea, so yeah, I kind of put in F-18s instead [laughs], because I make them up, so . . .

Russ: So this is a jet plane that you're seeing!

Melanie: Yeah, they're jet planes with a tapered nose and that kind of gray, dark gray steel with a . . .

Box 5.7

Melanie's and Eric's believability as subjects. "Auditory imagery" and "inner speech."

Russ: My skeptic detectors are pretty silent on this beep. I see little reason to doubt that Melanie was seeing an image.

Eric: I have raised some concerns about whether we should believe that Melanie's image had all the details she imputes to it. [See boxes 5.1, 5.2, and 5.4 and remarks in the transcript.] But could Melanie be *completely* mistaken, wholly devoid of imagery at or near the moment of the beep? It seems unlikely, but still I can't quite shake the thought that even such a radical mistake is a possibility.

Russ: It seems to me that you would have to have the same level of doubt about your own reports, then, Eric. When you were sampling some time ago, you said, I thought with confidence, that you had inner speech while reading. Do you doubt that, too?

Eric: I allow that I could have been mistaken in that way; but I confess that I find it harder to doubt myself than to doubt others. Maybe this is just normal human weakness. Or maybe accepting one's own judgments (in whatever domain), even when one knows that one is no smarter or more talented than someone else who reaches contrary judgments, is necessary to avoid a paralysis of skepticism. In my own sampling, in any case, I don't think I expressed the kind of confidence about the details of my reports that Melanie expresses here and throughout. Instead, I tended in my own reports to express considerable doubt.

Russ: I simply cannot agree that accepting one's own judgments is necessary. I think it is necessary to the advancement of consciousness studies to be *more rejecting* of one's own judgments, not more accepting, if those judgments are arrived at under roughly the same methods. And I don't think that leads to a paralysis of skepticism, but rather to a search for better methods. If you can find a better method and apply it to the situation of interest, then you are in a legitimate position to hold your own view to be better than someone with an inferior method. If you can't find a better method, then you should surrender to a legitimate "I don't know." Because I think there is legitimate reason to believe that DES is better than armchair introspection, I think my views of inner experience are better than yours.

I agree that, in your own sampling, you didn't express as much confidence as does Melanie. As I recall, I was more skeptical about your reports than I am about Melanie's. It seemed that you had unusually heavy theoretical baggage that needed gradually to be let go before you could attend to the phenomena that were actually occurring for you at the moment of the beep.

Box 5.7
(continued)

For example, you referred, early in your sampling, to your "auditory imagery," but the main features of your phenomenon were not primarily auditory, but much more centered on the act of creating the words, that is, more on the doing of the speaking than on the hearing. I found myself encouraging you to call this phenomenon "speaking" rather than "auditory imagery." For me to encourage a subject's choice of words is very unusual! Nearly always I prefer to use the subject's own words to my own. But your words didn't seem to be trying to reflect your phenomenon (that also is also very unusual); instead, they seemed to reflect some philosophical presupposition.

As I recall, while you weren't as confident as is Melanie, you did seem to come to accept the "speaking" nature of what you had originally called auditory-imagery. Without some external observer listening carefully, I doubt that you would have come to the realization of the important discrepancy between "auditory imagery" and "inner speaking."

Eric: I don't think I managed to abandon any presuppositions in that case. My shift toward accepting your phrasing was, as I recall, driven by the thought that imagery can be felt either as passively received or as actively created, and thus that both "inner speech" and "inner hearing" could be seen as forms of auditory (or mostly auditory) imagery. "Inner speech" thus seemed the more specific term—though I don't at all trust that I distinguished accurately between actively speaking and passively hearing.

I'm prompted to wonder whether in visual imagery there might be an analogous difference between active "inner sketching" and a more passive "inner seeing."

Thread: Bracketing presuppositions. Previous: box 4.10. Next: box 7.4.
Thread: Melanie's trustworthiness: General. Previous: box 4.9. Next: box 5.16.
Thread: Inner speech and hearing. Previous: box 4.11. Next: box 6.5.
Thread: Non-visual imagery. Next: box 7.9.
Thread: Retrospective and armchair generalizations. Previous: box 5.6. Next: box 5.17.

Box 5.8
Do children construct images slowly?

Russ: I have sampled with a few children, and they sometimes take minutes to create images. For example, I had a sample from a 9-year-old boy who had an image of a hole in his backyard with toys in it. I asked him whether this was an accurate portrayal of what was really in his backyard, and he said "Yes, but I don't have all the toys in it yet. If you had beeped me a few minutes later I would have had time to put all of the toys in the hole." This speaks to the possibility that image-making may be a skill, and you get better (faster) at it as you get older.

Eric: Or perhaps his report was driven in part by the assumption that if it takes a long time to put actual toys in a hole, then it must also take a long time to put imagined toys in an imagined hole? You weren't clocking him constructing images, and I'm disinclined simply to take his word for it.

Russ: That wouldn't explain the following teenager's image. She had an image of her school orchestra, seen and heard from her usual position as a violist. The orchestra was performing their contest piece. She had been repeating this image for a few days, over and over. At each repetition, she corrected some flaw in the performance: removing a violin squeak here and a clarinet squawk there; those corrections remained in subsequent images, so that at each repetition the orchestra sounded better than before. There was no question that the music she was hearing in her image was being performed by her orchestra, but the current performance was much better than her orchestra had ever sounded. I take this as being "playing" with the image for the same reasons that children play with blocks: they develop skills.

Thread: Visual imagery: Structure. Previous: box 5.6. Next: box 5.9.

Russ: This guy was ahead of his time! [laughs]

Melanie: [laughs] . . . with the little windows. I can't see pilots or anything like that, just the outline.

[On the substitution of F-18s for Stukas, see box 5.9.]

Russ: Okay. And in what way is this experience the same or different from the experience of the previous beep? In both cases you're reading and watching an image, which on the surface would seem to be sort of the same . . . [On the non-leading nature of this question, see box 5.10.]

Melanie: They're both the same in that they're both, again, still pictures. It's not like a movie going through my head. It's just a still picture.

Box 5.9
When is an F-18 a Stuka?

Russ: When pressed with detailed questioning, Melanie reveals that her imagined airplanes looked like F-18s, not Stukas. Should we be surprised by that? I don't think so. All representations are imperfect in some way. Even if Melanie were very familiar with Stukas, her imaginary Stukas would have some incorrect details such as the wrong sort of wheel covers, the wings slightly too low on the body, or the like. The fact that Melanie's imaginary Stukas were rather dramatically imperfect reflects Melanie's very limited familiarity with/interest in Stukas, not any fault or limitation in her inner seeing ability. She did not think "I'm supposed to be imagining Stukas, but because I don't know what Stukas look like, I'll use F-18s instead." She created a concrete, detailed, inner seeing that reflected her (low) level of knowledge about and concern for Stuka details.

That illustrates one way that inner seeing is markedly different from external seeing. If you're looking at a photograph of F-18s, you can pretend that they're Stukas, or mistakenly assume they are, but the fact will remain that they really are F-18s. In Melanie's experience, there is no pretense or error. She was simply illustrating a scene involving Stukas at precisely the level of her interest in/knowledge of Stukas at this moment. She's not seeing badly represented Stukas. She's simply illustrating Stukas.

I note in passing that Melanie never said that her imaginary planes looked like or were Stukas. She said she was reading about a formation of Stukas and was seeing "a line of military planes against a blue sky background." I take this to be a sign of Melanie's skillful attempts to provide faithful descriptions during the interview. She did not say they were Stukas; she did not say they were not Stukas; she did not say they were badly represented Stukas or that she had substituted F-18s. She said they were military planes against a blue sky, which is exactly the scene she was illustrating.

Thread: Visual imagery: Structure. Previous: box 5.8. Next: box 8.1.

Box 5.10
Non-leading questions

Russ: This "same or different" question is one of the most non-leading questions possible. It focuses Melanie directly on the phenomenon without preferring one explanation to another. It does not presume that all images are the same or that they are different.

Thread: Interview techniques. Previous: box 4.19. Next: box 5.12.

And then I would say that this picture was created much faster than the other one, because when the beep occurred, it was right at the beginning of a new chapter, of a new paragraph. So a huge scene change kind of just happened. Whereas in the one before, it was in the middle of a chapter and you had time, like you said earlier, to build up a scene.

Russ: Okay. And at the moment of the beep, do you have an awareness of this fastness? Or is this sort of a meta-description, given that we've stopped and . . .

Melanie: Meta-description. But I am aware of the sketchiness of it. Almost like . . . there's a feeling of . . . I'm ready to fill in other details. I don't know.

Eric: So what you're saying is in accord with—and you don't have to be at all in accord with what I was suggesting—so . . .

Melanie: Oh no, I really agreed with what you said before, because it feels very much like what I do.

Eric: Right, so it may take a certain amount of time to create a very detailed scene. So she seems to be saying that this scene is very sketchy, and that would make sense given that she had just started reading that paragraph.

[On whether Melanie is complying with a demand to report sketchy imagery, see box 5.11.]

Russ: Right.

Melanie: Although . . . I mean I don't know if this agrees with what you said or not, but at the same time I don't know how I could have filled in any other detail.

Eric: Um hm.

Melanie: It was just a very simple shot, almost, just to use . . .

Eric: So what about details like insignia on the sides of planes or shadows or those kinds of things?

Melanie: You couldn't. From the viewpoint you couldn't see any of that. It was just straight across. For instance, you couldn't see downwards, so you couldn't see shadows over land or sea. And then the plane that's right in front of you, it's very close in front of you, and you're just seeing a very tiny part of it, so you can't really see any insignia on it. Maybe the planes further in the distance, but I don't remember any insignia on them in that image.

Box 5.11
Complying with a demand for sketchy imagery?

Eric: We have just discussed the plausibility of the view that images are often sketchier than photographs and that it takes some time to build up a detailed image. Almost as though on cue, Melanie reports a sketchy image to fit the theory. As I have pressed Melanie on sketchiness, she has started to report more sketchiness in her imagery (from beep 1.3 to beep 2.1 to beep 2.2). While this could be coincidence, I find it suspect.

Russ: I think it's neither coincidence nor suspect. First, such synchronizations are rather common in my DES experience, and I used to marvel at it myself. Now I think it's a natural phenomenon that arises as follows. We commented earlier on the level of detail in Melanie's image because that was a quite detailed image, sufficiently detailed that it merited comment. Now either all of Melanie's images are that detailed, or such detail is somewhat unusual—that's why we commented. If the latter, then the next (or soon thereafter) image is likely to be less detailed, not because we commented on the detail but because one doesn't usually get many unusual things in a row.

It's the same phenomenon as the "*Sports Illustrated* jinx": many athletes decline to be on the cover of *Sports Illustrated* because, on average, athletes' performances just after a cover appearance are worse than just before. But it's not a jinx; athletes should not expect their subsequent performances to be as extraordinary as the ones that merited a cover story.

Thread: Melanie's trustworthiness: Interview pressures. Previous: box 5.1. Next: box 5.12.
Thread: Visual imagery: Detail. Previous: box 5.4. Next: box 7.8.

Eric: Um hm. Is it that you remember them as not having insignia, or is it that you don't remember whether they had insignia, or that you positively remember that there was no fact about whether they had insignia or not?

Melanie: I positively remember that there is no fact that they had insignia one way or the other, so I hadn't filled any in.

Eric: Okay, so that's the kind of thing when you said it was sketchy . . .

Melanie: Yes.

[Here we have excised a brief discussion of childhood imagery and scientific ignorance of the phenomena of reading. See boxes 5.3 and 5.9.]

Russ: So anything else about number 2?

Melanie: Yeah. I had a definite feeling of both sadness and dread. I've read the book several times before, so I knew what was going to happen; but just knowing that this invasion was going to happen, just a real feeling of sadness.

Russ: And is this sadness and dread two different feelings? Or is that the same . . .

Melanie: It was kind of merged into one—that's the best way I can think of to describe it.

Russ: So you're using two words to describe basically one feeling.

Melanie: Yeah, one emotion.

Russ: Okay, and this emotion is. . . . What does it feel like other than sadness and dread? Can you be more specific than that?

Melanie: Yeah, it's like a pressing on the lower . . .

Russ: And you've got your hand sort of on your chest. Is that where the pressing seems to be?

Melanie: Um hm, yeah.

Russ: And is it clearly there? Or does it seem like sort of all over with a center there? Or . . .

Melanie: I would say probably all over with a definite center feeling right at that spot.

Russ: Okay. And when you indicate that spot, you have your hands sort of outstretched covering whatever . . . six or eight inches.

Melanie: Yeah.

Russ: So we're not talking about a small . . .

Melanie: It's not like a knot, but it's a more diffuse area.

Russ: Okay. And this pressure, is this pressure going from the front backwards or from the inside out or the outside in or from all over inwards?

Melanie: I'd say outside in.

Russ: So there's as much pressure on the back as well? Or does it seem like it's on the . . .

Melanie: No, it's coming from . . . it's top to bottom kind of feeling but so it's outside here . . .

[On demands, see box 5.12.]

Russ: So the pressure is coming at you from the front?

Box 5.12
Melanie does not give in to all demands.

Russ: I sometimes ask questions, as here ("as much pressure on the back
... ?"), that are contrary to my current understanding of the subject's
experience, to provide demands in contrary directions. Here Melanie
demonstrates that she doesn't simply cave in to all demands.

Thread: Melanie's trustworthiness: Interview pressures. Previous: box
5.11. Next: box 7.3.
Thread: Interview techniques. Previous: box 5.10. Next: box 5.17.

Melanie: Yes.

Russ: As opposed to surrounding you in pressure.

Melanie: Yeah, it's not like a vise. It's more like a steady beat, I don't
know, almost as if you wanted to give someone CPR, that kind of pressing on someone's chest.

[On "subjunctifiers," see box 5.13.]

Russ: And is that pressing going sort of perpendicular to your body,
pressing right in like you were doing CPR?

Melanie: Yes. Um hm.

Russ: Okay. And hard pressure? Soft pressure? A little pressure?

Melanie: Enough so you could feel it and it's vaguely uncomfortable,
but not painful or super intense.

Russ: And how do you know that this pressure is sadness/dread as
opposed to something else?

Melanie: I think I just recognize it.

Russ: You just know.

Melanie: Yeah.

Russ: Your witness.

Eric: [laughs] Was there some other aspect to the emotional experience, besides the pressure?

Melanie: That was it.

Eric: That was it. So there wasn't any kind of feeling in your head,
or . . .

Box 5.13
Melanie's report of emotion more qualified than previous reports

Russ: Notice the number of phrases here that express some kind of doubt about her descriptions—phrases I call *subjunctifiers*. Here, for example, Melanie starts out by describing her emotion with confidence: "I had a definite feeling of both sadness and dread." But after that statement, she qualifies nearly everything she says about the experience with words such as: "kind of," "that's the best way I can think of to describe it," "it's like a," "I would say," "probably," "I don't know," "I think." Of the 136 words that Melanie utters during this description of emotion, 32 express some doubt about the accuracy of her statements. In most of Melanie's other reports, there are far fewer subjunctifiers. She is monitoring the level of accuracy in her own statements, and displaying her sense of uncertainty in a very deep way (all the way down to the grammar). Her uncertainty with respect to emotion shouldn't cast doubt on her credibility about images or inner speech; in fact, it should *raise* that credibility in that Melanie is displaying a nuanced evaluation of her own statements—she's apparently not shy about expressing doubt when there is doubt to be expressed.

Melanie is quite typical of DES subjects in having more difficulty describing the details of the experience of emotion than of other forms of experience. [See also beep 3.1.] This is still one of Melanie's early attempts at describing an emotion, and it's to be expected that she'll need a bit of practice before she gets it right. It may well be that if we sampled with Melanie for long enough for her (and us) to get really skilled at talking about her experiences, we may still have a level of imprecision or indecision about emotional experience. That could simply be the nature of emotional experience, or it could be a limitation of this method.

Eric: For the record, since it is relevant later, I get the sense that Melanie is reaching for words, but not that she means to be expressing much doubt about the experience itself. I'm worried that she doesn't very often explicitly express doubt where doubt might be appropriate. [See box 7.7.]

We should probably also remind the reader that in cleaning up the transcripts for readability, we have excised some of Melanie's (and our) dysfluencies, false starts, and hesitations throughout the manuscript. We tried not to do this when we thought they genuinely expressed uncertainty, but that is sometimes a difficult judgment to make. Readers interested in exploring this issue more carefully should look at the full transcript and/or listen to the interview audio at http://mitpress.mit.edu/inner_experience.

Thread: Melanie's trustworthiness: Subjunctifiers and confidence. Next: box 7.2.
Thread: Emotion. Previous: box 4.7. Next: box 5.15.

Melanie: No. It felt kind of general, kind of through my body, but very specific also in that one place.

Eric: So let's say that you were a subject in CPR training—I know this is dangerous and you wouldn't really do this [Melanie laughs]—but if someone were exerting pressure on your chest . . .

Melanie: Okay.

Eric: . . . in the way that you describe, would you be able to tell the difference between that and having the emotion?

Melanie: Oh, absolutely. Well, first of all they would be in two different places, because the sadness isn't really located near my heart. It's more near my sternum.

Eric: Um hm.

Melanie: And, yeah, there is some emotional quantity to it. It's not just the feeling of the pressure but . . . or maybe . . . no, that's not true. It *is* just the feeling of the pressure, but it's the pressure in a certain way that I just recognize instantaneously as being that combination of sadness and dread.

Eric: Um hm. So really it is just exhausted by the pressure. But the pressure is a kind of unique thing that couldn't have been caused by the outside environment.

Melanie: Yes.

Eric: But if you were somehow to construct an arrangement in the outside environment that would give you that . . .

Melanie: That would most closely mirror that feeling?

Eric: . . . then that would be exactly the same experience as having the feeling?

Melanie: Yes.

[For a criticism of the preceding exchange, see box 5.14.]

Russ: I'm not buying the answer to that question. My objection is that the question is too leading, I think.

Eric: Um hm.

Russ: Let me see whether I can rephrase it. So, judging from what you just said, if we could make the same kind of pressure, then that would come out to be [the experience of] sadness/dread.

Eric: Right.

Box 5.14
This exchange asks too much of Melanie.

Russ: I'm skeptical of Melanie's "Yes" answer here, Eric, because your "So really it is exhausted by the pressure" requires Melanie to draw a conclusion that I don't think she can safely draw. She can report the big things in her awareness, and she can report some smaller things in her awareness, but it goes beyond her ability to say that there is in fact nothing else in her awareness. There may well be other small things that don't rise to the level of reportability, but that nonetheless contribute to the experience of sadness/dread. There's a big difference between "nothing exists" and "nothing else occurs to me to report."

Eric: I agree. But if Melanie can't be trusted to distinguish what she forgets from what she positively asserts as absent, that undermines other of Melanie's reports as well, such as her assertion that there were no insignia on the Stukas and, in beep 1.1, that she is not visually experiencing the paper she is looking at. [See box 4.8.]

Russ: I accept your concern, but only if we recognize that it applies only to small details. I have confidence in the big picture: that she has an image of Stukas that look like F-18s and the image is not well articulated. I think it possible that her assertion about the insignia is a confabulation in service of that larger truth. Maybe the insignia were really there but some other details (e.g. the configuration of the canopy) were missing.

I think it is a serious mistake to be too concerned about small details. This point is worth making strongly because this mistake contributed to the downfall of the Introspectionist program of a century ago. The Würzburgers believed they had discovered "imageless thought." Titchener believed that all thoughts included images. Many years of introspection studies were aimed at trying to decide this issue, but neither side was convincing, and—in part because they couldn't agree—introspection was discredited. But Christy Monson and I (1993) showed that Titchener's and the Würzburgers's *observations* were very similar to each other—subjects in both laboratories sometimes reported thoughts that have no discernible imagery. However, Titchener and the Würzburgers had different explanations for that phenomenon. Introspection can provide the phenomenon, but it cannot provide the explanation.

If we ask such impossible-to-answer questions, we can destroy the ability to observe accurately. I return to this important discussion in subsections 11.2.1 and 11.2.2.

Eric: Here, perhaps, is a key source of our disagreement and divergence in approach. I'm greatly interested in such "details" as whether the experience of emotion is (or can be) exhausted by bodily sensations (box 5.15), whether there is constant visual experience (box 4.8), and whether thought is possible without imagery. My hope—which is still merely a hope and not yet a belief—is that DES, or some modified version of it (perhaps asking

---

Box 5.14

(continued)

the subject in advance to focus only on such matters), might give us insight into such major theoretical questions, which generally turn on what are from Melanie's perspective only small details of her experience.

When you're feeling relatively conservative and I'm feeling relatively liberal we may be pretty close to agreeing about what DES can deliver. But that may not be enough for what I really want.

Thread: Melanie's trustworthiness: Details. Previous: box 4.13. Next: box 7.3.
Thread: Limits of DES. Previous: box 4.10. Next: box 9.2.

Russ [to Melanie]:   Is that what you're saying?

Melanie: No. It's the closest approximation I can get to describing it.

Eric: Oh, that's interesting. I had thought I'd heard you saying the opposite.

[Here we've excised a brief discussion of whether Eric "badgered" Melanie into saying what she did.]

Russ: Yeah. I thought . . . I didn't think she was any longer in touch with the experience when she was answering your question. I didn't think she was trying to describe the experience any more. She was trying to answer your question.

Eric: Um hm.

Russ: And part of that comes from the experience of a lot of people talking about emotion. Her way of talking about emotion here was quite typical of many people. Not everybody, by any means, but of people who say about emotion "Well, I was having a pretty specific feeling, like somewhere between sadness and dread, and it had something to do, I guess, with my body. I'm not 100 percent sure, but it seemed like more or less in my chest, more in my chest than other places."

Eric: Um hm.

Russ: But I just don't think that she meant, or that others mean in that situation, that the feeling in her chest exhausts the whole deal. I think, you know, there is a literature that says that quadriplegics can have emotion even though they cannot experience bodily aspects.

Eric: Okay.

Russ: But maybe their experience is different—perhaps we ought to sample with some quadriplegics.

Eric: Right.

Russ: But what I am sure of is that for most people who are reporting the way Melanie just reported, the experience of emotion is beyond just what she is able to put into words about the bodily expression of it.

Eric: Right, yeah. You know, the James-Lange theory of emotion, I think, if I understand it correctly, is that emotion is a kind of sensation of your own bodily state.

[On the James-Lange theory of emotion, see box 5.15.]

Russ: Yeah, but I don't think it's true.

Box 5.15
The James-Lange theory of emotion

Eric: William James (1890/1981), following Carl Georg Lange (1885), asserts that emotion, or emotional phenomenology, is the feeling of the changes in one's body that are produced by the apprehension of a fact. Thus, he writes: "Common-sense says, we lose our fortune, are sorry, and weep; we meet a bear, are frightened and run; we are insulted by a rival, are angry and strike. The hypothesis here to be defended says that this order of sequence is incorrect, that the one mental state is not immediately induced by the other, that the bodily manifestations must first be interposed between, and that the more rational statement is that we feel sorry because we cry, angry because we strike, afraid because we tremble. . . . Without the bodily states . . . we might see the bear and judge it best to run, receive the insult and judge it best to strike, but we should not actually *feel* afraid or angry." (1890/1981, pp. 1065–1066)

Melanie's denial here that her emotional experience is exhausted by the feeling of pressure in the chest does not necessarily conflict with James' view, since the further aspects of her experience may consist of other bodily sensations (whether she recognizes this fact about them or not). But for a broader sense of just how complex and multi-faceted emotional experience may be, see Lambie and Marcel 2002.

On quadriplegics and the Jamesian theory in general see Hohmann 1966; Chwalisz et al. 1988; Damasio 1999; Prinz 2004.

Russ: Our DES studies do show that there are many people whose experience of emotion is *apparently* entirely in their heads.

Thread: Emotion. Previous: box 5.13. Next: box 6.2.

Eric: Yeah. I'm not inclined to buy that either. But it would have been interesting to me had Melanie avowed that [the James-Lange view]. But I guess you're saying that's not your experience, Melanie. Right?

Melanie: No. What I thought you were saying was that that was the closest approximation I could get to that feeling. That is what it is. But there's something missing in that.

Eric: Right.

Russ: People have a hard time describing how they experience emotion. Most people. Some people can tell you exactly.

Eric: So there's something else. But it's hard to say, hard to articulate in any way what that something else is.

Melanie: Right.

[The text from here to the end of this sample is transposed from a follow-up discussion we had while talking about beep 2.3.]

Russ: I'm not getting the impression, though, that there was something separate from the experience in her chest that led her to believe that this was sadness/dread. I didn't hear her saying that she was aware of something other than the pressure in her chest. Which she now seems like she's convincingly shaking her head to the negative about. I think she's agreeing with me that she was *not* aware of . . .

Melanie: There was no other feeling.

Russ: . . . anything specific other than what was going on in her chest, and yet what was going on in her chest doesn't seem to be enough to say that this is sadness/dread.

Eric: Um hm. So, okay, it's not that there is something additional, it's just that there's this one thing, and the best you can do . . .

Melanie: . . . is describe it.

Eric: . . . is describe it that way. Okay.

Beep 2.3

In lieu of the full transcript of the discussion of this sample, here is a description of this experience as Melanie conveyed it in the interview.

Melanie was standing in the bathroom and looking around, trying to make up a shopping list in her head. At the moment of the beep she had a mental image of a white pad of paper (the same writing tablet that she uses to write shopping lists) and of her hand writing the word "conditioner." Her hand in the image was in motion, and she could see the letters coming out from the tip of the pen. At the precise moment of the beep, the letter "d" (the fourth letter in "conditioner") was coming out.

At the same time, Melanie was saying in her inner voice "con-di-tion-er," slowly, in sync with the word as she was writing it in the image.

Also at the same time, she was aware that her toes were cold. This was a noticing or sensory awareness of the coldness that was present in her awareness at the last undisturbed moment before the beep. It did not seem to involve an explicit thought process.

The full transcript is available at http://mitpress.mit.edu/inner _experience.

Beep 2.4

Melanie: During this little time period I was brushing my teeth in the bathroom. I kind of was letting my mind wander, because it's such a banal thing that I do every day. I was aware of being slightly bent over the sink and aware of the kind of rhythmic motion of my hand, you know, brushing up and down and side to side. I was also aware of the kind of cold and gooiness of the toothpaste.

Russ: And is that it, in your awareness?

Melanie: Yeah.

Russ: And when you say you're aware of being bent over, so you're sort of . . .

Melanie: Like hunched over a little bit. I mainly could feel it in my spine, because it's not a super comfortable position to be in.

Russ: So this is like a bodily awareness or a kinesthetic awareness, something like that?

Melanie: Yes.

Russ: And at the same time you're aware of the brushing motion?

Melanie: Yeah.

Russ: And does that seem like a sort of separate awareness? You've got the bent-over awareness and you've got the . . .

Melanie: Yeah, they seemed very localized. Like the feeling in my back feels *in my back,* and the up and down motion I can feel in my mouth and with my hand and my arm, because I'm holding the toothbrush and moving it.

Russ: And the cold and gooiness?

Melanie: Another feeling that is very located, just in my mouth and everything.

Russ: And nothing else is going on at this particular moment?

Melanie: Nope.

Russ: Okay. The first day you were sampling, you said that when you were speaking you had the sensation of your mouth coming closed at the end of a sentence.

Melanie: Um hm.

Russ: Is this the same kind of deal, or a different kind of deal?

Melanie: Different.

Russ: In what way?

Melanie: I'm not so much feeling my teeth or my tongue or my lips or anything like that. It's much less specific, I guess.

Russ: Which is much less specific?

Melanie: This, brushing my teeth.

Russ: Okay.

Melanie: Because it just kind of feels all over. It doesn't feel like a deliberate movement. I'm not sure if that makes any sense.

Russ: And if I asked the same question about the bent-overedness portion of it and the hand movement portion of it, would you say the same thing?

Melanie: Yeah.

Russ: These are different kinds of phenomena from the . . .

Melanie: Um hm.

Russ: Okay, then I'm turning it over to you, Eric.

Eric: You started by saying your mind was wandering.

Melanie: Yeah. Well, I mean, that was the best way to say my mind was kind of empty [laughs].

Eric: Oh, okay, so that was . . . you were just . . .

Melanie: Pretty much absorbed in what I was doing.

Eric: . . . pretty much absorbed in that. Because you could think "your mind was wandering" could mean . . .

Melanie: Yeah, jumping to different subjects.

Eric: ... thinking about, you know, what you were going to do today or something like that, but that's not ...

Melanie: No.

Russ: Which, as an aside, is why I think content analysis is usually a waste of time. You know, the sort of mindless content analysis that people do when they try to count words like "mind wandering."

Eric: Um hm.

Russ: It's not what people say, it's what they mean. [Eric laughs] And I don't mean that at all in jest. I mean that as a straightforward way the world is. You've got to pay attention to what Melanie was saying here. She said her mind was wandering, and she was not actually referring to her mind and she wasn't referring to its wandering. [Melanie laughs] But other than that, she was trying to convey something, which was that she was paying attention to sensory awarenesses.

[On Melanie's not saying what she meant, see box 5.16.]

Box 5.16
People say things that are not true.

Russ: My subjects often say things about their experiences that are not true (as Melanie did here), but that fact does *not* increase my skepticism about the accuracy of the report. Most people have little practice talking about characteristics of their inner experience, and therefore are not likely to be very skilled in their descriptions. It is the function of the interview to help subjects "clean up" their descriptions.

   Melanie didn't really mean that her mind was wandering in the usual "daydreaming" sense of that term. She simply didn't have the practice skillfully to say that she was attending to sensory events. As she gets more experience in describing samples, she will likely make fewer and fewer such mistakes.

   Because of subjects' infelicity in describing their experience, both questionnaire studies and studies that accept written or oral descriptions without question are problematic. Melanie would have answered "Yes" to a questionnaire item "Was your mind wandering?" but that would have been misleading.

Thread: Melanie's trustworthiness: General. Previous: box 5.7. Next: box 7.15.
Thread: Loose language. Previous: box 4.1. Next: box 7.9.

Eric: Right.

Russ: And you know it's sort of a high art to figure out what people mean—you've got to ride along with them pretty carefully. It's hard for me to imagine a computer that could do it. It's a complicated deal. When she said her mind was wandering, she really meant something like "my mind had wandered away." [Melanie laughs]

Eric: So let's see. Again I guess I am going to diverge from the general DES method, but . . .

Russ: That's fine.

Eric: Is your sense, Melanie, that if you're just kind of attending to what you're doing when you're brushing your teeth as you normally do, and you're not thinking about other stuff, you're not distracted or planning the day or something like that, that your experience is primarily sensory like this? Or was this especially vivid, something like "Oh how interesting—this stuff is so gooey!"

Melanie: Of course, this is only one sample, but the best I can say is that I think this was primarily a singular case . . .

Eric: Ah.

Melanie: . . . because normally if, I don't know, if I'm not distinctly thinking about anything I'm not aware of how my legs are crossed or whether or not I'm sitting or lying down, or anything like that. So I was actually quite surprised when the beep caught me doing this because I didn't really think that I did this. [For skepticism about this claim, see box 5.17.]

Eric: Um hm.

Russ: Let me . . . I'm betting against her answer to that question having been accurate, which is why your question is not a standard question of the kind I would ask . . .

Eric: Okay.

Russ: . . . and the reason that I don't ask that kind of question is that I try not to ask the kinds of questions that I don't believe the answers to. But the reason that I don't believe the answer here is that she's two for four today on sensory awarenesses, the coldness on the bottom of her feet in the previous beep and the toothpaste here. It's a small sample, of course. But I think she just doesn't *remember* things like the coldness on the bottom of her feet or the gooiness of the toothpaste.

Box 5.17
People don't necessarily know what they frequently do.

Russ: Melanie makes a general claim about her experience here ("normally . . . I'm not aware of how my legs are crossed or whether or not I'm sitting or lying down, or anything like that") that she does not generally have sensory awarenesses of this sort. I call this kind of claim a "faux generalization" to distinguish it from a true generalization, which is an inductive characterization of an explicit series of observations. A faux generalization *looks like* a generalization, but in fact may not be the result of any inductive process whatsoever, instead being the result of cognitive processes such as availability heuristics, saliency, recency, and so on.

The facts of Melanie's sampling suggest that her faux generalization is far from true: she had sensory awareness in about half of her beeps (beep 1.1 of a rosy yellow glow, beep 1.3 of her mouth closing, beep 1.4 of the green screen, beep 2.3 of cold toes, beep 2.4 of being slightly bent over and of the cold and gooiness of the toothpaste, beep 4.1 of her body bobbing up and down, beep 6.1 of her eyes looking straight ahead, beep 6.3 of her lower lip and crossed arms). The careful reader may quibble about whether a beep or two should be added to (3.2, 5.1, 6.2?) or excluded from (1.1, 6.1?) this list, but in any case, Melanie apparently has frequent sensory awarenesses.

Many people, like Melanie here and including sophisticated individuals such as psychologists and philosophers, make faux generalizations about themselves that are far from true, even though they think they are true. DES therefore makes a clear distinction between characterizations of actually occurring moments and faux generalizations, crediting the first and discounting the second. As a result, I don't like to ask what Melanie "usually" or "typically" or "normally" does, because such a question invites her to make a faux generalization. Sampling can allow, over a long series of beeps, true generalizations about what a person usually or typically or normally does by simply counting the number of times the behavior occurs. Therefore, I think that if Eric's aim was to get a sense of whether there was some special "oh this is gooey"-ness about Melanie's experience or whether it was more a case of just attentively brushing her teeth, it would have been better for him to have asked this directly, rather than inviting Melanie to (faux) generalize.

Thread: Interview techniques. Previous: box 5.12. Next: box 7.3.
Thread: Retrospective and armchair generalizations. Previous: box 5.7. Next: box 8.5.

Eric: It seems to me that we should also bear in mind the possibility (I'm not saying that this is the case) that when the beep goes off you think "Okay, what was my experience? Was I having experiences of the bathroom? Oh, the bathroom floor is cold, my feet are cold. I guess I was experiencing that at the time"—letting your knowledge of your environment feed back into your impressions of what your experience was at the time of the beep.

Melanie: I'm not defending myself by any means. But I tried specifically to really focus on the moment of the beep and not what came afterwards, because of the discussion last time about how the beep would usually catch me towards the end of a thought. And I wanted to work on trying to hone that, and so I was trying to do that as best I could.

Eric: Right. I guess the concern I have is not so much directly temporal. You could be trying to reconstruct what's going on at the moment of the beep, or immediately prior to the beep, and not confusing it in any way with what's going on now, but noticing what's going on now and then deliberately thinking "Okay, was this going on a moment before?" And then because it's going on now and because you know certain things about your environment, you might infer that it was going on the moment before as well.

Russ: Well, I don't think Melanie can confidently say she doesn't do *any* of that. I think she just *did* confidently say she *tried* not to do that.

Eric: Right. And again, you know, I'm not saying that I have any specific reason to worry about that in this particular case. How do we partial out how much is due to a kind of reconstruction?

Russ: Right, but I think we can worry about that for every single sample: The beep came and she was reading. Well, she must have been having an image; here it is. The beep came when you were reading; well, you must have been talking to yourself in inner speech; here's what you were saying. What I think is that if you're careful, you don't get as far down that road as people are afraid that you might.

Eric: I'm not sure you can know how far down that road you're getting, though.

Russ: Well, I don't think there is an answer to that except that if all these things are made up at the end, you would think any subject's reports, from one beep to the next, would be a lot more similar to each other than they turn out to be.

Eric: Um hm. Well, I guess if the person is surprised by her own experience, that would at least suggest against the idea that she was constructing something to match her expectations.

Russ: Right. And here Melanie was slightly embarrassed to be reporting that all she was doing was paying attention to her back hunched and her gooey toothpaste or whatever. As you say, you'd wonder why somebody who was not reporting what was actually happening would report something that's mildly embarrassing. It's hard for me to believe that Melanie wasn't in some way paying attention to the gooiness of the toothpaste.

Eric: Yeah, it still feels like an open possibility to me.

Russ: And does it make a difference for you about Melanie's toothpaste or your, for example, inner speech while reading? Shouldn't you be equally skeptical that you had inner speech while reading as you were that Melanie was paying attention to the gooey toothpaste?

Eric: Well, just as a matter of what it's like to believe, you do kind of have to believe yourself in a way. But in principle I'm pretty skeptical about my own reports as well. [See box 5.7.] Now, I think I'm less skeptical about the imagery—her having at least some amount of imagery while she is reading—than I am about the toothpaste.

Russ: Why is that?

Eric: Partly because I think that there really is a special problem when you're talking about your experience in light of your knowledge of your immediate environment. You *know* that there's toothpaste in your mouth, right? So it's awfully hard, I think, to separate that knowledge from the experience when you're trying to figure out what your experience is.

Russ and Melanie: Yeah.

Eric: It seems likely that there's a lot of reconstruction in the memory of experience. It's hard to know whether your environmental knowledge is being used legitimately in the reconstruction or illegitimately. Whereas with an image that's happening while you're reading, because it's something that's not in the environment, it may be easier to keep your environmental knowledge out of it.

Russ: Yeah, I'm not totally convinced of that. At this particular beep she was aware that her back was slightly bent over, and she was aware of the rhythmic motion of her hand, and she was aware of the gooiness in her mouth, and seemed sort of equally aware of all of those things.

She wasn't saying that she was aware that her left foot was at 37 degrees from her right foot, or that her right leg was slightly bent, or that her left hip was leaning up against the sink edge, or any of the other myriad of things which were legitimate candidates, it seems, in the way that you just described them as being facts of her environment.

Eric: Right.

Russ: For some reason she selected these particular three facts of her environment.

Eric: Right. It could be that those are the most salient facts of her environment.

6 The Third Sampling Day

A technical malfunction destroyed the videotape of our interview on this day. A brief description of each sample is reconstructed from our written notes.

Beep 3.1

Melanie's boyfriend was asking a question about insurance letters. Melanie's focus was not on what he was saying but on trying to remember the word "periodontist." She was thinking "peri-, peri-," to herself, with the sense that this was the beginning of the word she was searching for. She described her experience as involving knowing that she knew the word and "waiting for the word to come." Although she initially said that she heard "peri-" in her own voice, she later felt unsure whether the word fragment was actually experienced auditorially or whether it was instead "slightly visual."

Beep 3.2

Melanie was walking to her car. She described herself as being dimly aware, at the moment of the beep, *that* she was walking toward the car. She said she had an indistinct visual experience of the car, sensing, roughly, its big black shape but not such details as its brake lights. At the center of her experience was a feeling of "fogginess" and worry. She described the feeling of fogginess as involving being unable to think with her accustomed speed and as feeling "out of synch." In addition, Melanie said that, at the moment of the beep, she was in the act of *observing* this fogginess. Her worry was felt as being behind the eyes, involving a heaviness around the brow line, although she thought her experience of worry was not exhausted by those bodily feelings. [See boxes 5.14 and 5.15.]

Melanie, Russ, and Eric extensively discussed varieties of emotional self-awareness. Eric suggested a threefold distinction among (1) what Russ calls a "feeling fact of body," which involves the bodily arousal and activity normally associated with an emotion (e.g., heart racing, furrowed brow, elevated galvanic skin response) without any corresponding emotional experience (if such a thing exists), (2) emotional states that are phenomenally conscious, part of one's stream of experience, but that are unaccompanied by special self-conscious attention to the emotion as it is going on, and (3) phenomenally conscious emotional states that are self-consciously apprehended as such; that is, emotions not only experienced but accompanied somehow by the conscious thought or recognition *that* one is having the emotion. Here are some examples:

(1) Feeling fact of body. Your heart races and you make a certain facial expression appropriate to anger, without any corresponding conscious experience of anger or of your heart's racing, or of your facial expression.

(2) Un-self-conscious anger. You feel angry in your normal way (with or without bodily arousal), without particularly attending to the fact that you're angry.

(3) Self-conscious anger. You feel angry, and simultaneously you are consciously thinking to yourself (in inner speech or in some other way), something like "Boy, I'm angry!"

Partly in the course of the discussion with Melanie at the moment of the beep and partly in subsequent discussions between themselves, Russ and Eric further refined this threefold distinction; some of these refinements appear in the accompanying boxes. [For a discussion of views that collapse (1) and (2) or (2) and (3) together, see box 6.1. On "feeling fact of body," see box 6.2. For additional discussion of varieties of self-awareness, see box 6.3.]

Melanie was surely influenced by our theoretical discussion. In the course of it, she asserted that at the moment of the beep she had an acute self-conscious awareness of the fact that she was feeling foggy and a lower-level but still to some extent self-conscious awareness of the fact that she was worried. She evokes the threefold distinction in later discussions as well, for example near the end of the discussion of beep 5.1. [On the difficulty of resolving these issues, see box 6.4.]

Box 6.1
Bodily emotion without emotional phenomenology? Emotional phenomenology without self-awareness?

Eric: There are two philosophical positions that might collapse my three-fold distinction (feeling fact of body, un-self-conscious emotion, self-conscious emotion) into two. The first, a version of a "rich" view of experience [see box 4.8, section 10.3, and subsection 11.2.1], holds that the bodily manifestations of emotion must be experienced in some way, though perhaps secondarily and peripherally, whenever they occur. William James, for example, writes that "*every one of the bodily changes* [associated with emotion], *whatsoever it be, is FELT, acutely or obscurely, the moment it occurs*. . . . Our whole cubic capacity is sensibly alive; and each morsel of it contributes its pulsations of feeling, dim or sharp, pleasant, painful, or dubious, to that sense of personality that every one of us unfailingly carries with him." (1890/1981, pp. 1066–1067) James holds that feeling those bodily changes *is* just feeling the emotion. On this view, apparently, a "feeling fact of body" in your sense, Russ, without experienced emotion cannot exist.

   A second view, the "self-intimation" view of consciousness, may some-what undermine the distinction between (2) and (3)—though perhaps that distinction can still be maintained as a difference in degree. According to this view, all conscious experience must be to some extent self-conscious, accompanied by some sort of ongoing epistemic awareness or apprehension of the experience *as* conscious. The relevant version of this view holds that this self-awareness must itself be consciously experienced (otherwise it would not be reportable through DES)—perhaps simply as part of the conscious experience itself. Brentano (1911/1973) appears to hold a self-intimation view; it has also sometimes been associated with Descartes. (See also Armstrong 1980; Natsoulas 1988; Van Gulick 2004; Gallagher and Zahavi 2005; Kriegel 2006.)

   Similar issues arise around other types of experience. For example, we might wish to distinguish unexperienced visual responsiveness (if that's possible), from un-self-conscious visual experience, from self-conscious visual experience.

Russ: I have repeatedly questioned DES subjects with respect to the self-intimation view, and can confidently say that most subjects do not experience some sort of conscious apprehending state separate from the emotion. Melanie seems to be a distinct exception to this rule. Most people who are experiencing emotion strongly deny, under the most careful of questioning, the conscious existence of an observer of their emotional state. Melanie, by contrast, occasionally did appear to have a separate observational part of her awareness; for example, of her lips coming together in beep 1.3, of the fogginess in beep 3.2, of the cognitive recognizing of her yearning to go scuba diving in beep 4.1, of her anxiety in beep 5.1, of her eyes looking

---

Box 6.1

(continued)

straight ahead in beep 6.1, of the bodily aspects of her feelings while playing video games in beep 6.2, and of her concentration in beep 6.3.

Thread: Self-Awareness: General. Previous: box 4.12. Next: box 6.2.

Box 6.2
Feeling fact of body

Russ: In what I call feeling fact of body, an emotion is understood as being ongoing in the person but not in experience at the moment of the beep. For example, a subject may be anxious, but at some particular moment she is engrossed in something else, and her anxiety is not in aware-ness precisely at the moment of the beep. And yet a half-second or so later, triggered by the onset of the beep, the subject may have a very clear sense that the anxiety actually was there, ongoing; she was just not aware of it at the moment of the beep.

What was ongoing, if the emotion was not experienced? Certainly part of it is physiological: If her heart had been racing with anxiety, it didn't immediately stop racing when she shifted her attention to something else. But more than that, apparently the physiological processes were organized or processed or structured in a particular, "emotional" way, and that orga-nization/processing/structure can continue even when the anxiety itself is not experienced.

I don't know exactly what this organization/processing/structure is, but consider an analogy from vision: At one moment, you are looking at a sea of Lakers fans and you cannot spot Jack Nicholson. Then you spot him. Then the game grabs your attention and Nicholson is no longer in your awareness at all. When you look back toward Nicholson a second time, you will spot him much more easily. Some visual organization/processing/struc-ture persisted while Nicholson was out of your attention and experience. So feeling fact of body apparently refers to both an ongoing physiological process and an apparently ongoing organizational process, so that when the beep sounds, the immediately-following-the-beep recognition is that the emotion has been there all along and that the experience is now return-ing to an ongoing emotional process.

The preceding paragraphs are speculative, going beyond the capabilities of DES to discover. DES is concerned only with what appears, not with what is behind the appearance. Purely from the standpoint of DES, it is perhaps possible that emotions do pop quickly in and out of existence depending on our attention.

Box 6.2
(continued)

Thread: Emotion. Previous: box 5.15. Next: box 6.3.
Thread: Richness. Previous: box 4.8. Next: box 9.1.
Thread: Self-Awareness: General. Previous: box 6.1. Next: box 6.3.

Box 6.3
Variations of self-awareness

Eric: The space between (2) and (3) is no simple spectrum, since people may be differentially self-aware of various of the physical and phenomenal aspects of emotion (the pounding heart, the surge of adrenaline, the angry inner speech, etc.).

Somewhat differently, I would also draw a distinction between skillful self-apprehension and acute self-consciousness. The skillful apprehension of emotion may be likened to a driver's skillful apprehension of the fact that she's seeing the road and the cars around her—an apprehension revealed by such things as her reluctance to take her eyes off the road, her glancing in relevant directions, her readiness to use the mirror or crane her neck when appropriate, etc. Such actions and dispositions reveal that she implicitly knows—or skillfully apprehends—that she's *seeing* the road, rather than (primarily) *hearing* or *reading about* it. (Of course we often—even usually?—implicitly know in this way that we're seeing when we're seeing. In this sense the "skillful apprehension" is quite ordinary.) All this may be, and apparently normally is, wholly unaccompanied by any *acute self-conscious reflection* on the fact that she is seeing the road. Skillful apprehension of an unpleasant emotional experience might similarly be revealed by coping strategies, by exiting the situation, by refusing a phone call from someone with whom one should appear cool, controlling oneself before a young child, etc.—i.e., by dealing in some skillful way with the fact that one is in a certain kind of emotional state—even before explicitly recognizing the presence of the emotion in yourself.

Thread: Emotion. Previous: box 6.2. Next: box 7.4.
Thread: Self-Awareness: General. Previous: box 6.2. Next: box 6.4.

Beep 3.3

Melanie was in her car, shifting from reverse to drive. Looking at the dashboard, she saw the word "brake" lit up and she realized the parking brake was still on. At the moment of the beep she was feeling exasperated at herself, hearing, in her own voice, the phrase "Why can't I . . .?"

Box 6.4
The difficulty of understanding self-awareness of emotion

Eric: The issues discussed in this chapter we've wrestled with repeatedly in our conversations since the time of this sampling session, at greater length and with more confusion than it seems fair to inflict upon the reader. The phenomena of self-awareness are difficult to grasp and discuss. Our talents and language are not well-suited for navigating this region. That is, I think, an intrinsically interesting fact; it also underwrites some of my hesitancy to trust Melanie's reports about her degree of self-awareness. [See also boxes 8.9 and 9.3.]

Russ: I think that the proper reaction to this difficulty is not simply to be hesitant to trust Melanie's reports, but to gain Melanie's differentiated cooperation, which is what we did. Our discussions clarified the distinctions for all three of us, and all three of us recognized the difficulties involved. Thus, when Melanie subsequently reported her self-awareness it was with a differentiated understanding of the issues. We conveyed to Melanie, and she (I believe) understood and accepted, that we needed to be extra careful in this area so as not to say more than was warranted.

Thread: Melanie's trustworthiness: Attunement to distinctions. Previous: box 4.5. Next: box 7.8.
Thread: Self-Awareness: Melanie's unusual. Previous: box 4.14. Next: box 7.11.
Thread: Self-Awareness: General. Previous: box 6.3. Next: box 8.6.

The beep occurred right after the word "I," and Melanie had the sense that the sentence, had it not been interrupted, would have concluded with a phrase something like "remember about the parking brake." She felt that even at the moment of the beep, before the sentence had been completed in her thoughts, she had the general sense of its entire meaning. She distinctly felt that the voice was heard, rather than actively spoken (in contrast to beep 3.1), almost as if it were a recording playing back in her mind—a fact she found surprising about this experience. She also felt that this episode of inner hearing was distinctly located in her head, moving from the region near her right ear toward the region near her left ear. Melanie said that the emotion of exasperation was also present at the moment of the beep but that she had no, or very little, self-conscious awareness of it *as* exasperation, although she felt uncertainty about this last point and about the issues involved in the self-awareness of emotion. [On the relationship between thought and inner speech, see box 6.5.]

Box 6.5
Thought and inner speech

Eric: People often suppose that when we think in inner speech we really are thinking *in* inner speech—that the speech is, in some robust sense, the *medium* of the thought, the thing that makes the thought conscious. (See, e.g., Carruthers 2005.) Although there is much I find attractive in this view, Melanie's experience as reported here raises a question for it. (Let me bracket here the distinction that Russ finds important, but to which most philosophers are insensitive, between "inner hearing"—which, strictly speaking, is what Melanie reports in beep 3.3—and "inner speech." See beeps 1.1 and 1.2.)

Generalizing from my own experience as best as I can recall it (and in a way I'm sure Russ will deplore), it seems to me that I often have some sense of what I'm about to say before I say it, or as I'm just beginning to say it—whether in inner or outer speech. Sometimes that sense is only very rough and inchoate; but in other cases, as perhaps like Melanie's here, it's fairly specific and developed. What's nice about this sample is that, since the beep interrupts Melanie mid-speech as it were, we can observe (if her report is accurate) that the conscious thought is already formed *before* the speech is complete. It runs, half-articulated, somewhat ahead of the speech (or hearing). Maybe, had the experience not been interrupted, Melanie would have completed the predicted sentence, catching up with the fully formed thought—or maybe even the thought would have departed quickly while the sentence completed itself with a kind of thoughtless inertia. In either case, if the thought is complete before the inner speech is complete, inner speech can't be the medium of the thought, can it?

Russ: I take my primary job as a DES explorer to be the describing of phenomena, not the explaining of what produces those phenomena, so I am somewhat reluctant to enter into this discussion. That said, I do agree that inner speech is probably not the (entire) medium of thought. My reasons: (1) As you point out, I do think there is an unequivocal phenomenological distinction between inner speech and inner hearing, the same phenomenological distinction as between speaking into a tape recorder and hearing your voice played back. In Melanie's example here, there *is* no inner speech, so experienced speech can't be essential to thinking; (2) unsymbolized thinking exists (Hurlburt 1990, 1993, 1997; Hurlburt and Heavey 2006)—I'm confident that people frequently think without any experience of words (spoken or heard), images, or other symbols; therefore experienced words can't be essential to thinking; and (3) the phenomenon that I call partially unworded speech exists (rarely), where the person is saying something in inner speech but one or several of the words are missing. "Space" is left for those words, as in "I should check the schedule for _____ Airlines." At the moment of the beep, there is an experienced hesitation between "I should check the schedule for" and "Airlines"; there

Box 6.5
(continued)

is no question that the missing word is "Southwest," but that word has not appeared in experience. That indicates to me that inner speaking is at least the coordination of two processes, one that creates the rhythm and another that creates the words themselves. (That is true for external speaking as well, I think.) There may well be an underlying thought process that creates both the rhythm and the word processes, but I know nothing of any underlying thing. By the way, while the sense-of-the-thought phenomenon you describe as characteristic of yourself exists in DES subjects, it is relatively rare.

Eric: Just to be clear, Russ: Are you saying that it's relatively rare for people to have a sense—I mean a conscious, but obviously not a linguistically articulated sense—of what they're about to say as they're beginning to say it? I'd have thought we *normally* have such a sense, though often only diffuse. Maybe you think we have that sense only dispositionally (so that we could, if asked, call up what we were about to say), but not as part of our conscious experience? (This might take us back to issues about the periphery and "richness" of experience. See box 4.8.) Or do you only mean that something like *pure* "thoughtless inertia" is rare?

Russ: Yes—the most frequent experience of inner speech involves simply the speech itself with no conscious sense of what is about to be said. When beeped while speaking aloud, most frequently DES subjects report no inner or outer experience at all. It's as if the act of speaking exhausts all their experience-making resources (whatever that means) so that there's no conscious sense of what they are intending to say or even of the words they are using to say it. They are speaking—nothing more.

Thread: Inner speech and hearing. Previous: box 5.7. See also subsection 11.1.3.

7 The Fourth Sampling Day

Melanie: Okay. I was having a conversation with my boyfriend over dinner regarding extreme sports, and kind of sports in general. I'm a really big scuba diver—it's one of my main hobbies and I absolutely adore doing it. And right before the beep went off, my boyfriend was saying something about how there are some sports that you can play in a rough and difficult way, but they don't wind up being life threatening, while there are other sports that you can play or do in a life-threatening manner. And so right at the moment of the beep, I was thinking about the comparison . . . well, just the notion of scuba diving and the possibility of its being life threatening. And what I was feeling was just this intense yearning and desire to go diving, because I miss it and I love it so much, as well as this feeling of being in the water, you know, where you're kind of bobbing at the top or surface of the lake or the ocean or something like that and you can feel the wave pick you up and drop you down, pick you up and drop you down.

Russ: So is that like two different sensations, there's the yearning to go and . . .

Melanie: One's very emotional, and one's more physical.

Russ: Okay. And is one of these more central to your experience or awareness or whatever it is we want to call that? Or are they sort of equal? Or . . .

Melanie: They're pretty much equal.

Russ: Okay, then let's start with one of them, and when we get done with that we'll move to the other one. So the emotional part. What . . .

Melanie: Just this desire to go, like this craving to go diving.

Russ: And what's that like?

Melanie: I feel it pretty much all over. It's really difficult to describe, because it doesn't feel like there's a location. It's just this *incredible* want, just to have the experience of going diving and going through the motions. I guess I can't pinpoint it to a location.

Russ: And is this a bodily thing—can you pinpoint it to your body? Or is it outside your body as well? Or in your head as well? Or . . .

Melanie: It's in my head as well.

Russ: And in the room as well? Or . . .

Melanie: No. It seems located just . . . it's in me, but it doesn't feel localized in a particular place. Like when I was worrying [beep 3.2] I said I could feel it especially behind my eyes and around my brow. This isn't like that. This is all-encompassing.

Russ: Okay. And when you say it's in your head as well as in your body, is it in your head in the same way as it is in the rest of your body? Or are you meaning to say that there was some more cognitive or mental or whatever aspect to it that's in your head?

Melanie: Probably more cognitive, I would think, because I knew what it was that I was feeling. [For concerns about this answer, see box 7.1.]

Russ: Okay. Then the feeling part, the bodily part, it's all over in your body, and it's hard to describe—I'm totally in agreement with that. But can we be *somewhat* more descriptive? Is it like pressure, pain, heat feeling? A twisting, turning . . .

Melanie: I guess twisting is actually pretty good. It kind of feels like just my entire body is being really twisted, in a way, kind of tense, with this craving.

[For more on subjunctifiers, see box 7.2.]

Russ: And when I said, and you bought into "twisting" as the alternative, and you sort of twisted with your hands, is this like one twist, like somebody has grabbed your ankles and turned you one way and grabbed your shoulders and turned the other . . .

Melanie: Yes.

Russ: . . . as opposed to a whole series of little twists?

Melanie: Yeah, it's not like the feeling, you know, when your esophagus is clumping down or anything like that, but it's just one general twist in your entire body.

Box 7.1
Is Melanie inferring rather than recalling?

Eric: Note that Melanie's statement here is structured like an inference from the fact that she knew what she was feeling to the conclusion that there was something cognitive going on in her head. That amplifies my skepticism here.

Russ: I agree that this statement is probably inferential. I disregard such statements (statements that include "because," "on account of," "usually," etc.) for precisely that reason. However, I don't think this provides reason to distrust Melanie's reports in general. Notice that this sentence also contains two subjunctifiers ("probably" and "I would think"), indicating that Melanie is a careful (although not perfect) reporter: she herself is discounting what she is saying; she is not entirely taken in by her theories. Like most other subjects, Melanie doesn't use subjunctifiers indiscriminately. [See boxes 5.13 and 7.2.] I have noticed over the years that even relatively uneducated people switch skillfully between declarative and subjunctive sentences when they switch between confident description and problematic reports.

One aim of DES interviews is to help subjects learn to give straightforward descriptions that they don't feel the need to subjunctify—and thus to eliminate theoretical and inferential statements.

Eric: Still, not all theory-driven distortions may be signaled in this way. For example, in beep 1.3, box 4.14, you, Russ, are skeptical—it seems to me rightly—of Melanie's awareness of her mouth closing at the end of a sentence. Yet her claim there appears straightforward and confident. It seems likely to me that all of Melanie's reports are to some extent affected—for good as well as for ill—by her general background theories and her knowledge or impressions of her own patterns of experience. I'm reluctant to rely much on the hope that straightforward descriptions are generally atheoretical and non-inferential.

Russ: First, I am skeptical of all reports; that skepticism is sometimes heightened for a variety of reasons, for example: because the reports are unusual (as in box 4.14); because the reports seem to be generalizations; because the reports contain subjunctifications; and so on. But a heightened level of skepticism does not imply a heightened level of disbelief (I came to believe that Melanie's mouth-closing awareness was probably true, for example). Heightened skepticism means that we should be especially careful to ask good questions, and perhaps that we should be on heightened alert to look for confirmations or disconfirmations elsewhere in the record. I do agree with the general notion that Melanie's reports are to some extent affected by her theories and her previous experience. The question is the size of the extent, and whether it can be held within satisfactory limits.

Box 7.1
(continued)

I also agree that not all theory-driven distortions are signaled. But some are (as here), and it is therefore possible to use those occasions to instruct subjects that we wish to avoid theories or inferences. We use a variety of techniques so to instruct: direct conversation, ignoring, and so forth. But I recognize that psychology and philosophy have used a variety of similar techniques without adequate success. However, the DES focus on the description of the single moment is substantially different from those previous attempts. At issue in this book is whether that single-moment focus, combined with the interview's focus on description of phenomena and repeated explicit and implicit avoidance of presuppositional theories, can be enough to limit the magnitude of the distortions. I think so.

Eric: Such instruction probably will reduce the use of phrases of the sort that tend to signal theories and inferences in favor of balder, more confident-sounding statements. However, it may do so not only through reducing the most blatant kinds of theoretical inference but also through encouraging a kind of blasé confidence or reluctance to show hesitation— or so I worry.

Thread: Melanie's trustworthiness: Influence of generalizations. Previous: box 4.18. Next: box 7.14.
Thread: Reconstruction. Previous: box 5.4. Next: box 7.6.

Box 7.2
More on subjunctifiers

Russ: Note that there are six subjunctifiers in this 29-word utterance: "I guess," "actually," "pretty good," "kind of" (twice), and "in a way." This rings my skeptical alarms, so I ask the following series of questions, which eventually lead Melanie to say that the twisting is more metaphorical than descriptive. That's part of the evidence that Melanie uses subjunctifiers skillfully to signal departures from simple description. That of course does not imply that a lack of subjunctifiers means that Melanie is being straightforwardly descriptive [see box 7.1]; it does mean, I think, that Melanie can be a nuanced reporter.

Thread: Melanie's trustworthiness: Subjunctifiers and confidence. Previous: box 5.13. Next: box 7.7.

Russ: And when we're talking about "one general twist of your entire body," is that like a metaphor? Or does it actually feel sort of like your body is being twisted physically?

Melanie: Probably more of a metaphor to explain the kind of tension that I feel.

Russ: So there's a tension, and to say that your body is tense, that would not be metaphorical . . .

Melanie: No.

Russ: . . . you're actually experiencing a tension in your body.

Melanie: Yes, definitely.

Russ: But that tension is not . . . it doesn't feel twisty in the sense that your feet are going to the right and your shoulders are going to the left, or clockwise and counterclockwise . . .

Melanie: No. But there's that kind of feeling all wrapped up about something and tense about something is there.

Russ: Okay. And is there any other way to describe the tension? From the inside out or from the outside in or . . .? [On whether Russ is creating too much pressure to be specific here, see box 7.3.]

Melanie: Yes. Inside out, in a way, almost feels like trying to . . . like there's something inside me trying to reach out for something.

Russ: And you're aiming forward with your hand . . .

Melanie: Yes. It would be out, away from my body. And it would be in a forward direction, not backwards, not out to the side. It felt very forward.

Russ: So like your body is going forward.

Melanie: Yeah.

Russ: And you're indicating it from your chest, sort of, but . . .

Melanie: It was more all over, you know, even like my knees and my toes and everything like that.

Russ: Okay. So like your whole body is trying to go forward. It feels like going forward.

Melanie: Yeah, reaching out.

Russ: And is that a metaphorical thing like the twisting thing, or is that more . . .

Melanie: No. That's more it.

Box 7.3
Is there excessive pressure for a specific description?

Eric: Note that Melanie begins by saying the feeling is "hard to describe." You persistently ask about it, Russ, and eventually (below) Melanie settles on a description that she thinks is not (too) metaphorical. I'm torn between applauding your persistence and worrying that you've pressured her into inventing something.

I suspect that most people have a deep-rooted reluctance to admit ignorance about something it seems they should know; and, to Melanie, it probably seems that she should know the details of her experience at the moment of the beep. Furthermore, she is now meeting with us to discuss the details of that experience. Consequently, she may feel considerable pressure to say something about the details. That pressure, plus the inherent difficulty of describing emotional experience (which you acknowledge in box 5.13), and the likely indistinctness of the memory [see box 7.5], may invite a kind of invention.

I'm not saying that Melanie would *deliberately* make things up. But she, and your other subjects, might react as locals do when asked directions by a tourist: Instead of accurately assessing how much they know and how much they don't, they simply give it their best shot—often feeling and expressing genuine confidence all the while, even if they are quite inaccurate. [For further support of this view, see box 7.7.]

Russ: It's probably impossible to be perfectly open, but I do think my interviews create a very unusual situation that may to a large extent mitigate the pressures you describe. Without being arrogant, I hope, let me say that I think that most psychological investigators don't take these issues as seriously as I do. I think it's possible—and I think I do it at least moderately well—to say "I'm interested in what your experience was, whatever it was, including nothing, and including 'Well I don't really know' and including 'it was so fuzzy that I can't really tell you about it.'" I'm happy to get any of these responses. I say such things over and over, and (I think) act entirely consistently with those intentions. Those intentions are (I think) pretty darn genuine, as the result of much work and practice. Consequently, I think most subjects understand that I really do want to know precisely what they are really experiencing at the moment of the beep—not more and not less. When subjects accept that that is true (which generally takes a while), it is often an extremely powerful event for them: *This guy really wants to know what is really going on with me!* They may never have received such a communication, and even if they have, quite likely never one delivered with such skill and consistency. Most subjects, as did Melanie, I think, experience this as a rare opportunity (for self-discovery, for genuine communication) and are motivated to a very high level of carefulness, far different from a local responding to a tourist.

As for persistence: If I quit asking for details before we all are satisfied that we understand each other to the limits of our abilities, then I have

---

Box 7.3

(continued)

conveyed by deed that I don't really care about Melanie's experience. I *have* to be persistent, not so much because the details themselves are important, but because the attempt to get the experience as exactly right as possible is important. The art of the method is to convey at the same time and with equal vigor that I don't want us to go too far.

It is possible (probably likely) that my persistence encourages some invention. At the end of a discussion, I generally explicitly acknowledge that pressure, and then say something like "Well, this is only one beep, and next time perhaps we can do better." And that is true, because it is likely that I have conveyed the genuine aim for accurate description of detail, and therefore won't have to be quite so persistent the next time.

So while perhaps I can't completely eliminate your concern here, I do think it applies only in a limited way, and at the margins.

I feel very confident, for example, not only that Melanie was yearning to go scuba diving, but also that her yearning was experienced at least in large part as her body leaning, reaching forward (as she says below).

Thread: Melanie's trustworthiness: Details. Previous: box 5.14. Next: box 8.1.
Thread: Melanie's trustworthiness: Interview pressures: Previous: box 5.12. Next: box 8.1.
Thread: Interview techniques. Previous: box 5.17. Next: box 8.6.

Russ: So this is more descriptive of what the sensation actually feels like . . .

Melanie: Yes.

Russ: . . . and the twisting is more . . .

Melanie: A metaphor.

Russ: . . . a way of trying to describe the degree of tension, or something like that.

Melanie: Yeah.

Russ: Eric, do you want to ask more about that, or shall I press on to the other half of it?

Eric: [laughs] Boy, it's so hard to know what to make of all this. It's such a funny description. I'm not saying that, I mean . . .

Russ: What's funny about it? And we're not taking it personally or critically or whatever, but what is it about it that you find hard or funny or whatever?

Eric: I guess my inclination is to read it as pretty metaphorical, even what Melanie is saying is less metaphorical. Umm. Like your toes reaching forward, and . . .

Russ: And if you take the whole thing as metaphorical, what do you make of Melanie's seemingly confident distinction between twisting as being metaphorical and reaching forward as being not metaphorical?

Eric: You know, I'm not sure what to make of it. I don't know.

[On whether people are mostly alike, see box 7.4.]
   [Here we have excised a discussion of people's loose language in describing experience. See boxes 4.1, 5.16, and 7.9 and section 3.3.]

Russ: Okay. But Melanie is saying it's like her body is reaching forward. And that is a description of the sensations in her body, not a metaphor. A metaphor could use exactly the same words. She could say "It's like my whole body is reaching forward" where that really means is "I want something and I want it bad, and I'm trying to convey to you that I want it bad and I'm using these words that don't have anything to do with the experience. It's like my whole body wants it."

Eric: Right.

Russ: But that, I think, is what she's *not* trying to say here. What she *is* trying to say is that there's something about her body that leads her to say in as descriptive a way as she can say "my body is reaching forward."

Melanie: [nods].

Eric: Right.

Russ: She has assented to all of that.

Eric: [laughs] Yeah. How much of this did you note at the time that you were making notes after the beep, Melanie? And how much of this is stuff—phrases or words—that you're only generating now?

Melanie: Umm, most of it I'm probably generating now. [For a concern about this, see box 7.5.]

Eric: And are you generating it, do you think, on the basis of a sharp memory of the emotional experience? Or are you kind of re-creating the emotional experience now and then kind of observing it now as you're reporting? How would you describe that process?

Melanie: Remembering the way it feels like. Because the way I took my notes was to engage my memory to think about the experience . . .

Eric: Um hm.

Box 7.4
Are people mostly alike?

Russ: Eric, you apparently find some of Melanie's reports relatively easy to accept, such as her images and inner speech. But you find other reports more difficult, like her report of bodily yearning here. I worry that you find this description more problematic because you yourself don't have access to that particular kind of experience—that you fall victim to the if-I-don't-do-it-then-others-must-not-do-it-either syndrome.

Eric: That's probably right, at least in part—but too strongly put. This is a key issue. I do think that there's prima facie reason to suppose that people are mostly similar, except where there are gross differences in behavior or physiology. The burden of proof, then, should generally be on the person who says that two apparently normal people are radically different inside. Consequently, when someone says something about her experience that seems vastly different from what my own experience is, that does give me grounds for suspicion about the claim. Of course, for a skeptic like me, this issue gets complicated with questions about self-trust. How much should I trust my own judgments about what seems familiar and what seems alien?

But let me now say that I feel like relenting a bit on the skepticism here. In retrospect now, it does seem to me somewhat familiar and reasonable to suppose that a strong yearning might sometimes be accompanied by something like a feeling of forward impetus, or a readiness to move forward—perhaps as a kind of broadly distributed motor imagery of moving forward.

Russ: In my view it is a large mistake to "think that there's prima facie reason to suppose that people are mostly similar." Whether or not people's experiences are similar is exactly the issue, and should be decided on a flat playing field, not one tipped in the direction of some preconception.

I have sampled with some people whose inner experience is characterized almost exclusively by inner speech; with others whose inner experience is characterized almost exclusively by images, or by sensory awareness, or by unsymbolized thinking, or by feelings; with others whose inner experience is characterized by a combination of all those; with some whose inner experience is characterized by many simultaneous events; with others whose inner experience is characterized almost exclusively by one event at a time; and so on. So, yes, I think people are importantly different when it comes to inner experience. I accept that I have a burden of showing that that is not hogwash, and I have been trying in a variety of ways (including inviting you to participate in this project) to shoulder that burden. But I must say I have been sampling with substantial skepticism for 30 years, and I'm 99.99 percent sure that I haven't been duped in all those observations.

Box 7.4
(continued)

As for your relenting because the feeling of impetus in yearning now seems familiar: I cannot say strongly enough how risky I believe is the appeal to familiarity. If-I-do-it-it-must-be-possible is just as dangerous as its opposite.

Eric: You seem to be assuming here that your species of experience sampling is the best method—the "flattest playing field," as it were. But if one is attempting to assess the validity of experience sampling itself, then one has to think about whether its deliverances are plausible. There is no way to do this other than to bring in antecedent (that doesn't mean unchangeable) opinions, thoughts, or preconceptions that arise from sources other than experience sampling. Since I think it is antecedently plausible that people with similar physiology and behavior have largely similar basic forms of experience, if your results suggest otherwise, in my view that casts suspicion on those results.

Russ: I don't simply *assume* that DES is the flattest playing field; I've become convinced of it after 30 years of (I think) careful investigation. I may well be mistaken; that is what is at issue in this book.

One of our central disagreements is what to do when a DES result conflicts with your antecedent plausibility. You think the conflict itself is evidence against DES. I think that such antecedent plausibilities are a primary cause of the unproductive history of the science of inner experience. The list of antecedent plausibilities that sophisticated people have held is very long: all thinking is in words; all thinking is in images; images don't exist; images always exist; emotions always exist; and so on. Therefore I think you should bracket your plausibilities (holding them neither to be correct nor incorrect). If you (antecedently) think that everyone's inner experience is mostly the same, then you should question Melanie extra carefully but open-mindedly on those points, not simply hold your plausibility against her.

Thread: Bracketing presuppositions. Previous: box 5.7. Next: box 7.13.
Thread: Emotion. Previous: box 6.3. Next: box 7.9.
Thread: Human similarity and difference. Previous: box 5.3. Next: box 7.12.

Box 7.5
A concern about introducing unrecorded details

Eric: If right after the beep Melanie didn't think particularly about whether it was kind of twisty or forward-reaching or pay attention to what parts of her body were involved—if she didn't flag these particular facts at the time, but rather just the intensity of the feeling (which is what she emphasizes in her initial description)—then I am reluctant to trust her memory of that detail of the experience, especially since she comes to this description so late in the interview. It seems to me that such aspects of one's experience evaporate pretty quickly if one doesn't specifically note and label them as soon as they've happened (as I argued in section 3.3). If there is a pressure to unwittingly invent details [see box 7.3], this report seems like a plausible candidate for having been invented.

Russ: How to ask the subject to record is a dilemma. There's good reason to keep the recording task the property of the subject, to be used in whatever way the subject finds effective. For example, the eyewitness testimony literature holds that it's best to let witnesses tell their stories their way at least at first, and hold probing questions to later. If we were to tell Melanie how to take notes, we would (a) substantially impose our presuppositions about what to pay attention to, (b) interfere with her own natural way of remembering, and (c) weaken the subject's co-investigator responsibility. Sometimes I do give subjects explicit note-taking instructions, and inspect those notes, but that is always only after the do-it-the-subject's-own-way has raised questions. Maybe the best way to allay your concerns would be to sample for more days during which you may give whatever instructions you like.

I agree that *some* of what Melanie says here is probably not accurate—she's describing a hard-to-describe phenomenon and hasn't yet had much practice at it. However, the equivocation about details should not be held against the big picture, as I said in box 5.14. Here, I'm *quite* confident that she is yearning, and that this yearning is somehow bodily. I'm *pretty* confident that it's in some way a going forward. I'm *not very confident* that we understand what the "twisting" part is.

I'm quite sure that we have trained Melanie to pay attention to her emotional experience (among other kinds of experiences) in ways she hadn't done before we embarked on this endeavor, but that training is probably not complete. So I think she does now at the moment of the beep pay more careful attention to her emotional experience than she did before, and that tomorrow and the next day she'll pay more accurate attention than she did today.

Thread: Melanie's trustworthiness: Memory. Previous: box 5.4. Next: box 7.6.

Melanie: . . . and I guess the way I'm trying to do that is to put myself . . . to remember the exact situation and exactly how it felt.

Eric: Right, although it's interesting that you . . . that there's an incomplete sentence there, which is "you put yourself. . . ." You might say that there are two ways of remembering. One is a kind of abstract remembering that doesn't involve imaginatively putting yourself back in the situation you were previously in, and the other involves kind of putting yourself in the situation in imagination, and then kind of provoking some of the old reactions. Like I remember at one point when we were talking about an image, you said something like that you were reconstructing the image as you spoke to us about it. [See beep 2.1 and box 5.4.]

Melanie: Um hm.

Eric: That's a kind of way of remembering by actually doing something now that you know to be similar to what happened in the past, and then reporting on what's going on now.

Melanie: That's not what I'm doing now.

Eric: That's not what you're doing in this case.

Melanie: Uh uh [No].

[Here Eric and Russ discuss "reconstruction" and the extent to which Russ is pressuring Melanie. Some of this discussion has been condensed into boxes 7.3 and 7.6.]

Eric [after agreeing that Russ is remarkably open about different alternative descriptions of experience]:   But there's one type of answer that you haven't particularly laid space for, and that I haven't heard Melanie say. I don't know if she said it at all, or certainly not very much. That answer is "I can't remember it to that level of detail." If you're not reporting on a reconstruction of the experience, and especially if you took only pretty sketchy notes at the time, you'd think that there would be a level of detail you wouldn't get. You wouldn't be able to remember all the details exactly right. So then an accurate report would involve recognizing that you didn't remember one thing or another, and an inaccurate report might involve filling in some aspect of the experience that you don't actually accurately remember.

Russ: Yeah. [to Melanie] Would you feel comfortable in saying "I don't remember?"

Melanie: Yes. In fact I think I have.

Russ: I think you have too, actually.

Box 7.6
Recalling and reconstructing

Eric: I seem to be working with a somewhat inchoate sense of "reconstruction." As I use the term at the end of day 2, "reconstruction" means something like using present knowledge (or opinions or theories) to infer, or to guide one's opinion about, what is likely to have been the case. In this broad sense of "reconstruction," probably all memory for past events is to some extent reconstructive (the classic articulation and defense of this view is Bartlett 1932/1995)—though the extent to which a particular report is reconstructive may vary, as well as the extent the opinions guiding the reconstruction are well-founded.

In this passage, I'm using "reconstruction" to mean something more specific: attempting to re-create the experience, then reporting on the re-created experience, with the expectation that what is true of it will be true of the original experience. Melanie here denies that she is re-creating the yearning in this way. I'm not sure I believe her; I think she could be doing that without realizing it. Robert Gordon (1986, 1992) and Alvin Goldman (1989, 2006), for example, argue that thinking about another's mental states often involves imaginatively putting oneself in the other's shoes, perhaps without even being aware that one is doing so. Could Melanie likewise be imaginatively putting herself back in the morning's situation and to some extent re-experiencing the emotion, either actually or hypothetically (if that makes sense)?

This may seem perverse, but I think, partly for reasons described in box 7.5, that her claim here may be *more* believable as a reconstruction than as simple recall.

Russ: I know of no way absolutely to eliminate the possibility that she is reporting on a re-created experience. However, we can reduce the potential for errors due to reconstruction by (1) stressing the difference between a recollection and a reconstruction and valuing the former over the latter, (2) keeping the interval between the event and its report as short as possible, and (3) where desirable, encouraging the subject to write more detailed accounts immediately after the beep.

So I accept that our "discovery of Melanie's experience," the end result of the DES interview, is (roughly speaking) X percent Melanie's experience at the moment of the beep, Y percent Melanie's incorrect reconstruction during the interview, and Z percent our own presuppositionally mistaken overlay over Melanie's reports. The object is to employ a method that keeps Y and Z as small as possible.

For many purposes, and this responds to your "perverse" comment, the size of Y is not terribly important, because X + Y is still uniquely Melanie. If Melanie uses a newly (re-)created image in place of an original image, we still find out something about the characteristics of Melanie's *images*. You, for a contrasting example, are more likely to use inner speech to

---

Box 7.6
(continued)

re-create an original inner speaking. As long as we keep Z small, we might be able to understand something of the important differences between Melanie and you, all the while recognizing that both of you are giving re-created (X + Y) reports.

Thread: Melanie's trustworthiness: Memory. Previous: box 7.5. See also section 10.4 and subsection 11.2.4.
Thread: Reconstruction. Previous: box 7.1.

[On whether Melanie admits ignorance, see box 7.7.]

Melanie: Especially on the second day, when I had a lot of mental images [beeps 2.1 and 2.2]. I remember there were a couple times, and I think it was mainly you, Eric, who were asking the questions, when I several times said I wasn't sure, or I didn't know. Oh! For example, when I had that scene in that book in my head, when there were people standing on a road talking, and one of the characters was dressed in an army uniform . . .

Eric: Right.

Melanie: . . . but I couldn't tell you what shoes he was wearing.

Eric: Right.

Melanie: And I remember saying I didn't remember or I didn't see that.

Eric: Right. But there's a difference between those two. And maybe you did say you don't remember for some things—I don't want to say you didn't [laughs] say it *ever*. But there certainly is a difference between saying "I don't remember whether I saw, or had an image of, one particular shoe or another," and "I remember that the image did not specify what type of shoe he was wearing."

[On underspecification vs. failing to remember, see box 7.8.]

Russ: Yeah. I think it's part of my expectation that not remembering is okay, and I think I convey that to people that I work with. And I think, maybe not perfectly, but I think I convey that pretty well. You may have a different view of that, Eric, but I think there's the implication by the

Box 7.7
How often does Melanie admit ignorance?

Eric: In fact, reviewing the transcripts, I find that Melanie explicitly admits ignorance or uncertainty about what was going on in her experience at the moment of the beep for the most part only when it comes to finding the right *words* to express her experience. Prior to this discussion she never explicitly admits ignorance about even the smallest details of the experiences themselves, except maybe in beep 3.1. The only clear exception to this tendency in the preserved transcripts is when, later in this discussion (and so possibly as a result of the present conversation), she disavows knowledge of whether she was in an up or a down phase in the cycle of imagined bobbing in the water. You have pointed out that Melanie sometimes uses "subjunctifiers" that implicitly suggest a lack of confidence [see boxes 5.13 and 7.2], but generally her hesitations are resolved.

I find it difficult to believe that Melanie could accurately remember all the details of her experiences she confidently reports. This undermines my trust in Melanie's confidence.

Russ: I think you overstate when you say she "never explicitly admits ignorance about even the smallest details of the experiences themselves." For example, in beep 1.3 she said about the image of the shed "I can see more than just the outline of the objects in the room but beyond that I couldn't tell you the grain of the wood, or, you know, where one board stops and the next begins." In beep 2.1 she said about an image of the soldier "I know that he's standing [but] I couldn't tell you what directions his feet are pointed in." It seems to me that she quite capably and unabashedly admits ignorance about details when she is in fact ignorant.

I have agreed that all subjects, including Melanie, confabulate details to some degree. [See box 5.14.] But Melanie shows herself to be quite careful, so I don't think that degree is very high.

Eric: Both of the cases you cite are cases in which I interpret Melanie as admitting a certain amount of indeterminacy in the image, *not* admitting ignorance about her own experience. The two admissions are very different, as I emphasize in box 7.8.

Russ: I think Melanie in both cases is ambiguous about whether there is indeterminacy in the image or ignorance about her ability to recall the details. In fact, I think the disentanglement of such discriminations is often exceedingly difficult if not impossible to do in practice. You are correct to point out that the two admissions might have very different philosophical ramifications, but it is a large mistake to make too much of a distinction that is by its nature unreliable. (I will return to this issue in subsections 11.2.1 and 11.2.2.)

Thread: Trustworthiness: Subjunctifiers and confidence. Previous: box 7.2. Next: box 7.8.

Box 7.8
Melanie's conflation of underspecification and lack of memory

Eric: There's a crucial difference, central to our discussions of the nature of imagery on day 2, between failing to remember what type of shoe the soldier was wearing and remembering that the image did not specify the type of shoe. The latter involves no ignorance whatsoever about the imagery experience itself: It is a clear memory of the fact that the image was vague in a certain respect.

My sense at the time was that Melanie's grasp of this distinction was somewhat tenuous, which seems to be confirmed by her comment here. Perhaps this supports the point of box 5.14, that we should be very cautious in trusting even apparently sophisticated subjects regarding the kinds of "details" on which most major disputes about the structure of conscious experience tend to hang.

Russ: I think you oversimplify the possibilities when you differentiate between only two: (a) the image was clear but was forgotten and (b) the image was nonspecific and remembered clearly. I think, based on my DES work, that there is (x) a continuum of clarity of inner seeing, (y) a continuum of detailedness of inner seeings, and (z) a continuum of accuracy of remembering. Your (a) is at the clear/detailed/forgotten corner of my cubic space; your (b) is not adequately specified in my space: it could be somewhere along the unclear half of x and/or along the not-very-detailed half of y, along with the accurate end of z.

I understand Melanie to be saying (and originally to have said on day 2) something like (according to my cubic model) "I don't know what kind of shoe, and I don't know why I don't know. It could be because it wasn't specified, or because it wasn't clear, or because I can't remember."

Eric: I admit this is a possible interpretation, though I interpreted her differently. In any case, the point remains that there is no detail, however trivial, that she has *clearly* and *explicitly* said she doesn't remember.

Thread: Melanie's trustworthiness: Attunement to distinctions. Previous: box 6.4. Next: box 8.9.
Thread: Melanie's trustworthiness: Subjunctifiers and confidence. Previous: box 7.7.
Thread: Visual imagery: Detail. Previous: box 5.11. Next: box 8.2.

hesitancy of the way I ask questions, if nothing else, that "I don't remember" is okay.

Eric: Yeah. [But see box 7.3 for a concern.]

Russ: The fact of the matter is, I think Melanie *does* not remember some things, and fills in the blanks "on the fly" as we talk. I think that's the way it is. And I don't believe Melanie can possibly have access to that, because that would require her having a veridical recollection of the scene and comparing the two recollections [Eric laughs], which I think is just not possible. So I think that Melanie is doing the best that she can, and I think that she's less than perfect, and if she is perfect then she'll be walking across the fountain on the way out of here. But I doubt that she is.

Eric: [laughs] Right.

Russ: So it's a matter, I think, of keeping the imperfections at a manageable level, and by "manageable" I mean a minimal level. So I think Melanie, for example, when she says "My whole body is reaching forward," well, the fact of the matter is that at that particular moment it probably wasn't her whole body. Maybe there was a quarter of a square inch on her left hipbone that wasn't going forward, or something. And so to say "My whole body was yearning forward" is an oversimplification of the fact of her experience. But from my point of view, everything we ever say about anything is an oversimplification of the fact, and the object is to have it be a non-substantially-misleading oversimplification of the fact.

Eric: Yeah.

Russ: In fact, it would probably be more accurate for Melanie to say "My whole body was leaning forward" than it would be for her to say "My whole body was leaning forward except for this square centimeter on my left hip which I wasn't really noticing at the time" because that wasn't what she was doing at the moment. It wasn't like she was putting a sheet of graph paper over her body and counting off the square centimeters that were leaning forward. She was into the scuba thing. [For Russ's elaboration of these ways of speaking, see box 7.9.]

[Here we have excised a brief discussion of Melanie's degree of accuracy, the openness of Russ's questions compared with those of other investigators (see box 5.1), and Eric's supposition that people are generally similar (see box 7.4).]

Box 7.9
The language of accurate reports

Russ: This is an important but little-discussed point. There is an emotional way of experiencing, and to convey emotion accurately you have to use an emotional way of speaking. There is also an analytical way of experiencing, which is different from the emotional way of experiencing, and with it goes an analytical way of speaking. It is probably impossible to convey an emotion accurately in the analytical way of speaking. I think Melanie's "whole body" example is a good one. Perhaps a more accessible one is the lover who says "I love you forever" or who says "I think I'll probably love you forever but the base rate of forever-loving is pretty small, so it's probably more accurate to say that I feel like I'll love you forever but it's quite possible that I'm mistaken." Which statement more accurately conveys the emotional state? I think the first, even though it's quite probably not true in an analytical sense because the base rate of forever-loving *is* pretty small. The second is more analytically true, but doesn't do justice to the emotion.

In this important sense, then, getting some of the details wrong may be the *only* way to convey something accurately; and conversely, getting the details all correct may in a fundamental sense *misrepresent* the experience.

Eric: "I'll love you forever" *expresses* an emotion (as "Ow!" expresses pain), but doesn't *describe* it; "I feel like I'll love you forever," in contrast, describes the emotion with (a certain degree of) cool accuracy. It seems that we should be aiming for the cool description of emotions in such interviews, rather than the expression of those emotions.

I think you could make the point about the centimeter as follows: Probably Melanie's feeling of reaching forward (if it existed at all) involved a general sense of her whole body reaching forward but not a specific sense of every cubic centimeter individually reaching forward. Perhaps Melanie's motor imagery here leaves those details unspecified in the way that her visual imagery seems sometimes to leave certain details unspecified, as we discussed earlier (in beeps 1.3, 2.1, and 2.2). I see no need, then, to interpret her "whole body reaching forward" statement as a misrepresentation or an "emotional way of speaking."

Russ: I think it is our (Eric's and my) job to provide a somewhat cool description of Melanie's experience, including her emotional experience. Melanie's job is to provide us faithful access. If she can provide such access and at the same time provide a cool description, so much the better. But I would much rather have her simply express herself in an intelligible way (e.g., say "Ow!") and let us provide the cool characterization, than have her confound her experience with the attempt to be cool.

Thread: Emotion. Previous: box 7.4. Next: box 8.5.
Thread: Loose language. Previous: box 5.16. Next: box 8.6.
Thread: Non-visual imagery. Previous: box 5.7. Next: box 7.15.

Eric: I guess I have some inclination to wonder whether the difference between people who describe their emotions one way or another might be a difference as much in reporting as in the actual experience. I'm not sure how you settle that kind of thing. It would be interesting to see if there were some other kind of measurable difference—a total fantasy, but some kind of physiological measure of what's going on in the emotion that differs between the people, or if you could do some kind of cognitive test that might reveal a difference.

Russ: Right.

Eric: What you were talking about with imagery and reading, for example. [See box 5.3.] I guess I have a general tendency to be somewhat skeptical about verbal reports without some kind of other something to back them up.

Right: Right. And I can appreciate that. But I think that the skepticism is justified particularly because psychology has done such a poor job of asking for verbal reports.

Eric: Yeah.

Russ: If we had done a better job, then maybe you wouldn't have to be such a card-carrying skeptic.

Eric: [laughs] Yeah. You know, it's not a skepticism that I think most people find natural. It's a skepticism that's grounded in reading history of psychology and reports about experience, and seeing vast differences that don't seem to be very plausible and that aren't backed up well by other kinds of evidence.

Russ: Right.

Eric: So it's partly that experience that makes me nervous about reports in general. But that experience has been informed by methodologies that are different than the one that you are using and that have faults that you avoid or seem to be at least partly avoiding.

Russ: So, what I think has happened is that you and I have gone down rather similar roads in our skeptical apprehension of the history of inner experience reporting. The road that I've taken is "I think it might be possible to do it better."

Eric [to Melanie]:   I hope my skepticism isn't too dispiriting or discouraging or something like that.

Melanie: Nope.

Eric: You seem to have skin of Teflon about it, so that's good.

Box 7.10
Melanie's reaction to skepticism

Russ: I don't think people react at all negatively to honest skepticism. On the contrary, if the conversation is honestly aimed at discovering the truth (and discussing the limitations and risks of the reports is part of that), DES subjects almost never find bluntly stated skepticism at all discouraging or dispiriting. In fact, perhaps surprisingly, they seem to relish skeptical reactions to their own reports as if they have a deep understanding of the necessity of skepticism as essential to accessing human truth.

People do react negatively to most expressions of skepticism, because most such expressions are not actually skepticism but dogmatic opinions of ideologues disguised as skepticism. In those cases, the negative reaction comes not from the skepticism but from the dishonest expression. I think Melanie senses that this is not your attitude, Eric.

Eric: Still, being frank about my skepticism feels a little awkward to me, and unless Melanie is exceptional, it's hard to believe that it's not at least a little awkward for her, too. There's something easier, smoother, more socially comfortable about accepting the confident reports of someone you're interviewing. Not doing so, maybe, feels awkward because it conveys to the subject the sense that she's being judged, rather than trusted and treated as a collaborative equal.

Russ: I am 100 percent confident (from repeated personal experience) that it is possible to express the most heightened, doubtful, "that's very, very, very hard to believe" kind of skepticism without engendering the kind of awkwardness that you describe. The key, I think, is the honesty of the skepticism, the wholeheartedly honest recognition of the depth of the chasm between "that's very, very, very hard to believe" and "I don't believe that."

For more on this, see section 10.5.

Russ: She doesn't believe a word you're saying, Eric! [All laugh.]

[For Russ's comment on the reaction to skepticism, see box 7.10.]

Eric: Well, that's good! So you said something about the emotional experience being through your whole body but also in your head.

Melanie: Yes.

Eric: The aspect in your head was more cognitive.

Melanie: Right.

Eric: I'm wondering if you could say a little more about that.

Box 7.11
Self-awareness of emotion

Eric: Although we do not press Melanie much here on her assertion that she was aware of her emotion as it occurred, this is a major theme of some later discussions (beeps 5.1, 6.1, 6.2).

Thread: Self-Awareness: Melanie's unusual. Previous: box 6.4. Next: box 8.8.

Melanie: Well, there isn't very much to it. The reason that I say it was more cognitive is that I could recognize the feeling as being that of yearning and of wanting, and that was the cognitive part that was involved.

Eric: Right. And why do you say that the cognitive part was in your head?

Melanie: Because I didn't think that recognition occurred anywhere else. It wasn't as though my chest recognized it as wanting. It was my head that recognized it as that.

[Here we have excised some remarks by Eric on the location of thought in ancient China and Greece. See box 7.12.]

Russ: Did you mean to say that it's "in your head" or "in your mind" or "a mental thing"? Or are all those things interchangeable? Or none of the above?

Melanie: Well, there wasn't any aspect of "Oh, I heard a voice in my head" or "I saw words running through my head." There wasn't any of that at all. It wasn't inner speech, or anything like that. But it felt upwards in my body, it felt like it was in my head, or in my mind. I find it difficult to make the distinction there.

Russ: So this recognizing that this is "yearning" seems to be physically located in your head . . .

Melanie: Yes.

Russ: . . . not. . . . So you meant to be giving a physical, "headly" description here . . .

Melanie: Yes.

Russ: . . . as opposed to a metaphysical, "mentally" description.

Box 7.12
Do we think in our heads?

Russ: Some of my subjects are very explicit about *where* things are experienced, and some aren't. If subjects experience a process that we could call "cognitive" (inner speech, knowing, imaging, etc.), they may or may not report that that experience takes place in a particular location. But if cognitive processes do have a location, they are almost always in the head.

Perhaps surprisingly, many people who, in sampling, use locutions like "it was in the back of my mind" intend that phrase to be understood not as a metaphor but as a simple description of a phenomenon, meaning "I sense this to be taking place in the back of my skull, maybe an inch inside the posterior portion of my cranium." And when they report this, they often look at me quizzically, as though noticing for the first time the non-metaphorical nature of this expression. Melanie provides an example of this in beep 5.1.

Eric: The fact that the brain drives cognition does not of course imply that cognition will be *experientially* located in the head: Compare the case of pain, which can be referred anywhere in the body, including amputated limbs, even when its physiological basis is elsewhere. So why should we locate cognition experientially in the head instead of, say, the chest or nowhere at all? People in ancient China (also, famously, Aristotle, who described the brain as an organ for regulating temperature) generally believed that the heart was the locus of thought. It seems natural to suppose that they located cognition in the heart in part because that is where they experienced—or at least thought they experienced—it as occurring.

Is it possible that the actual phenomenology of the location of thought has changed over time, shifting with our growing knowledge about the functions of the organs? I don't think we should entirely dismiss this possibility, but I'd wager against it. More likely, I think, the phenomenology of thought has remained roughly the same over the ages, and Melanie's report is driven more by her knowledge of the function of the brain than by accurate recall of her experience.

Russ: My guess is that if there is a cultural distinction between where thinking takes place, that might well be due to a difference in what is meant by "thinking." What a Westerner might call the "deepest of thoughts," the deepest personal apprehensions, are in fact typically experienced by my (Western) subjects as taking place in the heart. But those are rare, and the far more frequent thoughts are usually experienced in the head. If those deepest of personal apprehensions are what the Easterners meant by "thinking," then I think my DES subjects would agree that thinking is in the heart. Of course, this conversation cries out for cross-cultural sampling studies, which have not been done.

Box 7.12

(continued)

Eric: I'm pretty sure the terms we generally translate as "thinking" (e.g., "si" in classical Chinese) have broader application than that; although in the Chinese at least, there may not be as clear a distinction between thought and feeling as we often make in the West (see Wong 1991; Shun 1997).

Thread: Human similarity and difference. Previous: box 7.4. Next: box 8.8.

Melanie: Yeah. I wasn't reaching for the metaphysical there. That's where I felt it was located. But there wasn't anything more to it than that.

Russ: So there was a mental knowing that . . .

Melanie: Of what I was feeling.

Russ: . . . that was happening independent of the beep.

Melanie: Yes.

Russ: That in our alternate reality [in which there was an identical Melanie without the beeper], that Melanie would have known that she was yearning.

[On self-awareness, see box 7.11.]

Melanie: Yes.

Russ: And that knowing seemed somehow to take place in your head.

Melanie: Um hm.

[Here we have excised a discussion by Russ and Eric of the topics covered in box 7.12 (whether people think in their heads), in box 4.1 (what "thinking" is), and in box 7.13 (bracketing presuppositions).]

Russ: Okay. So the other half . . . are we done with the emotional half here, fifty-six minutes into the discussion?

Eric: [laughs] Yeah.

Russ: The other half . . . I've forgotten what it was. It was something . . .

Box 7.13
Bracketing presuppositions

Russ: I think we have conveyed to Melanie pretty adequately that it would be okay for this kind of thinking to take place in her head, or outside her head, or in front of her head, or in her left toe, or nowhere at all, if that's how it seemed to be. I think the core of the method involves the serious bracketing of such presuppositions and carefully listening to what people are saying, not allowing your own preconceptions to get in the way.

"Bracketing presuppositions" means taking them out of play, acting as if they may or may not be true, allowing them to be examined fairly, letting the evidence support or contradict them with equal acceptance. This is difficult—partly because people's presuppositions are generally more stubborn and insidiously influential than they think—but I think it must be adequately performed if one's aim is to obtain faithful accounts of inner experience, using whatever method. Otherwise, the investigator is likely to find precisely what was expected and little or nothing else. I believe that one must attempt to suspend *all* presuppositions. Doubtless it is impossible to be entirely successful in this, but it is definitely possible to move closer and closer to that ideal. I do believe that with practice we can get better at it, in the same way that with practice we could become better violinists.

Your task, Eric (and the reader's as well), as I see it at least in part, is to try to evaluate, as best it can be evaluated, to what extent I was (or we were) successful in bracketing presuppositions in my (our) interactions with Melanie, and to what extent the process enabled Melanie to bracket her own presuppositions. I think we did a pretty darn good job of it. Because I think the skillful bracketing of presuppositions is of fundamental importance in investigations of inner experience, then our investigations of Melanie are fundamentally different from and fundamentally better than other investigations.

Eric: Certainly bad science can, and does, arise from excessive bias and unwillingness to examine one's presuppositions frankly. However, it's impossible to set all presuppositions aside and do anything that looks like inquiry. The art of asking questions, forming and testing hypotheses, and exploring the data requires a background sense of what is plausible and what would be startling, what would profit from further inquiry and what would not, a sense of the benefits and limitations of one's techniques, of how an inquiry might end and when we should finally accept a hypothesis under test, and so on—and all of that requires at least initial working, though possibly revisable, suppositions about how things stand in one's field of inquiry. Francis Bacon (1620/2000) advanced the ideal of a pre-suppositionless science in the seventeenth century, but I think the majority of philosophers of science today are right to follow Kuhn (1962/1970), Lakatos (1978), Longino (1990), and others in rejecting that ideal.

Box 7.13
(continued)

For example, at the beginning of today's interview, something guided your choice of the word "sensation" to describe Melanie's experience, something impelled you to ask whether one aspect of the experience was more "central" than another, etc. An interviewer (if it is possible to imagine one) with no knowledge whatsoever of experience could not have asked such questions. I do find you unusually open-minded, and you probably would have gone along with Melanie had she rejected the word "sensation" or insisted that the question of whether one aspect was more central than another made as little sense as the question of whether one aspect was the square root of the other. But of course there are—how could there not be?—pre-existing frames and conceptions you are initially inclined to apply. It is illusion to think one can set them aside; the most one can sensibly aim for is to hold them lightly. Furthermore, I'm not sure we *should* always hold them lightly, if they are well grounded (as Kuhn, Lakatos, and Longino have emphasized). But that's a tricky issue.

Thread: Bracketing presuppositions. Previous: box 7.4. Next: box 8.3.

Melanie: Feeling of bobbing in water.

Russ: Oh, the feeling of bobbing in water. Right! And do you mean to say that your body was . . . or . . . what do you mean to say?

Melanie: Well, I wasn't physically, in actuality, bouncing up and down. But that's what it kind of felt like. I could imagine the waves picking me up and dropping me off, and picking me up and dropping me down, like that.

Russ: And when you say you "could imagine" that, there's another subjunctive . . .

Melanie: It is a subjunctive, because it's not like I felt the water. I felt the motion, not the actual water [quizzical tone]. I don't know if that makes sense.

Russ: So, are you saying that in some way your body is imagining itself going up and down and you're experiencing that up-and-downnessing?

Melanie: Yes. And it's the motion. It wasn't a thought about the water or anything like that. And it wasn't feeling the water kind of, you know, hitting the swimsuit or lapping away or making a noise or anything like that. It was directly the motion of bobbing up and down.

Box 7.14
On the word "because"

Russ: Melanie is using the language of causation here (*"because* if you're bobbing . . ."), and when people do that it opens the possibility that they are not describing the experience but instead explaining what the experience *must be* (cf. box 7.1). What makes it difficult is that this language is ambiguous. Melanie's language here can be interpreted as the result of a reality demand, as if she had said "in the real water you feel it on the top of your body, therefore I must be feeling it on the top of my body now." But it is also possible to interpret Melanie's statement as simply as a way of communicating to us about the phenomenon, as if she had said "Yes, I'm feeling it only in my upper body, and I want you to understand that, so I'm going to appeal to *your* sense of reality." So Melanie's statement here can be interpreted either as signaling that she's inferring more than recalling this aspect of her experience or as a use of causative language as a way of communicating to us. I don't think we can determine which is the case here from this utterance alone. But her explanations coming shortly allay my worries somewhat.

Thread: Melanie's trustworthiness: Influence of generalizations. Previous: box 7.1. Next: box 9.3.

Russ: And is that motion in your body?

Melanie: It felt more like my upper body, because if you're bobbing at the surface like a cork the lower half of your body is under water, so you don't really feel that. [For some worries about this statement, see box 7.14.]

Russ: Okay.

Melanie: So it was mainly just, I don't know, maybe from about my ribcage up.

Russ: And with your hand you're gesturing up. Do you mean to say that at the moment of the beep you're going up? Or are you going up and down, or down . . . ?

Melanie: I couldn't narrow it down that specifically.

Russ: So there's something about the upper portion of your body . . .

Melanie: Yes, that's feeling an up-and-down motion.

Russ: . . . that's feeling an up-and-down motion, and it's impossible to say which of those motions, which phase, is going on at the moment of the beep.

Box 7.15
Should we believe Melanie's report of kinesthetic imagery?

Russ: My skeptical receptors are pretty quiet here.

Eric: I don't see any particular reason to doubt this aspect of the report, apart from my general concerns about the method. It *could* be an invention, but nothing in the transcript especially points in that direction. However, it is interesting that she would report kinesthetic imagery of bobbing simultaneously with (what I take to be) motor imagery of yearning forward.

Melanie's trustworthiness: General. Previous: box 5.16. Next: box 7.16. Thread: Non-visual imagery. Previous: box 7.9.

Melanie: Yes.

Russ: Okay. And. . . . [pause] So without trying to be too personal here, when we're talking about the upper body, your hands are under your breasts. Are you talking about the surface of your body being lifted?

Melanie: Yes.

Russ: So it's not like your whole body going up? It's like your breasts being . . .

Melanie: Oh no, no, no. It would be the whole upper body.

Russ: Inside and outside?

Melanie: Yes.

Russ: Okay. So your whole torso, your whole upper torso . . .

Melanie: Is being lifted and then being dropped down.

Russ: Okay.

[Here we have excised a brief discussion by Russ and Eric of the believability of this report. See box 7.15. For a discussion of an aspect of the experience we may have left out, see box 7.16.]

Beep 4.2

In lieu of a full transcript of the discussion of this sample (available at http://mitpress.mit.edu/inner_experience), here is a description of this beep as Melanie conveyed it in the interview.

Box 7.16
Did we leave out an aspect of the experience?

Eric: In her initial description of the experience, Melanie says that at the moment of the beep she was "thinking about the comparison [of scuba diving with other sports] . . . and its possibility of being life threatening." She mentions that first and might be interpreted as juxtaposing or contrasting it with her feeling of yearning and her sensation of bobbing. Neither we nor Melanie seem to have picked up on this in the interview. Maybe her "thinking" was just this yearning and/or bobbing? Another possibility is that the "thinking" refers to an episode of inner speech (or some other type of thought) that concluded prior to what is described here and so provides a kind of background for it.

Thread: Melanie's trustworthiness: General. Previous: box 5.15. See also chapters 10 and 11, passim.

Melanie was reading a book. At the moment of the beep she was reading about one of the characters who steals the joker from decks of cards, and simultaneously she was having an image of a playing card with a joker on it. The card brand in her image was Bicycle, and the image was of a joker who was dressed in a Harlequin costume with a jester hat and pointy shoes, a jumpsuit that has colorful triangles on it, as well as a big bicycle wheel. (The fact that the image did not correspond very well to an actual Bicycle joker was of little importance to Melanie or to us.)

Looking back after the beep, Melanie was aware of the emotions of concern and resentment ongoing in her body at that time, but they weren't experienced by her at the moment of the beep. Russ calls this phenomenon of emotions that seem to be ongoing as bodily processes (e.g. fists clenching, face flushing, heart pounding) but which are not in experience at the moment of the beep "feeling fact of body." [See box 6.2.]

8 The Fifth Sampling Day

Beep 5.1

Melanie: For the first beep, I was thinking about the fact that I have an appointment at 11:15 this morning, and it's all the way across town from here. So I was feeling a little bit of anxiety about getting there on time. I also had a mental image in my head of me sitting in my car and driving my car, and being stopped at a red stop light at just a generic intersection. It wasn't a specific street or anything like that. I was seeing this image as though I was in the driver's seat looking out the car window. I could see the stoplight and the road stretched out in front of me, and then could see my hands on the steering wheel.

Russ: So the image. Is this just like you were looking, like you were actually in the car?

Melanie: Like I'm in the car. You could see the, you know, the frame of the car where the window stops, and out of the corner of my eye I could see the passenger seat that was empty.

Russ: And do you take that to be *just like* being in the car, or is it in some way different from being in the car?

Melanie: Just like it.

Russ: So in no discernible way is it different . . .

Melanie: No.

Russ: . . . it might have been different but you didn't discern it?

Melanie: Right, exactly.

[For Eric's skepticism about this remark, see box 8.1.]

Russ: And you said you saw cars ahead of you, and stop lights and . . .

Box 8.1
On how one starts questioning

Eric: Here's another instance of the sort described at the end of box 5.1. The way you first ask the question—"Is this just like you were looking, like you were actually in the car?"—may provoke Melanie too casually to equate her imagery experience with her normal sensory experience. Once she does that, she may then have to provide vision-like details if she isn't to undermine herself. Perhaps a different line of questioning, one that didn't *begin* by asking Melanie for a general judgment of this sort, would have produced a different description in the end.

I don't want to make too much of this. You are certainly not overtly pressuring Melanie to say her imagery experience was just like the experience of being in the car—if anything, you pressure her the opposite direction by evidently being unsatisfied with her answer until she modulates it a bit (to "it might have been different but [I] didn't discern it"). However, social psychological research and research on testimony has shown again and again that subtle variations in the phrasing and order of questions can have a large effect on subjects' responses.

Russ: I think the transcript makes my questioning appear somewhat more forceful than was the actual interview, which includes pauses and uncertainties not rendered in this transcript. But more importantly, Melanie had already given, in her opening description of this beep, an unambiguous account of a visual experience: "I had a mental image in my head," "I was seeing this image," I could see the stoplight," and "could see my hands on the steering wheel." She had already given an unambiguous account of being as if in the car: "of me sitting in my car and driving," "seeing . . . as though I was in the driver's seat," "see the stoplight and road stretched out in front of me," "see my hands on the steering wheel." So I think "Is this just like you were looking, like you were actually in the car?" is a pretty even-tempered question; my "just like" gives Melanie the opportunity to withdraw from (add ambiguity to) her earlier statements or to reiterate them.

I accept the possibility of the influence of truly subtle factors, and return to this discussion in subsection 11.2.5, where I will discuss why I think truly subtle pressure might not be as risky as you think it is. Furthermore, it strikes me as plausible that you're raising this issue here is in the service of your presupposition against clear imagery. I think that is indeed a risky strategy, and I will return to this discussion in subsection 11.1.7.

Thread: Melanie's trustworthiness: Details. Previous: box 7.3. Next: box 8.2.
Thread: Melanie's trustworthiness: Interview pressures. Previous: box 7.3. See also subsection 2.3.1, section 10.5, and subsection 11.2.5.
Thread: Visual imagery: Structure. Previous: box 5.9. See also section 3.2.

Melanie: No, I just saw the . . . it was like being stopped at an intersection. So I saw the two roads crossed. There was one heading straight out in front of me . . .

Russ: Like the road that you were on, continuing?

Melanie: Yeah, and then there was the other road running perpendicular to that, perpendicular and straight through the intersection. So I could see kind of buildings (they weren't specific), buildings on the corners—apartment buildings or high rises, Las Vegas high rises—and the stop light that you get at the . . .

Russ: So there were buildings on the corner?

Melanie: Um hm.

Russ: But they weren't specific buildings?

Melanie: No.

Russ: So you couldn't say this was the Plaza Suites or that it was . . .

Melanie: Or it was Jones Street or something. No, I didn't know what street it was.

Russ: Okay. And is this like a still picture? Or is it like a moving picture? Or are you driving through?

Melanie: Still picture.

Russ: "Still" like snapshot still? Or still like you're at an intersection and just don't happen to be moving, but it would be a movie if you happened to be moving?

Melanie: It was snapshot still.

Russ: Color? Black and white?

Melanie: In color.

Russ: And accurate color as far as you know? The stop light's red . . .

Melanie: Yeah, and the desert colors and all that kind of thing, um hm.

Russ: So accurate colors, except not accurately portraying any particular intersection.

Melanie: Right.

Russ: Okay. Any other details of the visual portion of this experience that we ought to be asking about?

Melanie: I can't think of any.

Russ: Eric, do you want to ask about that portion?

Eric: Sure. I'm not quite sure what you mean when you say they weren't specific buildings or it wasn't a specific intersection or road. Was it that the buildings were kind of generic looking?

Melanie: Yeah, they were. They were, you know, rectangular buildings with windows, but I couldn't have said "Oh that's the building that's on the corner of Jones and Flamingo, so I must have been driving down Flamingo at the intersection with Jones." I don't know any of that.

Eric: So although the buildings had a specific appearance . . .

Melanie: Right.

Eric: . . . they weren't familiar?

Melanie: Right.

Eric: Or let's say . . . conceivably could there be an intersection in the world that looks exactly like that?

Melanie: Conceivably, yes.

Eric: Yeah, so it's not that the buildings were kind of hazy or something like that?

Melanie: No. The scene was detailed and clear, but it just wasn't representative of anything that I've seen here.

Eric: Um hm.

Russ: And clear all the way around? Like not just clear looking forward but clear to the sides? Like if you were really parked at an intersection I would think . . .

Melanie: No. It was clear straight ahead. I mean I couldn't tell you like what cars were parked on the street running perpendicular to the one I was on, you know, waiting for the intersection there.

Russ: So the apartments that you're talking about are on the street ahead of you?

Melanie: Yeah, they're the ones that are across the street, on the other corner.

Russ: Okay. Sorry, Eric.

Eric: Um hm, that's fine. So you said there were other cars that were in the image?

Melanie: Um, I couldn't tell you that.

Eric: So you don't know whether there were other cars?

Melanie: Nope.

Eric: So, just to get clear on what that means: It could be that the image may or may not have had other cars in it, and you just can't remember that fact; or it could be that the image somehow under-specified whether there were cars there; or maybe there are other possibilities, too. Which way would you describe it, or how would you describe that?

Russ [after a pause]: She's looking quizzical. I would ask the question more from a process rather than an entity perspective.

[The following six conversational turns summarize a somewhat longer conversation.]

Russ: So I might ask, if I were trying to get at the same thing: Was it that you didn't see cars? Or was it that you just didn't notice whether you were seeing cars or not?

Eric: Um hm.

Russ: She's still looking quizzical. Well, what I was reacting to in wanting to reframe the question was what seemed to be the presupposition that there's some inner screen somewhere, or some neurological equivalent of an inner screen, on which we create images. And then there's some inner equivalent of a spectator in which we look at those images. And those neurological processes could be more or less independent, so that you could have a clear image and a lousy seer or a clear seer and a lousy image or any combination thereof. I don't want us to fall into the trap of assuming that. [For further discussion of this point, see box 5.5.]

Eric: I agree that's a trap, and I hope my question didn't assume or imply that. What I was trying to get at was the difference between her imagery experience being indeterminate regarding the presence of cars, and her definitely remembering that fact, and her simply not remembering well enough what her imagery experience was to say whether there were cars in it.

Russ: My guess from watching Melanie is that all this conversation has little to do with what her experience of the moment is. [Melanie and Eric laugh.] And I think the reason for that is that for her to be able to accurately answer any of these questions, she'd have to have a veridical copy of the image and compare what she was reporting to what was actually happening, which of course she doesn't have. [For a qualification of this, see box 8.2.]

Eric: Okay.

Box 8.2
Would Melanie need a veridical copy to answer Eric's question?

Eric: I think you've overstated your point here, Russ. Melanie could answer this type of question without facing the epistemically impossible task of comparing her memory of the image to a veridical copy of the image. She does, in fact (as I interpret her; I know you disagree in box 7.8), answer analogous questions in beeps 2.1 and 2.2 (saying that she positively remembers indeterminacy in the position of the soldier's legs and in the presence or absence of insignia) and she goes on again to answer this type of question below. I don't know whether we should believe these answers, but I do think that at least in principle a person might be able to remember whether an image, or some aspect of it, was sketchy or indeterminate.

Russ: The phrase "I couldn't tell you [whether there were other cars in the image]" is ambiguous—purposefully, strategically ambiguous, I think—between (a) "I couldn't tell you because I don't remember" and (b) "I couldn't tell you because the image no more specified whether there were cars there than it specified whether the Tower of Pisa leans right or left." I don't think we can unequivocally determine which option to support: Too much hinges on too small details.

Thread: Melanie's trustworthiness: Details. Previous: box 8.1. Next: box 9.6.
Thread: Visual imagery: Detail. Previous: box 7.8. Next: box 8.3.

Russ: So what I hear her to be saying is something like "I'm confident that I was seeing, that this was a visual experience. And I'm confident that in this visual experience was my hands on the steering wheel and the frame of the car I'm looking out. And I'm confident that there was the road and the stop light. And I'm confident that there were buildings that looked like real buildings and that I had no reason to think that these were sketchy or schematic buildings, but I don't know which buildings or which intersection. And there may or may not have been cars—that I don't know." And beyond that, it seems like we've gotten pretty much to the limit of what she can say.

Eric: Yeah, right. I assume she's nodding [laughs].

Russ: She is!

Melanie: Yes [laughs].

Russ: She looks happier now than she did five minutes ago.

Eric: [laughs] That seems fair. Maybe there is no way to determine from our vantage point now whether what she's not confident about is a result of the failure of memory over time or a result of its not being there in the experienced image immediately prior to the beep.

Russ: And I think that's true. I think we just can't make that determination, and she's nodding as if she agrees to that.

Eric: Right.

Melanie: Well, I would say that my inclination would be towards those cars weren't in the image. I was looking straight ahead; I didn't see anything out of my peripheral vision. I was mainly concentrating straight ahead. I can see room for the explanation of that, that there was an entire picture with things that could be in my peripheral vision. But all I was concentrating on, and all that was "in my awareness," quote unquote, was directly straight ahead of me.

Eric: Um hm. Although I would have thought that the buildings would be more peripheral than the cars on the street in front of you.

Melanie: Well, no, because I was pulled up, like I was the first car at the stop light.

Eric: Um hm.

Melanie: So there wasn't a car in front of me; that wasn't a question. There weren't any cars ahead of me; I could tell you that. Like there weren't any cars waiting at the stop light across the street. But it's on the perpendicular road of this intersection that I couldn't tell you, where looking at those cars really would be more peripheral than the buildings would be.

Eric: Um hm, right. So the cars on the street you were crossing would be more peripheral. But any cars on your street, even if they were, say, parked by the curb a couple of blocks ahead of you on the street . . .

Melanie: Right. Those weren't there, I can tell you that. Those weren't there. There weren't any cars directly ahead of me. It was just the road.

Eric: So the road was in a way strikingly empty?

Melanie: Yes.

Russ: Or at least empty.

Eric: [laughs] Or at least empty. Maybe "strikingly" . . . yeah, okay. So maybe that means it wasn't strikingly empty. I think the reason I said "strikingly" here was that it would be striking, in retrospect, if there was a road big enough to have a stoplight, and straight, and you can see all the way down it, and there were no cars coming or going on it in front of you and no cars parked on the sides.

[Here we have excised a discussion of Eric's use of "strikingly." See box 8.3.]

Russ: We can obviously revisit this later, but it seems pretty convincing to me. And are we ready to move on to the other portion of this experience?

Eric: I guess so, yeah.

Russ: Which was the feeling of anxiety as I recall. What was that like?

Melanie: It was more at the back of my mind. It wasn't as clear, I'd say, as the image was, this feeling of anxiety. It was almost as though I was monitoring myself again, like one part of me—kind of me in the back of my mind—was monitoring what I was feeling at that time and noticed that these thoughts about what I was going to do this morning, and the fact that I had this appointment and everything this morning, went from being an idle thought to something I became quite focused on. It was after the beep that I noticed I was actually a little bit more tense, after I thought about it, than before. But it was just a general feeling of anxiety about wanting to be there on time.

Russ: Okay. So I'm a little confused about this experience. Is the feeling of anxiety a head kind of thing? Or a body kind of thing? Or both or neither one?

Melanie: Both.

Russ: And what do you mean? What's the body part? What's the head part?

Melanie: The head part is knowing that it was anxiety that I was feeling.

Russ: So there's some kind of cognitive awareness . . .

Melanie: Yeah.

Russ: . . . cognitive understanding, apprehension, not in the negative sense, but the seeing of anxiety?

Melanie: Right. And then bodily, it was just focusing more, much more intently on something. That was the main bodily aspect of it.

Russ: So your body seemed focused?

Melanie: Yeah.

Russ: On anything in particular?

Melanie: Just the thought.

Russ: And the thought being this image of the car or the thought of . . .

Box 8.3
"Strikingly" and bracketing presuppositions. Detail in imagery.

Eric: I think my agenda in asking this question was a suspicion that Melanie may have conflated the absence of a fact with the fact of an absence. The use of "strikingly" then, was to motivate Melanie to reflect on whether there really was a positive fact of the absence of cars, which might have been a striking feature of the image if true.

Russ: I certainly agree that it's possible that Melanie has conflated the absence of a fact with the fact of an absence. And I agree that it is legitimate to attempt to discover, to the best of our abilities, whether such a conflation has taken place.

But there was no hint of strikingness in Melanie's description, so this question may reflect a presupposition that if an inner seeing (an "image") includes a feature that would be unusual in reality (such as an empty major road), then the discrepant feature must be or is likely to be striking. My work shows that that is simply not the case. Inner seeings do *not* follow the same rules as seeings in reality. We've had at least one pretty clear example already from Melanie: She was seeing Stukas that actually looked like F-18s (beep 2.2; box 5.9). In reality, that would be striking, but in Melanie's inner world, it was quite matter of fact. Similarly, it makes sense to understand that Melanie was not interested in the "carlessness" of her intersection representation, and therefore that was not apprehended as being at all striking.

Such unbracketed presuppositions cloud our ability to hear what Melanie is saying and diminish our effectiveness in helping Melanie to describe accurately. She responded "Yes" to your question, despite the fact that there was probably nothing striking at all about the carlessness of her innerly experienced road at the moment of the beep.

Eric: I hope I was not presupposing what you suggest. I continue to worry, however, that Melanie overspecifies the detail in her imagery. This worry arises from a general inclination to think that people often overdescribe their visual imagery when they ascribe this level of detail to a momentary image. Such overdescription may come in part from analogizing images to photographs [see box 5.2] and in part from something like the "refrigerator light phenomenon" for imagery coupled with reconstruction in the reporting [see boxes 4.18, 4.20, and 5.4].

This worry, too, is based in "presuppositions," I suppose. But without such presuppositions, how can one have a sense of what warrants suspicion, so one knows where to press and where to accept? Although I go astray with the question here, I do think that Melanie probably would not be acknowledging as much indeterminacy in her images as she now does had my suspicion of the specificity in her reports in beeps 1.3 and 2.1 not led me to press her on the matter in a way that you did not. Have I simply bludgeoned Melanie into adjusting her reports toward my preconceptions? I hope not, but it's a tangled issue.

Box 8.3
(continued)

Russ: In my thinking, bracketing does not mean ignoring antecedent senses of plausibility. I think it is legitimate to ask with special care about issues that you think (antecedently or presuppositionally) warrant suspicion. The object of bracketing is (a) to avoid the bludgeoning to which you refer (and I think we did avoid that with Melanie); and (b) to be open to answers to those specially careful questions that go in a direction opposite to the presupposition. In these interviews, for example, despite your careful questions, Melanie consistently describes substantially more image detail than your presupposition would have expected. It seems to me that that you should let that weaken your confidence in (not eliminate completely, to be sure) your presupposition.

Thread: Bracketing presuppositions. Previous: box 7.13. Next: box 8.5.
Thread: Visual imagery: Detail. Previous: box 8.2. See also section 3.2.

Melanie: The thought of this appointment.

Russ: So there was a thought of the appointment?

Melanie: Um hm.

Russ: Well, maybe we should start there.

Melanie: Uh, okay.

Russ: What was the thought of the appointment about?

Melanie: Stepping back a little bit, what I was doing last night was kind of running through things I have to do today . . .

Russ: Okay.

Melanie: . . . and I remembered that I had to come here at 9:30, and then the next thing that came into my head was that I had this appointment at 11:15. And then I was thinking in my head that that appointment is all the way across town. And that's when I started feeling the anxiety. And at that exact moment, after thinking that this appointment is all the way across town, this mental image slipped into my head of seeing the intersection of the car and driving all the way across town, and having an anxious feeling of worry about getting there on time.

Russ: Okay, and so is the thought "I've got this 11:15 all the way across town," is that still there or is that here and gone by the time of the beep?

Melanie: Here and gone.

Russ: But the anxiety that that sort of aroused . . .

Melanie: Is there.

Russ: . . . or engendered is still there?

Melanie: Um hm.

Russ: And in what way is that there?

Melanie: It's lingering. I'm not fully engaged in it, but it's still there like at the back, kind of at the fringes of my thoughts and feelings.

Russ: And is it possible to say what it feels like? what it thinks like? what it . . .

Melanie: I couldn't tell you at that time, but probably I had my brow furrowed and was staring at something pretty intently. But I didn't know this at the moment of the beep.

Russ: Okay, so at the moment of the beep there was a sense that you were anxious?

Melanie: Um hm.

Russ: And that sense was partially bodily and partially . . .

Melanie: Mental.

Russ: . . . mental. And the mental seems to be in the back of your mind, you said?

Melanie: Yeah.

Russ: And when you say "back of your mind" your hands are going . . .

Melanie: Yeah, it actually felt like it was in the rear of my head [laughs].

Russ: Okay. So there's some mental process that seems like in the rear of your head?

Melanie: Um hm.

[See our discussion of the back-of-the-mind phenomenon in box 7.12.]

Russ: So this isn't a feeling in the back of your head . . .

Melanie: No.

Russ: This is a mental process that seems like it's in the back of your head, which is this awareness of . . .

Melanie: Of being anxious.

Russ: . . . being anxious.

Melanie: Um hm.

Russ: So it's not just that anxiety is in your body, but that there's a mental . . .

Melanie: Cognitive aspect of knowing that I'm anxious.

Russ: . . . cognitive aspect of knowing that you're anxious.

Melanie: Um hm.

Russ: Okay. [to Eric] Your turn.

Eric: So were you actually having the thought "I'm anxious"?

Melanie: No. It's not like inner speech or inner hearing or anything like that. It's just this knowledge that I'm anxious, if that makes sense.

Eric: Right.

Melanie: Like a mental or bodily knowledge. I'm not saying to myself "Oh I feel anxious right now" or anything like that. And I don't hear rattling in my head or in my mind, or having a thought saying that I feel anxious.

Russ: Is this a mental knowledge of anxiety?

Melanie: Yes.

Russ: So some cognitive, or thoughtful, or whatever . . .

Melanie: Right.

Russ: . . . understanding of that . . .

Melanie: Yes, but it's not like having the words pass through my head or anything like that.

Eric: So would you say that you're not just having the experience of anxiety, but that there is some kind of awareness of that experience?

Melanie: Yes.

Russ: And that that "some kind of awareness" is pretty hard to articulate.

Melanie: Yeah.

Russ: It's clearly not in words . . .

Melanie: Right, and it's not something that I'm hearing or reading or seeing.

Russ: But it's also not *not* there either. It *is* an awareness. So there's some cognitive understanding of being anxious.

Melanie: Yes.

Russ: Okay. And the bodily portion of being anxious isn't apparently much more differentiated than the thought portion?

Box 8.4
On the use of the word "experiencing" here

Russ: I shouldn't have used the word "experiencing" here, since I'm trying to ask whether the body is undergoing anxiety *without* that fact being part of her inner experience. However, I think Melanie knew what I meant, as the subsequent dialogue indicates.

Melanie: It wasn't until after the beep.

Russ: Okay.

Melanie: After the beep I noticed that I was a little bit tense, but not before.

Russ: And so at the beep was there in your awareness any . . .

Melanie: No.

Russ: So at the very precise moment of the beep is it true to say that really the only portion of the anxiety was the *knowledge of* the anxiety?

Melanie: Um hm.

Russ: So what's happening is that there is something in your body, which is experiencing anxiety, but you're not aware of that. [On the use of "experiencing" here, see box 8.4.]

Melanie: Right.

Russ: But there's also some kind of a thought process that knows that that process is going on, and you are aware of that.

Melanie: Um hm.

Russ: Okay, she seems confident in that now.

Eric: [laughs] I'm confused. So . . .

Russ: So shall I summarize the way I understand it?

Eric: Okay, yeah, why don't you?

Russ: A second or so before the beep she had been thinking "Oh I've got this appointment across town. That's going to be tight," or something like that. And that had caused, I guess, a wave of anxiety that was probably in her awareness, but we didn't beep her then so we don't really know that for sure. So now at the moment of the beep there is apparently a bodily process that's related to this anxiety, but that bodily process seems to be outside her awareness. When beeped and called to take a look at it, she can see "Aha, yeah, there's some anxiety going on

---

Box 8.5
Knowledge of anxiety without the experience of anxiety. Judging others by oneself, continued.

Russ: Possibly Melanie experienced herself as being anxious at some past time, and that emotion-experience started a thought process that has "out-lived" the emotion-experience for a moment. Or possibly Melanie has two fairly separate and parallel processes, one cognitive and one emotional, and her cognitive process may be able to understand herself as being anxious without *ever* having experienced the anxiety.

Such things may seem impossible or improbable. I myself certainly don't experience anxiety that way (as far as I know). But that seeming improbability is a presupposition about the way anxiety takes place. Bracketing that presupposition means not judging others by oneself, not presuming that what Melanie says is wrong.

Eric: Maybe such things are common; I don't know. However, as I argue elsewhere [box 9.9 and section 10.6], I think it makes sense to be warier of—I don't say completely reject out of hand—Melanie's reports when they don't jibe well with the results of other approaches, including one's "armchair" sense of one's own experience. Am I thereby "presuming" that what Melanie says is wrong? I don't think so: I'm just not ready to buy uncritically every report that survives the interview process.

Thread: Bracketing presuppositions. Previous: box 8.3. Next: box 9.9.
Thread: Emotion. Previous: box 7.9. Next: box 8.8.
Thread: Retrospective and armchair generalizations. Previous: box 5.17. Next: box 8.7.

---

in my body." But what is *in* her awareness is some kind of thoughtful apprehension of the anxiety process. So even though the anxiety process isn't in her awareness directly, the thought about, the recognition of, the knowledge about that, *is* in her awareness in a not particularly articulated way that seems somehow to be in the back of her head, a mental process in the back of her head. And then all at the same time is what seems to be the center of her attention, which is the image of the intersection. [looking at Melanie] She seems to be pretty happy with that reconstruction. [On the possibility of experiencing the awareness of anxiety without the anxiety itself, see box 8.5. On Russ's use of "awareness" here and elsewhere, see box 8.6.]

Eric: Hmm . . . so I guess I'm wondering . . . let's see, um . . . so you had some anxiety but you say that you weren't experiencing the anxiety then? You didn't have an experience of it?

Box 8.6
On Russ's use of the word "awareness"

Eric: Here, and often throughout these interviews, Russ, you use "in awareness" as synonymous with "innerly experienced" or "in consciousness." I think that phrase invites confusion between a *phenomenal* and an *epistemic* sense of the word "awareness." Thus, in one sense, the phenomenal sense, to say that a thought was "in awareness" is simply to say that it was conscious or experienced. In another sense, the epistemic sense, to say that a thought was "in awareness" is to say that one is aware *of* the thought—that is, that one stands in some particular epistemic relationship to it, that one knows in some way that the thought is occurring.

Some philosophers have argued that awareness in the first sense is necessarily accompanied by, or tantamount to, awareness in the second [see box 6.1; Rosenthal (1986) and Lycan (1996) emphasize that this awareness might itself be nonconscious], but that is a substantive philosophical thesis to which I don't think you want to be committed.

Russ: I don't want to be committed to that or any other tightly defined thesis. My methods simply don't address such issues.

There is no perfect word or phrase to describe the phenomenon I am after; each locution has its advantages, disadvantages, connotations, and theoretical implications. I therefore explicitly try to use a variety of phrases more-or-less interchangeably, thereby indicating that I do not favor any one set of advantages/connotations/implications: "Is . . . in your awareness?" "Do you experience . . . ?" "Is . . . in your inner experience?" "Are you paying attention to . . . ?" as well as, once the subject has the general idea, more neutral phrases like "happening" or "going on with you." My subjects are almost never confused by these terms and, like me, treat them interchangeably. It is clear enough what the questions are about that the particular label is irrelevant.

Eric: I see your motivation. I wonder, though, whether using all these terms interchangeably may invite certain responses. Using "aware of the emotion" and "experienced the emotion" interchangeably may invite the view (e.g., in Melanie?) that we are always epistemically aware of our experiences; using "paying attention to" and "experiencing" interchangeably may invite the view that we only experience what we attend to (box 4.8), or it may suggest that the interviewer is only interested in the objects of attention.

Is it so abundantly clear what your questions are about? I think it *is* abundantly clear that central features of one's experience immediately prior to the beep are the principal topic of discussion. But maybe it's too much to expect Melanie to be accurate about matters such as exactly how to characterize her self-knowledge, the existence or non-existence of a periphery of experience, indeterminacy versus forgetting—issues that may require some theoretical discussion before one sees exactly what's at stake

---

Box 8.6
(continued)

and what one particular answer or another *means*, exactly. [See also box 5.14.] Even if Melanie can eventually be brought to see what is at stake, commitment to one answer or another early on in the process may frame and bias later discussions.

Russ: The "fact" of my DES interviewing with many different people is that most people who report emotion do so in your phenomenal sense with no epistemic reference; they say things like "At the moment of the beep I was feeling anxious" and confidently deny any experience (cognitive or otherwise) of a separate observation of that emotion. I ask about that distinction with other subjects with at least the same care and probing as we did here with Melanie.

   Thus Melanie's report here (and elsewhere) is quite different from those of most other DES subjects. Therefore I don't think it's true that my questions "invite" the report of epistemic awareness. It is of course possible that Melanie interpreted my (our) questions in a different way from that of most subjects, and that the questions did in some way "resonate with her proclivity to give epistemic reports." But another possible explanation is that Melanie's experience is quite different from that of most others.

Thread: Self-Awareness: General. Previous: box 6.4.
Thread: Interview techniques. Previous: box 7.3. See also section 2.2.
Thread: Loose language. Previous: box 7.9. Next: box 8.9.

Melanie: Well, I was experiencing it. I don't know. We're coming again into this whole quandary between consciousness, awareness, experience, you know, picking the right word out. [See beep 3.2 and box 8.6.]

Eric: Right.

Melanie: My body was experiencing it somehow. But the way I found out how it was experiencing it wasn't until I reviewed what I was thinking about after the beep took place, when I noticed that I was a little bit tense and much more focused on this thought that I was having than the idleness of the thought that had come before. But at the moment of the beep I wasn't aware of that tension and I wasn't aware of that focus, but I *was* aware of the fact that I was feeling some anxiety.

[Some of Russ's and Eric's remarks from the following discussion have been excised for brevity; the principal themes are addressed in the boxes.]

Eric: I remember a discussion of emotion in a previous sample where you were feeling aware of the emotion at the same time it was going on. [See beeps 3.2 and 4.1.]

Melanie: Um hm.

Eric: Now in that case I thought that you had said that you had both the emotion itself—the emotional experience—and (although maybe these two things aren't separable) the awareness of the emotion, maybe not integrated with the emotion itself. Whereas here maybe you're saying you just have the awareness without the underlying thing?

Melanie: Yeah.

Russ: And my sense of it is that for Melanie that's part of what is the emotion. It's not like there's the emotion that's in her body, and then there's an analytical thing that's watching the emotion. It's that the emotion in her body and the watching of it are sort of wrapped up together as the emotional experience. This is the way Melanie experiences emotion—as both a bodily and a mental watching kind of thing. And that might be different for Melanie than for some other people, but that's her version of emotion.

Eric: Right. I don't know. I guess I'm somewhat skeptical still. I'm not saying that that's impossible, but it would seem to me—my first guess would be—that a lot of times we have emotional experiences, but normally we aren't really attending to those emotional experiences as we're having them. Now there are probably cases in which we think "Oh, you know, I'm angry. Why am I angry?" But most of the time you're just angry, or sad, or anxious, or whatever, without thinking about that fact at the same time that it's going on. So it seems to me a little funny that Melanie seems to be reporting in general that she's thinking about the emotion as it's happening. And it seems in this case even a little funnier that she's kind of thinking about the emotion but there isn't the underlying emotional experience at all. I'm not saying it's impossible, but I guess I'm not wholly convinced.

Russ: Well, I'm pretty sure I don't do it that way, and it sounds probably like you don't do it that way. But that doesn't necessarily mean that Melanie doesn't do it that way.

Melanie: Because I mean I was just . . . sorry to interrupt . . .

Eric: That's fine.

Melanie: . . . but I was just saying that in most, if not all of the cases when I have been experiencing an emotion there's a mental component tied into it. There's both going on at the same time.

Russ: Right. And that's not the way most people are. That's the way Melanie happens to be. That's part of what makes Melanie Melanie as opposed to June or Sally or something. [Melanie and Eric laugh.] So we've got to make sure we're talking about the idiographic Melanie rather than people in general.

Eric: Yeah, right, and I'm not sure how much variation there is between people. But it's such a complex set of issues. [See box 7.4.]

Melanie: I was remembering that we've talked about the different kinds of emotion [see beep 3.2]. There are emotional processes in the body; and there is the experience of the emotion itself; and there is the cognitive awareness that you are having the emotion. I remember when we were having that conversation I had a lot of trouble understanding the experience of emotion without any cognitive . . . without knowing that you're feeling anything. That made no sense to me until I really tried to work it out, and finally I figured it out: "Oh! I guess that sometimes people must just feel the emotions!" But even then I had trouble. How do you feel anger without knowing that it's anger? It's something I still have trouble comprehending in some ways.

Russ: Right, so you're at an opposite sense of where Eric is. Eric is thinking "Well, how can you have emotion *and* have the thought [every time]?" And you're thinking "How can you have emotion *without* having the thought?"

Melanie: Yes, exactly.

Russ: And I think that's the deal. You grew up doing it your way, and he grew up doing it his way and you both assume that everybody does it the same as you.

Melanie: [laughs] Yeah, exactly.

Eric: [laughs] I'm not sure exactly where we ended up with this, but at least my thought at the time had been that maybe there were three different levels at least conceptually possible. One or more may not be possible in reality, or not very common in reality, but they're at least conceptually possible. Those three are first what I think Russ calls an emotion fact-of-body, which would be just the fact that, say, your heart is racing or you're tensed up; and then there is a second level which would be having the kind of subjective experiences that are associated with that kind of emotion; and then the third is an awareness, a kind of meta-cognitive awareness, of the fact that you are having that emotion. My thought would be that when you get to the third level, the meta-cognitive awareness of the emotion as it's going on, that that would be . . .

Russ: That's different from what Melanie's reporting here.

Eric: It is?

[Here Russ and Eric enter a long discussion about levels of self-awareness and the connection between awareness and experience [see beep 3.2 and box 8.6]—a discussion in which we fail to agree on the last point at issue above, and in which we sometimes misunderstand each other (but not productively enough to merit detaining the reader). Melanie does not comment. Against armchair introspection, see box 8.7. For Russ's description of how most people experience emotion, see box 8.8. On whether Melanie's emotional experience is different from others', see box 8.9. Because of the length of this discussion, we examined only this one beep from Melanie's fifth sampling day.]

Box 8.7
Against armchair introspection

Russ: There are two main reasons that I am strongly opposed to armchair introspection. First, and less important, is that armchair introspectors don't agree with each other. Eric, for example, believes that there is visual experience present (nearly) all the time. [See section 10.3.] Many others, including John B. Watson (1925) and Baars (2003), believe that inner speech is present (nearly) all the time. Still others believe that people experience a continuous stream of affect (D. Watson 2000). And so on. I see no reason to prefer one account to the other.

Second, and more important, is that many of my subjects come to disbelieve some aspects of *their own* armchair introspections as a result of their sampling. Melanie is a rather typical subject in this regard. For example, Melanie's armchair version of herself was unaware that she paid direct attention to her sensations: She was surprised that she noticed the cold of her feet (beep 2.3) and the gooiness of the toothpaste (beep 2.4), for example. Melanie herself, very like most other subjects, didn't reject the accuracy of her DES observations; she rejected the adequacy of the armchair version of herself. I don't believe I have *ever* had a subject who, when confronted by such a discrepancy said "I think my armchair view was right and the DES 'discoveries' were incorrect."

There are some subjects whose armchair versions turn out to be quite accurate—their samples fit nicely in their armchair framework. Thus, I am not claiming that armchair observations are not true. I'm claiming that they are *often* not true, and I have not figured out a way, other than DES, to

Box 8.7
(continued)

discern which are true and which are not. In my experience, the size of the discrepancy between the armchair version and the DES version does *not* depend on the level of sophistication of the subject or the confidence of the armchair observer.

Eric: I'd be the first to agree that armchair generalizations about conscious experience are often quite radically mistaken; this is common ground between us. It also seems likely to me that many of your subjects have a better understanding of their own experience after having sampled with you than before, though it wouldn't surprise me if they walked away with some false impressions as well—as, for example, Melanie might if she now thinks she experiences emotion very differently from how most other people experience it. [See box 8.9.]

It would be a mistake, though, I think, to treat sampling interviews as a silver bullet methodology against which all other methods must be tested for validity. *All* methods for studying conscious experience, including DES in my view, are seriously problematic: The stream of experience does not admit of straightforward measurement. The best we can do in reaching our final judgments about experience is to balance considerations from a variety of doubtful sources, including both sampling interviews like this one *and* armchair introspection.

By the way, the view that there is nearly constant visual experience (which I do tentatively accept) need not be taken as contrasting with the view that there is nearly constant inner speech and/or emotional experience, if one holds that the stream of experience is rich. [See box 4.8.]

Thread: Retrospective and armchair generalizations. Previous: box 8.5. See also subsection 11.1.7.7.

Box 8.8
How most people experience emotion

Russ: I think it would be useful here to summarize how most of my subjects experience emotion, as revealed by my sampling procedure. I am convinced that the differences I describe here are not merely variations in report.

First, nearly all subjects make a clear, unshakeable distinction between thinking and feeling. They may use different words, but the distinction seems obvious to them. When pressed for the source of this obviousness, they are typically frustrated and say something like "Well, this is thinking and that is feeling!" as if that were an irreducible fact of experience.

Second, some people experience emotion as being primarily in their bodies; others experience emotion as being primarily in their heads. Here again, these descriptions are made with confidence. Furthermore, subjects who report that emotions are in their heads are not at all confused about the distinction between thinking and feeling. "They're both in my head, but one's thinking and the other is feeling!"

Third, some people's emotion seems to be entirely cognitive. That is, they think their feelings. They don't *feel* angry; they *are* angry in some cognitive way. (This is not necessarily the same as saying they feel the emotion in their heads.)

Fourth, even if emotion is experienced in the body, it is difficult for many subjects to pin down exactly how or where in the body it is experienced, although a minority experience extremely clear bodily referents for their emotion, such as "deep in my chest, right here (points), in a region about the size of my fist, and then with less intensity throughout the rest of my chest."

Fifth, many subjects report emotion frequently or almost always; many other subjects report emotion not at all or rarely.

Sixth, most subjects who experience emotion (either in the body or the head) explicitly deny the existence of some cognitive/mental/thoughty monitoring/appraisal/observation of their emotions. Unlike Melanie, most of the time they simply feel their emotions.

Seventh, emotional processes can be ongoing in the body without being immediately noticed. I call such emotions "feeling-fact-of-body." [See box 6.2.]

Eric: I guess I'm still inclined to think that some of this might be variation in report only, rather than variation in the underlying emotional experience. [See box 8.9, the transcript of beep 6.4, and section 3.3.] But how to sort out which is which? Well, that's the big stumper—*the* essential issue we need to address before consciousness studies can get traction as a science. You may think you've figured it out, Russ, but I'm still flailing!

Thread: Emotion. Previous: box 8.5. Next: box 8.9.
Thread: Human similarity and difference. Previous: box 7.12. Next: box 8.9.
Thread: Self-Awareness: Melanie's unusual. Previous: box 7.11. Next: box 8.9.

Box 8.9
Is Melanie's emotional experience different from others'? Emotional self-awareness.

Eric: Melanie has become convinced, on the basis of our discussions of this sample and a few others, that her emotional experience is different from most other people's in being more analytically self-aware (e.g., beeps 3.2, 5.1, 6.1, 6.2; see also box 9.3). While I would not be surprised to find that Melanie is in some way more self-conscious or self-observational than most people, I find it difficult to imagine that her emotional experience is as radically different from others' as seems to be implied here—i.e., that she never, or hardly ever, has an emotional experience without also reflecting on the fact that she is having that experience, while most people simply feel their emotions and only rarely reflect on those emotions as they occur. [See Russ's sixth remark in box 8.8.]

Emotional experience is at least sometimes hard to describe (as Russ mentions in boxes 5.13 and 8.8). The connection between self-awareness and consciousness is a tricky one, both to understand and to articulate. [See beep 3.2 and the accompanying boxes. Also see boxes 8.6 and 9.4.] Melanie might easily get tangled up here, especially if she is driven by a theory or self-conception and consistently overdescribes the extent of self-awareness in her emotional experiences—or consistently uses language that we misinterpret as signaling a higher-than-usual self-awareness. This is dangerous and confusing territory, and I wonder whether subjects might seem to have big individual differences only because they slip into different patterns of describing what really is the same thing, just because it's so murky.

So, for example, there seems to be a space between having a "feeling fact of body" with no accompanying emotional experience at all (box 6.2) and having vivid emotional experience accompanied by an acute self-conscious thought about that experience. I cut it into three levels (beep 3.2, transcript), but maybe it's more like a continuum—maybe even a continuum in two different dimensions: extent or intensity of experience, on the one hand, and self-awareness or self-knowledge of that experience on the other (with "feeling fact of body" being zero on both dimensions). Maybe these dimensions are separable, maybe not. My guess is that, given the difficulty of thinking through and articulating such issues (to what extent, or in what way, was I "aware of" my anxiety at the moment of the beep?) subjects might find ways of speaking that work well enough to get the approval of the interviewer—ways of speaking they then repeat in describing future experience. But these different ways of speaking may not reflect real, underlying differences in the overall structure of their experience.

I suppose it seems likelier to me that something like this is going on than that Melanie's emotional experience is constantly attended by self-reflection in a way radically different from mine or other people's.

Box 8.9
(continued)

Russ: To be fair, I am at least as convinced as is Melanie on this point. If Melanie sees herself as different from others, she probably learned much of that from me. I think we have evidence on a number of fronts that Melanie, unlike many or most others, has a distinct self-aware or self-observational characteristic.

Melanie has a separated self-awareness for many of her experiences, not just her emotional experiences. For example, she was specifically aware of her mouth closing as she talked in beep 1.3. That is a quite unusual characteristic of the experience of speaking.

I see no positive evidence that Melanie is confused about the terminology of self-awareness and substantial evidence that she understood the distinctions and was not confused. But I accept that with any single subject, one cannot be sure.

Eric: We ourselves were confused! (See our last three conversational turns and the concluding bracketed remark.) I'm *still* confused.

Thread: Emotion. Previous: box 8.8.
Thread: Human similarity and difference. Previous: box 8.8. Next: box 9.9.
Thread: Loose language. Previous: box 8.6. Next: box 9.4.
Thread: Melanie's trustworthiness: Attunement to distinctions. Previous: box 7.8. Next: box 9.6.
Thread: Melanie's trustworthiness: Unusual claims. Previous: box 4.14. Next: box 9.3.
Thread: Self-Awareness: Melanie's unusual. Previous: box 8.8. Next: box 9.3.

Beep 6.1

Melanie: Okay. Some of these were taken from last night, and some were from today. I was in a restaurant with my boyfriend having dinner. We were talking about the All-Star Game that was on last night, discussing how this year is this whole new thing where whichever team, National or American, that won the All-Star Game would get home-field advantage for the World Series. And we were trying to remember how they divide up the games in the World Series between the National and American fields. He said, although he thought it was wrong, that they did it three games in one place, two games in another place, and then two games somewhere else. And then I said "But that doesn't make any sense because that means that one stadium gets the World Series games five times if you play all seven games." And then the beep went off. So the beep happened right when I said "that means one stadium gets the World Series five times" *beep*.

Russ: You were saying that out loud?

Melanie: Um hm.

Russ: You were in the midst of saying "that means. . . ." And what, if anything, is in your experience other than your saying this.

Melanie: A feeling of conviction that what he said was wrong.

Russ: And can you tell us more about this, how you know this is a feeling of conviction, what it feels like, and . . .

Melanie: Um . . . I think probably being a little bit more assertive in what I'm saying is part of it, and just a certainty that I'm right.

Russ: Okay. So if an unbiased observer were watching your conversation, would that observer be able to say "Well she's being definitive here"? Are you saying that there are characteristics of your voice that . . .

Melanie: Yeah.

Russ: Okay. So these are externally observable characteristics.

Melanie: Um hm. And although it certainly wasn't in my awareness at the time, I probably leaned forward a little bit, kind of, so there was body language.

Russ: Okay. And was there anything other—I think you said that there was but I don't remember what it was now—anything other than the certainty in your voice that led you to . . .

Melanie: I can't really get any more specific than this, just the feeling of knowing that what I was saying was correct.

Russ: And is that feeling of knowing, is that describable in any more detail? Mental? Physical? Bodily? . . .

Melanie: It's mental. It's not physical or bodily. It's definitely mental but . . . beyond that, no.

Russ: So it's not just that your voice is more definitive. There is some awareness beyond just the recognition of the characteristics of your voice that you are right about this.

Melanie: Yes. Um hm.

Russ: Okay. But we're not finding any way to describe it other than this is some kind of a mental event.

Melanie: No.

[For brevity, we have excised, here and elsewhere in this sample, some of Russ's confirmatory repetitions of Melanie's statements.]

Russ: Okay. And is there anything else going on at this particular moment in your awareness?

Melanie: I was looking at the person I was speaking to, and I was aware that I was looking at him, but there wasn't anything else, like I couldn't tell you what particular part of his face I was looking at, and there wasn't some bit of me noticing what I was seeing. I just know that I was looking at him.

Russ: And when you say "you know that you're looking at him," does that mean in a retrospective sense?

Melanie: No, it means that I know that my eyes are pointed straight forward.

Russ: At the moment of the beep you know that your eyes are on him.

Melanie: Yeah, I'm not looking down and I'm not looking up, I'm looking straight ahead.

Russ: Okay.

Melanie: Which ties into the whole feeling of certainty . . .

Russ: Leaning forward looking at him.

Melanie: Yeah, and feeling of asserting something.

Russ: Okay. So there is at the moment of the beep some awareness of looking straight ahead . . .

Melanie: Straight ahead.

Russ: . . . at this guy. Okay, and anything else?

Melanie: That's it.

Russ: Eric?

Eric: So you said that you knew your eyes were pointing straight forward. Would you describe this as more knowledge about your eyes, then, or knowledge about the thing you're seeing? Or . . .

Melanie: Probably knowledge about the eyes as opposed to what I'm seeing.

Eric: So in a way it sounds like, it would be analogous to, say, bodily knowledge that you're faced a certain direction or something?

Melanie: Yeah. More like that than looking directly at something. And picking up what I was looking at. Because I could have been staring at anything, or looking at anything, but I just knew that I was looking straight ahead. [On whether she was having visual experience, see box 9.1.]

Russ: And is that part of the feeling of leaning forward, leaning into these words in some . . .

Melanie: Um hm, definitely.

Russ: So it's not like you knew that your body was intensely focused forward, and, separately from that, you knew that you were looking forward.

Melanie: Um hm.

Russ: It was that those things were the same or those were coordinated?

Melanie: Coordinated, yeah.

Box 9.1
Was Melanie having visual experience in this sample? Intermediate states of consciousness.

Eric: I wonder what Melanie would have said had I asked her whether she had visual experience at the moment of the beep. Is it possible to know self-consciously that you're looking at something without actually experiencing the thing you are looking at? Perhaps that would be analogous to knowing you have an emotion without experiencing the emotion (box 8.5)?

Russ: I think our questioning here left a bit to be desired, but my understanding is that Melanie was self-consciously aware of looking straight ahead, rather than simply aware of looking at the person. That interpretation may diminish the apparent contradiction that you point to in this instance.

Two comments: First, as we have noted elsewhere, Melanie's self-awareness here is somewhat unusual in DES subjects; see boxes 6.1 and 9.3. Second, I do think, based on my sampling studies, that some people some times (not often) do have the kind of awareness that you describe: self-conscious experience of looking at something without actually experiencing the thing being looked at. (Here, as always, when I say "without actually experiencing" I am not making the I-think-impossible distinction between "totally not experiencing" and "too-slight-to-be-noticed experiencing.") Most often, looking at and seeing are highly correlated, experientially inseparable processes, but DES shows that that is not always the case.

Eric: Let me add one thought to your parenthetical remark. On the one hand, there's the tricky methodological question of differentiating between "no X" and "an undetectable X." On the other hand, there's an issue about whether the phenomena of consciousness might be *intrinsically vague*—whether there might be states of mind that are somewhere *between* conscious and nonconscious, so that it makes no more sense to draw a sharp line separating the conscious from the nonconscious ones than it does to draw a sharp line dividing "tall" men from those that are not tall (at exactly 5'11", say). I see no reason to suppose that "in-between" states, not definitively conscious, not definitively non-conscious, can't exist. Furthermore, given gradualism in the phylogeny and development of brains, there seems to be excellent reason to suppose consciousness would emerge gradually. So maybe "peripheral" experiences (per box 4.8) exist somewhere in this nether zone?

Yet, for some reason, I can't quite embrace that idea. *If* Melanie has any wisp of visual experience here—no matter how peripherally, inarticulately, fuzzily, inattentively—then it seems to me that (reportably or not) she did indeed have visual experience, in a peripheral, inarticulate, fuzzy, inattentive way. Either her visual consciousness is a total blank, or she has some hazy beginnings of visual experience. I see no "in between" here. Thus, it

---

Box 9.1
(continued)

seems to me that "being conscious" is more like "having money" than "being tall." Having money comes in degrees. One can have more or less. But having even one cent is having money; and this is discretely different in kind from having not a penny.

However, I'm perfectly willing to acknowledge that my inability to conceive of genuinely indeterminate, in-betweenish cases of consciousness may say more about my (our?) *concepts* of consciousness than about the actual structure of the world.

Russ: Your distinctions are too fine for me or my subjects to know anything about. But if you're into metaphor, I think of consciousness as being more like a frozen lake. Sometimes it's clearly liquid, sometimes clearly solid, but sometimes, as when it's patchy or slushy or when there's a slight film of ice not strong enough to support an ounce, whether it's "frozen" comes down merely to the details of the definition.

Thread: Richness. Previous: box 6.2. See also section 10.3 and subsection 11.2.1.
Thread: Sensory Experience. Previous: box 4.18. Next: box 9.7.

Russ: Coordinated processes.

Eric: Oh, that's funny. Maybe I misheard what you said before. But I thought that you had said that it was only after the beep that you realized that you were leaning forward, that that wasn't part of your experience at the time of the beep.

Melanie: Well, no, that's right. I didn't know that I was leaning forward; I did know that I was looking straight ahead and I assume that I was leaning forward.

Eric: Um hm. So you say, then, that you had an experience having to do with, maybe your eyes being pointed forward at the time of the beep, and then after the beep you had an experience of which that was a part, which is a kind of general kind of feeling of leaning forward. Is that what you're conveying?

Melanie: Yes, that expresses it exactly.

Eric: I don't think in previous beeps you've described an experience of feeling certainty or feeling uncertainty about anything you've said.

Russ: I'm agreeing with that.

Melanie: Yeah.

Box 9.2
Is Melanie's external speech generally accompanied by certainty or uncertainty?

Russ: Melanie is making a general statement about herself based on very few samples, so it may well be a faux generalization. [See box 5.17.] I think we have to suspend judgment until we have more evidence.

Eric: Below, I suggest that this issue is something that could be explored in further interviews. Now, however, I wonder whether it might be the sort of fine theoretical issue that hangs on details of the subject's report (was there a faint sense of confidence or not? do we always experience some degree of certainty or uncertainty when we express things to ourselves or others?) that may be beyond the scope of this method.

Thread: Limits of DES. Previous: box 5.14. Next: box 9.10.

Eric: So is your sense that this is different from your reports about other things that you said in that respect?

Melanie: Well, there aren't many other times when I report that I've actually *said* something. [Beep 1.3 is the only case.]

Russ: Right.

Melanie: Usually it's inner speech or inner hearing.

Eric: Right.

Melanie: And when it's inner speech or inner hearing there isn't certainty or uncertainty, one way or the other. It's just kind of a thought meandering through my head, for lack of a better word. [On this statement, see box 9.2.]

Eric: I don't know whether we'll meet again, but it would be interesting to see whether that's a general feature of your experience of talking, that was maybe particularly salient in this case because it was so strong, or whether it's something that is generally absent.

Russ: Melanie has said sort of all along that she has something like an analytical portion of her, which is watching what she's doing while she's doing it.

Eric: Right.

Russ: And it seems like this is part of that, or similar to that kind of process to me. She's nodding to that.

Eric: Huh.

Russ: When you said, Melanie, that this is "I'm right," is there an affect that goes along with that? Like "I'm right" triumphantly? Or is it "I'm right" declaratively? As a matter of the fact of the world, this happens to be one fact that's right . . .

Melanie: Yeah, declaratively more than . . . I don't feel like I won anything and I don't feel superior or anything. It's just a fact.

Russ: So this is a stamp of correctness . . .

Melanie: Right.

Russ: . . . more than a stamp of victory.

Melanie: Yeah, it has nothing to do with anything victorious at all.

Russ: Okay. Do you have other questions about this piece, Eric?

[Here we have excised some confusion between Russ and Eric regarding Melanie's purported self-analyticity.]

Eric: When I was doing my own beeping, especially at the beginning, I think I was quite bad at determining the exact moment of the beep. So I'm wondering what your feeling is about the precision with which you're locating what's going on immediately before the beep. I'm wondering whether you're kind of gathering up a bunch of stuff that's in the general time vicinity of the beep and putting it all together as the thing that's going on at the moment of the beep. [See box 4.13.]

Melanie: Well . . . I certainly tried to be as accurate as possible. That's probably the only answer I can give with any certainty. But beyond that, I think if I were just doing that kind of "sum up" process, I could add a lot more to it. There is a lot more going on in those seconds right before the beep, because I was looking around the restaurant and I could add in little bits and pieces about that too, or things that caught my eye, or things that I was aware of hearing in the din of the other people there. But I can say with certainty that at the moment of the beep I wasn't hearing the other people in the restaurant; that wasn't in my awareness, although it had been at one time before.

[On the possibility of a periphery of experience, see box 4.8.]

Eric: Um hm.

Melanie: And I wasn't aware of what was on the TV screens around us, even though I had been just a moment before that because it had something to do with what we were talking about. But right in that moment before the beep it, none of that was there, and I know that.

Russ: So is your question, Eric, something like this: "Is it your opinion, as best that you can give your opinion (and we recognize there's limitations to this), that it seems that if we could take some kind of recording of your experience and then play back this experience, there would be sort of two things going on simultaneously in this recording . . .

Melanie: Yeah.

Russ: . . . There would be the speaking, and the analysis or the conviction?

Melanie: Yeah. I think that at any time you might try to record my experiences that you would have that specific duality between what I'm doing or what I'm thinking or what I'm saying and this analytical part of me that's watching what I'm doing or what I'm thinking or what I'm saying.

[On Melanie's possible attachment to seeing herself as self-analytical, see box 9.3.]

Eric: Um hm. I'm remembering also now something that you had said when we sampled the speech act by you before [beep 1.3]. At that time you said that you had the experience—now I'm not going to remember exactly what it was—something like your closing your mouth or the feeling of vibrations in your throat or . . .

Melanie: Oh right. Yes.

Eric: At that time I think you made a generalization that you thought that was fairly typical for you.

Melanie: Um hm.

Eric: Would you say in this case there was also that kind of stuff going on?

Melanie: No, not here.

Eric: Do you still accept that generalization though?

Melanie: I would certainly say it happens pretty often.

Eric: Um hm.

Russ: Let me ask a related question. Does the thing we're calling the analytic process, the "I'm right" part, seem like the same kind of a process as the noting the sensations in your mouth . . .

Melanie: Yes.

Russ: . . . or does it seem like a different kind of process?

Box 9.3
Is Melanie attached to seeing herself as self-analytical?

Eric: I worry that Melanie is by now—and perhaps earlier—attached to a self-conception that she is unusually self-analytical. This, of course, raises methodological concerns.

Russ: Suppose Melanie is attached to such a self-conception—which I'm not sure is the case. If we were asking her to *generalize* about her experience (as she does here), it is likely that that self-conception would lead her to select or invent instances that confirm her theory. But in experience sampling, Melanie is confronted with single, concrete instances. Just as having a theory that stop signs are red will not prevent you from recognizing that a particular stop sign is brown if you attentively view a brown stop sign, so also I think if a single, immediately occurring, sampled experience doesn't include a self-analytical feature, Melanie's self-theory probably will not insert one.

Eric: If the stop sign goes by quickly, I might see it as red, if that is what I was expecting, even if it is actually brown. Experience flows quickly, degree of self-awareness is a particularly murky issue, and she generally reports it (when she does) as only a secondary feature of her experiences.

   There's an opportunity for the refrigerator-light error here, as well. [See box 4.18.} If she is wondering now whether she is generally self-analytical, that may itself create a presently occurring self-analyticity that seems to confirm her theory.

Russ: Note, though, that Melanie doesn't allow her self-theory about experiencing the mechanical aspects of speech [see beeps 1.2 and 1.3 and boxes 4.11 and 4.14] to influence her judgment below (near the end of this sample) that they are not occurring in this particular case. Instead, the influence is the other way around: the particular observation alters her general self-theory (narrowing "quite often" at beep 1.3 to "pretty often" here).

Thread: Melanie's trustworthiness: Influence of generalizations. Previous: box 7.14. See also section 10.4.
Thread: Melanie's trustworthiness: Unusual claims. Previous: box 8.9. See also section 10.6.
Thread: Self-Awareness: Melanie's unusual. Previous: box 8.9. Next: box 9.4.

Melanie: A similar process, if not the same.

Russ: So if that's true, then that seems like the answer to your question, Eric. When she said, back a while ago [beep 1.2], "It seems to me like I do this kind of thing a lot" [she actually said at beep 1.2 ". . . often. Quite often."], you and I thought that what she meant by that was she pays attention to the vibrations in her mouth. But what she really meant was a somewhat broader thing, which would include things like monitoring herself for correctness, or whatever.

[Here we have excised, and above we have trimmed, some further discussion of the timing of the beep.]

Beep 6.2

[Melanie begins by expressing some embarrassment over the fact that she was playing a video game, a rare event for her. Russ and Eric reassure her that there is nothing to be embarrassed about.]

Melanie: I was playing it with someone, and the beep came right after I said "You're crowding me" in a joking manner. The beep came right after I finished saying that. And at the moment of the beep I was still smiling from having said that remark in a joking manner, and I felt just *happy*. I was just very happy.

Russ: And when you say that you were still smiling . . .

Melanie: Um hm.

Russ: . . . is that smiling in your awareness?

Melanie: Yes, I knew I was smiling.

Russ: So you were aware of the smiling.

Melanie: Um hm.

Russ: And when you say you felt happy, is that also in your awareness at the moment of the beep?

Melanie: Yes, definitely.

Russ: So this is not looking back when the beep goes off and saying "What's going on with me?"

Melanie: No. I knew that . . .

Russ: It's "I'm happy and I know it."

[For a comment on the preceding exchange, see box 9.4.]

Box 9.4
More on Russ's use of "awareness"

Eric: This is a good example of an exchange in which "awareness" seems to blur between its phenomenal and epistemic meanings. [See box 8.6.] You, Russ, maybe meant to be asking about "awareness" in the phenomenal sense: as in, was your smiling and your happiness part of your experience at the moment of the beep? Melanie takes this to be a question about whether she *knew* (in some self-analytical way?) that she was happy and smiling at the moment of the beep.

Russ: I disagree. I meant the question in the phenomenal sense, and I think Melanie understood it in the same phenomenal sense. She does use the word "knew," but goes on to clarify that what she meant was not cognitive, but rather that the lightness in her chest was in her experience at the moment of the beep. I don't think we adequately clarified here whether or to what extent this sample is an example of her self-analytical stance, but we do so below.

Eric: I take Melanie's statement "Very kind of lightweight inside . . ." to be an attempted clarification of the feeling experience only (the "I'm happy" part) not a clarification of what she means by her claim that she *knew* that she was happy (the "and I know it" part).

Russ: The words "and I know it" are mine, not Melanie's, and they illustrate that the interview process is imperfect. I was referring, probably too obliquely, to the children's ditty "If You're Happy And You Know It (Clap Your Hands)." Certainly that ditty asks children about their phenomenal, not their epistemic, awareness, and I meant the question in the same way. I agree with you, Eric, that my question raises an unfortunate (but I think pretty small) ambiguity: we don't know how Melanie interpreted it. However, I think there is no evidence that she understood me to be asking the epistemic question.

Thread: Loose language: Previous: box 8.9. See also section 3.3.
Thread: Self-Awareness: Melanie's unusual. Previous: box 9.3. Next: box 9.5.

Melanie: Yes.

Russ: And how do you feel, what is this happy feeling?

Melanie: Very kind of lightweight inside, you know, just no pressures, nothing to worry about, just feeling good and feeling happy and almost feeling healthy in a way.

Russ: And when you said "lightweight inside," you went like this, sort of referring to your chest?

Melanie: Yeah, it's like in your lungs, almost like when you have a balloon in your lungs or something like that. Not when you feel choked up, because you can also use that to express that, but just really light-weight, like there's no pressure. It's easy to breathe, it's easy to think and to talk all at the . . .

Russ: But sort of mostly in your upper torso, does that mean . . .

Melanie: Yes.

Russ: . . . neck to midsection?

Melanie: Yeah, um hm.

Russ: So in some other places you've said that you have feelings that were in your head [maybe beeps 1.1 and 5.1, depending on how you interpret them]. This one wasn't so much in your head?

Melanie: No. This felt all over. But at the same time if I had to just give it a place where it was, it started like around, you know, midsection or upper torso.

Russ: And now it sounds like we're maybe confusing what was happening in the physiology and what was happening in the experience. So at the moment of the beep [snaps fingers], are you more aware of your midsection as opposed to other portions of your body?

Melanie: Yeah, yes.

Russ: So you're feeling this lightness from . . .

Melanie: Upper torso.

Russ: . . . upper-torso-ness in your awareness.

Melanie: Yes.

Russ: And anything else going on in your experience?

Melanie: Just that.

Russ: You're playing the game but you're not really paying attention to the game?

Melanie: Well, we weren't playing. It was kind of . . . we were switching off taking turns, so there was like a pause, you know, and so I was kidding around to the person I was playing with. And at the moment we didn't have to punch a button or something like that, and so it was just like a little break.

Russ: Okay, and are your eyes aimed at the computer screen still?

Melanie: They were down, but I wasn't really paying attention to where they were located.

Russ: And by "down" do you mean at the computer screen? Or . . .

Melanie: No. It was like an arcade game, so I would say that the screen was kind of straight ahead and the controls were downward, so I was looking toward the controls.

Russ: But they weren't really in your awareness?

Melanie: No.

Russ: Your eyes were aimed at them but you weren't really paying much attention to what your eyes were . . .

Melanie: . . . doing.

Russ: Right, okay.

[Here we have excised a brief discussion of Melanie's physical situation.]

Eric: So I think that we had said that it was at least conceivable at one point that you could have an emotional experience but not have knowledge at the time that you're having the experience, or attentiveness to the experience at the time it's going on.

Melanie: Okay, yeah.

Eric: And you would say *this* would be a case in which you were having the experience *and* you were attending to the experience.

Melanie: Yeah. I was happy, and I knew I was happy.

Eric: And you said you knew you were smiling. Is this an awareness of your facial posture . . .

Melanie: Yeah.

Eric: . . . or is it kind of like . . .

Melanie: It was more like I could feel the smile.

Eric: It's an awareness of having your face in that position . . .

Melanie: Yes, I think the latter. I could feel that I was smiling, like feel a little tightness in my cheeks—that whole sort of thing that I go through with smiling.

Eric: Um hm.

Russ: And is that part of the awareness of the lightness in your upper torso? Or does that seem like it's different for you?

Melanie: Similar, again.

Russ: And in the beep that we were just talking about, when you were talking aloud, you were aware of facial, mouthful things, oral things. Is this the same or different from that?

Melanie: It's the same.

Russ: So there's what we were talking about as being a sort of an analytical kind of a thing.

Melanie: Um hm.

Russ: So the noticing of the smile is part of the analytical, part of the self-aware . . .

Melanie: Part, yeah.

Russ: . . . part. And is the awareness of the body also part of the self-aware part? Or . . .

Melanie: Um hm, it's like I'm monitoring what's going on at that moment in my body.

Russ: Okay. So it's not just that it's going on in your body and you're noticing it, but you're noticing it in an analytical sense. Is that correct? Kind of self-awareness . . .

Melanie: Yeah. Almost [laughs wryly] like there's this other little being that's taking notes about what's going on.

Russ: Um hm.

Melanie: That sort of awareness.

Russ: So theoretically, but apparently not for you or at least not very often, it might be possible for a lightness feeling in your body and a smile to take place, and you might know that it would be happening, and you could recognize it and feel it happen, so to speak. But this experience has something on top of that which is . . .

Melanie: A knowledge of what's going on.

Russ: . . . and it's sort of in an analytical or self-monitoring kind of way?

Melanie: Yeah. Um hm.

Russ: Okay.

Box 9.5
Consolidating Melanie's sense that she is self-analytical

Eric: Here you and Melanie are refining and consolidating the idea that Melanie is exceptionally self-analytical—that, unlike most of us, she normally observes her own life or experience in some detached way as it is going on.

I remain unconvinced that Melanie has the radically different kind of inner life that this would seem to suggest. The issues around self-awareness are tricky and the opportunities for miscommunication and distortion ample. [See box 8.9.] In some sense, of course, we are all constantly attuned in some way to ourselves, though it's difficult to articulate what exactly this involves. Could Melanie be misreporting, or we misinterpreting, this normal self-attunement as something unusually self-conscious?

I'd probably need to see some kind of evidence not based on self-report before accepting that Melanie differs from the rest of us in this particular way.

Russ: While I think "exceptionally" and "radically" are a bit too strong, I don't think the issues are tricky enough to overrule my sense that Melanie's self-analytical experience is different from most other subjects with whom I've sampled at least as carefully as Melanie.

Thread: Self-Awareness: Melanie's unusual. Previous: box 9.4.

[Here a further discussion of self-awareness, mostly between Russ and Eric, is excised. For Eric's concerns about this exchange, see box 9.5.]

Beep 6.3

In lieu of the full transcript of the discussion of this sample (available at http://mitpress.mit.edu/inner_experience), here is a description of Melanie's experience at the moment of the beep as she conveyed it in the interview.

At the moment of the beep Melanie was still playing the arcade game, standing in front of the arcade machine with her arms crossed, concentrating on what was on the screen. She was very aware of the fact that she was concentrating, and in particular she was noticing that her brow was furrowed, that she was worrying (chewing on) her lower lip, and that she had her arms crossed. She was also aware of the way her feet were placed and the way she was standing. All these bodily manifestations were part of the feeling of concentrating, but they did not exhaust that feeling. [See box 5.15.] She described it as like an inner camera watching what she was doing and taking stock of it. This self-monitoring was similar to that in other samples [e.g., beeps 3.2, 5.1, 6.1, 6.2], only more so than usual. The content of the video screen was, she said, only about 20 percent of her awareness.

Beep 6.4

Melanie: I was at home. We had some flowers on our kitchen table, and I had taken them to the sink in the kitchen to throw them out because they had gone dry. Right before the beep I had taken the bulk of the flowers out of the vase and tossed them in the trash. Then right before the beep, I was leaning over the sink and picking up the remaining petals and collecting them in my hand to throw them in the trash. I was thinking that those flowers had lasted for a nice long time. It was just kind of an idle thought that was inner speech.

Russ: As in, quote, Those flowers lasted for a nice long time, unquote?

Melanie: Quote, They lasted for a nice long time.

Russ: Okay.

Melanie: And at the moment of the beep my awareness was split between being focused on picking up the petals and on hearing the echoes of "nice long time" in my head.

[On Melanie's carefulness here, see box 9.6.]

Box 9.6
Melanie's carefulness

Russ: Notice that Melanie is carefully distinguishing between before the beep (throwing out flowers), right before the beep (picking up petals and inner speech), and the moment of the beep (picking up petals and hearing echoes). Melanie also corrects my quotation of exactly what she had said in inner speech. This kind of care increases my confidence in Melanie's report.

Thread: Melanie's trustworthiness: Attunement to distinctions. Previous: box 8.9.
Thread: Melanie's trustworthiness: Details. Previous: box 8.2. See also section 10.4, section 10.5, subsection 11.2, and section 12.2.

Russ: So you had said in inner speech "They lasted for a nice long time" *just prior* to the beep?

Melanie: Um hm, not at the beep but just prior to it.

Russ: But in some way the "nice long time" portion is still there. Is that right?

Melanie: Yeah, it was. The best I can liken it to is an echo.

Russ: And is this a hearing experience? You called that a hearing experience; do you mean that to be taken literally? Or . . .

Melanie: It was. The "nice long time" bit was. The "it lasted for a nice long time," quote unquote, was inner speech, but this was much more like inner hearing.

Russ: Okay. And when you said it in inner speech, was that in your own voice?

Melanie: Yes.

Russ: And when you're hearing "nice long time," is that still hearing your own voice?

Melanie: Yes.

Russ: And do all of these things sound the same? Because there's your real voice, and then there's the innerly spoken voice, and then there's the heard voice, are they . . .

Melanie: No, they sound the same. [Compare beep 1.1 and box 4.2.]

Russ: Okay. And "echo." I want to understand what you mean by "echo." An echo gets softer and softer; did you mean to imply that? And echo sometimes is repeated and sometimes once but . . .

Melanie: No, it didn't get softer and softer, it's almost like [quizzically] it got blurrier and blurrier. Not in terms of visual blurry, but a sound blurry [again quizzically], where it just started overlapping itself until it just came to this jumble in which you can't make any noise out. It sounds really weird but . . .

Russ: So are you saying that you said in inner speech something that was quite clear . . .

Melanie: Um hm.

Russ: . . . "It lasted for a nice long time," and then there's "nice long time," "nice long time," overlapped with "nice long time" . . .

Melanie: Yeah.

Russs: . . . then "nice long time" overlapped with "nice long time" overlapped with "nice long time" . . .

Melanie: And it keeps going.

Russ: . . . until there's sort of several of these things going?

Melanie: Yeah.

Russ: Okay. And is it possible to say how many of these things?

Melanie: No . . .

Russ: And is it possible . . .

Melanie: I think at the moment of the beep it had only been a couple.

Russs: So the part about overlapping a long time would be sort of speculating about what would have happened if this had gone on undisturbed . . .

Melanie: Um hm.

Russ: . . . that there would have been more of these things included?

Melanie: Yeah, because it started to overlap, and then overlap a little more. Not a couple, so there were about three or four that echoed in there.

Russ: Okay. And at the same time as these overlapping inner hearings are taking place, you're seeing petals . . .

Melanie: Yeah, and picking them up, and so focused in the motions of: There's a flower petal, reach my hand down, pick it up, and put it in my other hand.

Russ: Okay. Do you mean that in a cognitive sense? Or in a somehow thinking that I should pick up this petal?

Melanie: No.

Russ: So it's a . . .

Melanie: It's just what I'm doing.

Russ: . . . it's your arms are going and petals are coming up. That kind of thing.

Melanie: Yeah.

Russ: And that kind of thing could happen in awareness, and it could happen outside of awareness.

Melanie: It's in awareness.

Russ: So you're directedly, consciously, so to speak, in awareness . . .

Box 9.7
Melanie's experience of activity

Eric: I don't think we pushed hard enough on this aspect of Melanie's description. Did this activity involve visual experience, tactile experience, feelings of motor control, or all or none of these? (At some point, pushing on such issues would be asking too much of Melanie, of course.)

Russ: I agree that we did not push hard. My DES experience leads me to speculate that had we pushed harder, we would not have arrived at a much different description, because such "doings" are generally difficult or impossible to describe with more detail that what Melanie has done here. However, because we didn't push, I cannot be confident about that.

Thread: Sensory experience. Previous: box 9.1. See also section 10.3.

Melanie: Yeah, oh there's another one. Yeah.

Russ: ... but you're not saying "Oh there's another one"?

Melanie: No.

Russ: You're examining the sink ...

Melanie: Right, and then just going and picking up all of the ones there, collect them all out of the sink and throw them away.

[On whether we should have asked more here, see box 9.7.]

Russ: Okay, and you said your awareness was "split." Did you mean to imply evenly split? partially split? 80–20? 90–10? ...

Melanie: It felt pretty evenly.

Russ: Your turn, Eric.

Eric: So, the echoes that you're hearing of your inner speech. At first I was inclined to take the idea of an echo pretty metaphorically ...

Melanie: Um hm.

Eric: ... like there may be some pretty vague sense in which a thought can still be with you even after you've finished saying it in inner speech.

Melanie: Right.

Eric: But you don't mean that. You mean something much more like an echo, where there's actually a repetition ...

Melanie: Yes.

Eric: ... of an auditory thing that's going over and over again.

Melanie: Yes.

Russ: In sort of the same way as if we all decided in a minute here, to say "nice long time" all at the same time. You would start at one time, and I would start a little bit later, and Eric would start a little bit later than that, and we'd all say "nice long time." That's what it sounded like?

Melanie: Yeah.

Russ: Except that it would be all your voice.

Melanie: Right.

Eric: So it probably takes about a second to say "nice long time." So if you're talking about having the echoing repeating, you're talking about something that's happening over the course of several seconds? Or I remember your saying at some point earlier on that in your inner speech things are speeded up [beep 1.1; see boxes 4.4 and 4.5].

Melanie: Yeah. It felt instantaneous. Or not instantaneous but incredibly, you know, microseconds apart. I mean in a very, very short span of time, so it all felt like it was happening all at once.

Russ: And does that mean that it felt like the speech was speeded up? Or did it just feel like the whole experience happened at the same time?

Melanie: No, it didn't seem like it was faster than normal speaking. It just felt like it was all happening at once.

Russ: And so is what you're saying, basically, a physical impossibility here, because Eric is right, these things take a second or so, that some overlapping has got to take a couple of seconds, if it was going to happen in reality. But it's not happening in reality . . .

Melanie: No.

Russ: . . . it's happening in your imagination, so this seems like it happens . . .

Melanie: Very fast.

Russ: . . . more or less instantaneously, even though in reality . . .

Melanie: It couldn't.

Russ: Okay. I don't know how she could do that either [all laugh], but that doesn't mean that she can't.

Eric: Right. It seems to me that it can't *literally* seem both that it's repeating multiple times, one after the other, and that it's instantaneous. It seems like the seeming of repetition must involve at least some little time gap between the starts of the various . . .

Box 9.8
Mozart's claim to hear a symphony instantaneously

Russ: In a letter in 1789, Mozart wrote: "... my subject enlarges itself, becomes methodised and defined, and the whole, though it be long, stands almost complete and finished in my mind, so that I can survey it, like a fine picture or a beautiful statue, at a glance. Nor do I hear in my imagination the parts *successively*, but I hear them, as it were, all at once (*gleich alles zusammen*). ... Committing to paper is done quickly enough, for everything is, as I have said before, already finished." (Holmes 1979, pp. 317–318)

As I have frequently said above, I am highly skeptical of retrospective generalizations, even from a genius such as Mozart. Nonetheless, there is some corroborating objective evidence (e.g., Mozart is known for his great speed in written composition and his ability to hear another pianist play an extended piece once and then Mozart himself to play it in its entirety from memory without error). But the point here is not that we should believe Mozart's account, only that we should not hold too tightly to our presuppositions about the nature of musical experience and thereby be open to credibly examined surprising views. (As an aside, Mozart himself, at the beginning of the paragraph before the cited portion, uses by my count eight subjunctifiers, a reflection of his honesty in the generalization attempt.)

Thread: Rules of inner reality. Previous: box 4.16.

Melanie: It did. I didn't mean instantaneous, but it felt like mere microseconds apart. Very fast.

Eric: Right.

Russ: And I disagree with the implication of your statement. I don't think that's an impossibility.

Eric: Um hm.

Russ: Mozart, for example, said—I've never sampled with him unfortunately, which would have been a pretty cool thing to do [all laugh]—that he heard a whole symphony at the same time.

[For an elaboration of the Mozart reference, see box 9.8.]

Eric: Um hm.

Russ: And you would be saying that's impossible because these things are temporal and there are entrances and exits and whatever ...

Eric: Right.

Russs: . . . how could you hear those things at the same time? Somehow he could do it. It would be interesting to know whether that was really true—I don't know whether it was or not. But it seems like we have to suspend the laws of physics if we're going to understand what *experience* is like.

Eric: Right. But it doesn't seem to me like this is just the laws of physics. I mean, you know, maybe it is conceivable. Maybe I'm being narrow-minded—the Mozart story has kind of a nice ring to it. But it does seem to me like if you're imagining a symphony auditorially, you have to imagine one note ending and another one beginning after it's ended. I don't think that's a matter of physics. If it's true, it's a matter of what a symphony is.

Russs: Not to Mozart.

Eric: If all the notes come at the same time, it's not a symphony even in imagination.

Russs: But not to Mozart, apparently. And you'd think he'd know!

Eric: Maybe I'm being too narrow about this, but the thought I was having was that it's a violation of the laws of physics to go floating off the floor, but you can certainly imagine that coherently.

Russs: Right.

Eric: But I'm not sure you can coherently imagine an instantaneous symphony in the same way.

Russs: Well, I've got the advantage probably of having sampled with a bunch of other people. Time is a pretty screwy thing in the sense that it's not at all uncommon for people to report things that seem to violate the laws of temporal sequence. The example we've got going here is a pretty good example.

Eric: Um hm.

Russs: And I've asked as many skeptical questions as you've asked over many years of doing this kind of stuff, to try to say "Well, you know, it can't possibly be!" And people like Melanie stick pretty much to their guns and say "Well, you know, maybe it can't be. But that's the way it seemed. It seemed like there was a long thing happening but it didn't seem like it took a long time to do it."

Eric: Right.

Russs: And so the laws of experience are somehow different from the laws of physics. But, you know, a skilled moviemaker can capture an event that takes a long time to actually occur, can capture that in some kind of implied way. If a moviemaker can do that in the really restricted medium of a movie, Melanie ought to be able to do it better in her own experience.

Eric: Yeah, well maybe so.

Russ: Here again, I'm not saying what it is that she did and what it is that she didn't. But it's part of what I call "bracketing," that it's not fair to discount her experience on the basis of what must happen in reality, because her experience is not reality.

Eric: Yeah. Well, for some reason I can find more sympathy with the idea that something could go quickly and not seem sped up—you know, go much more quickly than it would in reality. So when Melanie says that her inner speech happened quickly, more quickly than normal speech, but it didn't seem that she was talking fast [beep 1.1], that doesn't bother me as much as what seems to me saying that the echoes were *instantaneous* does, which Melanie actually denies in this case.

Russ: Yeah. It seems to me that if we took a regular piece of audio tape and played it back at double speed, it would of course be twice as high in pitch and take half as long. And if we did this kind of thing often enough, we could probably become quite skilled at hearing the original speaker as if the original speaker were actually speaking in his normal voice, even though in actuality it's going higher and faster. And so I think Melanie can develop a shorthand that does even better than that about her own voice.

Eric: Right. Now. . . . see, I think I'm much more inclined than you are to see people as similar in their basic experiences. [See box 7.4.] So for me it seems to be that the default is what my opinions about what my own experiences are. [On the appropriateness of such a default supposition, see box 9.9.] I am, of course, as I acknowledge and would even argue, kind of ill-informed and mistaken probably in many respects about my experiences. But the following seems to me like a possibility. I had a sense from some of my samples of having a thought that was expressed in inner speech somehow continuing to linger with me for some short period after the inner speech was completed, and it's hard to characterize exactly what that experience is.

Russ: Right.

Eric: So it would seem to me possible that someone attempting to characterize that would think of the metaphor of an echo, which is kind of a nice metaphor. But then she might buy into the metaphor too much and start to attribute to her experiences the literal features of an echo,

Box 9.9
Should unusual reports be held to a higher standard of evidence?

Russ: You have every right to wonder about this, and to question Melanie carefully when she is reporting something that strikes you as unusual or alien. But bracketing presuppositions means suspending your default presupposition that people are the same. It means being as happy to discover that Melanie really had echoes in her experience as to discover that she did not.

Eric: I think it's a question of reasonably having a higher standard of evidence for some claims than for others. It doesn't make sense to treat all claims as equal, regardless of their initial plausibility. If some experience is very common, then all else being equal we should be readier to believe her report of that experience than a report of some previously unheard-of experience. Compare: If someone says she saw a car doing 90 miles per hour on the freeway, all else being equal we should be readier to believe that than if she says she saw a car doing 190. It's not that we should *never* believe the latter, just that the standards are rightly higher.

Russ: I agree that it makes sense to have some sensitivity to prior probabilities. However, the point hinges importantly on "all else being equal." If someone says "I saw a car doing 90" as the result of casual curbside observation, and someone else says "I saw a car doing 190" as the result of sophisticated radar equipment readings, then you should not necessarily be readier to believe the first observation than the second. Casual introspective or retrospective generalization is like curbside observation, and rigorous experience sampling interviews are like sophisticated radar equipment (I think). Prior probabilities based on casual observation shouldn't be taken to impugn careful observations conducted by a considerably more sophisticated method.

Eric: So then the question becomes: Is descriptive experience sampling, followed by careful interview, sufficiently superior a method that it should trounce evidence from all other sources? I guess I still don't take that to be established. [See my concluding remarks in sections 10.1 and 10.6.]

Thread: Bracketing presuppositions. Previous: box 8.5. See also section 10.6 and subsection 11.1.7.
Thread: Human similarity and difference. Previous: box 8.9. See also section 12.1.

imputing them backwards and erroneously into the experience, like I think people in the 1950s erroneously attributed to their dreams black-and-whiteness because it seemed natural to compare dreams to movies. [For an extended discussion, see Schwitzgebel 2002b. See also box 5.2.]

Russ: Right.

Eric: Right, so I guess I have a suspicion that that would be what was going on in this case.

Russ: Yeah, and I think it's okay to have that suspicion and that you ought to inquire about it as carefully as you can, but not just assume it.

Eric: Right.

Russ: And as part of our conversations here I have come to the notion that there's a fundamentally important deal about the difference between thinking that everybody's the same and thinking that everybody might not be the same.

Eric: Yeah, yeah, I think that's a big deal, all right. People give very different reports of experience, and I guess I have just a general bias toward the default presupposition being that people are the same. You would have something to overcome, some burden of proof before you could say "Wow! You know, people really are as different as they seem from these reports!"

Russ: Yeah. But let's put it this way. When I sample with people, people say things that would never in a million years occur to me to say.

Eric: [laughs] Right. See, I guess my overall inclination is to think that experience is elusive and gone in a second. So it's hard to remember. And in addition, it's hard to articulate. We don't have good words for talking about it. We don't usually think about it or talk about it. It's hard to describe, hard to conceive, hard to categorize the things that are going on in experience. So we reach for different ways of speaking about it, different kinds of metaphors, and because people reach in different ways and reconstruct in different ways and employ different categories to deal with their experience, it can give the impression that people's experiences are very different, where they may actually be pretty similar.

Russ: Yeah, I can appreciate that. But I've tried to be as absolutely, scrupulously careful as I can to distinguish between what's metaphorical and what's not, and to give people the out of saying "Well I don't really know." And yet, when I do that, people come out to be a lot different.

[On whether people know when they are being metaphorical, see box 9.10. On "first-person" science, see box 9.11.]

Box 9.10
Do people know when they are being metaphorical?

Eric: It's natural to suppose that people know when they are being metaphorical—and many times they do know. But I do also think that people can be taken in by their own metaphors without realizing it. Thus, I think it is possible—and something that probably *cannot* be resolved by further questioning of Melanie—that Melanie is being taken in by her own metaphors when she says here that she experienced an echoing, or when she says in beep 5.1 that her recognition of herself as being anxious was experienced as literally in the back of her head, or when she says in beep 1.1 that her feeling of humorousness was accompanied by a "rosy-yellow glow."

I'm not sure how we can settle the issue of how metaphorical such statements are; but I think we cannot simply trust Melanie on this matter, even after she has been carefully questioned.

Russ: I agree that people are often taken in by their own metaphors, but, as I have stated repeatedly throughout this book, I think the risk is greater when dealing with general opinions than when dealing with specific moments carefully examined.

I disagree that this cannot be resolved by further questioning of Melanie. It may be true that we cannot resolve the "metaphoricity" of this particular beep, because the being-taken-in might have already happened. But we can (and did) discuss the taken-in-by-metaphor notion here, so that *next time* Melanie will be more alert to the notion at the time of the beep. I think we also did that more or less adequately at beep 1.1 and beep 5.1, as well as elsewhere, so I have more confidence in Melanie here than you apparently do, but I accept that that is a matter of judgment. My solution to your skepticism here would be to sample further, as often as it takes, to see whether or not we get enough evidence to satisfy us that Melanie has become skillful enough not to be taken in by her own metaphors.

Furthermore, if Melanie is taken in by an echo metaphor, wouldn't we expect her to describe repetitive, rather than the uncharacteristically overlapping, echoes?

Thread: Limits of DES. Previous: box 9.2. See also subsection 11.2.1 and section 12.2.
Thread: Influence of metaphors. Previous: box 5.2.

Box 9.11
Is DES an example of irreducibly "first-person" science?

Eric: Alvin Goldman (1997, 2001) and David Chalmers (2004) have asserted that the study of consciousness requires distinctively "first-person" or non-"public" methods, involving introspective self-judgment—methods different in kind from and irreducible in principle to the "third-person," "public" methods of the other sciences. Dennett (2002) has disagreed, asserting that consciousness studies should and can be every bit as objective and third-personal as the other sciences, relying only on "public" data such as brain measurements and transcripts. This debate has captured the attention of consciousness studies researchers and the interested public, because it seems to concern the fundamentally important question of *how to study consciousness*—what sorts of methods can and cannot, should and should not be implemented. So, looking back on these dialogues, the question seems to arise: Are we using here a "first-person" or a "third-person" method?

Actually, I don't know. Nor do I care, much. The seeming centrality of this debate to the methodology of consciousness studies is an illusion. One looks in vain for any genuine prescriptive differences, any study or method permitted by Goldman or Chalmers, forbidden by Dennett (as Dennett himself notes). The dispute really concerns only the *description* of introspective methods. Should we describe the interviews in this book (per Chalmers) as "irreducibly first-personal" because they depend on Melanie's attunement to her subjective experience? Or should we describe them (per Dennett) as "third-personal" and "objective" because what we are doing is analyzing spoken utterances, in principle available to all, and hypothesizing about what might lie behind them?

Each way of speaking highlights important aspects of the study of consciousness. But the more important question for consciousness studies—what *should* be the central methodological question—is *when* and *under what conditions* and *to what extent* people's reports about their experience are trustworthy. That, of course, is the topic of this book.

Russ: I could not agree with you more, Eric! Fascination with the Goldman-Chalmers-Dennett debate has misdirected consciousness researchers away from what you rightly call the central question.

Yet let me also say that I consider DES to be a first-person-plural method: *We* (Melanie, you, and I) examined Melanie's inner experience and evaluated her/our characterizations thereof. To be sure, only Melanie had access to the experience we sought to examine. However, only I had experience with a method designed to identify specific moments, focus attention on those moments, bracket presuppositions, avoid faux generalizations, and so on; and you brought your own perspective that changed and illuminated things. Thus, Melanie, you, and I together did what none of us could have done alone. But my use of the term "first-person" here is not intended to imply a position in the Goldman-Chalmers-Dennett debate. I want only to emphasize the value of the skilled investigator–willing participant alliance.

III Reflections

10 Eric's Reflections

Eric Schwitzgebel

Melanie makes a number of interesting claims in these interviews—claims which, if true, reveal much about one person's stream of conscious experience. But the question is, *are* her claims true? What license do we have to believe them? In my mind, this is the first and most central question that must be answered.

Let's grant from the outset that Melanie is a sincere and conscientious subject, Russ a careful and even-handed interviewer. What they deliver is probably about as good as can reasonably be expected from open interviews about sampled experiences. If we reject it, we reject the method in general—and in its wake surely also a plethora of related but less careful approaches. We then either resign in defeat or face the difficult task of specifying some *better* way to garner reports about spontaneously generated emotion, imagery, and the like. If, on the other hand, we are justified in accepting what Melanie says about her experience, then perhaps, by repetitions of this method, we can make some headway in the vexed field of consciousness studies. In the merit or failure of these interviews, we can glimpse a possible future of the discipline.

My position is this: We should tentatively accept the most basic claims Melanie makes about her experiences, pending further evidence. However, we should view the details she provides, even plausible details confidently asserted, with a high degree of skepticism. So, for example, in beep 5.1, I think we should tentatively accept—as more likely to be true than not—that Melanie had visual imagery of an intersection and also a feeling or recognition of anxiety sometime roughly around the moment of the beep. We should, I suggest, accept this *tentatively*, barring countervailing evidence. (Such evidence is not available in this case but could include such things as later recantations or physiological or facial measures suggestive of a different emotional state.) However, even without specific countervailing evidence, I think we should be very wary of the details. I don't think we should accept, even tentatively, what Melanie says about the specifics of the image, about the level of detail in the image, about whether she was actually *feeling* anxiety at the moment of the beep (as opposed to just "knowing" that she was anxious without an anxious feeling), about what this knowledge or feeling of anxiety was like, about whether she is right to deny the presence of other experiences at the moment, etc. We should, I think, withhold judgment about the accuracy or inaccuracy of such assertions, absent further physiological or behavioral evidence of some sort for or against them. The details of Melanie's reports *may be* true. But, without some further corroboration, we should not cite them as serious support for particular philosophic or scientific theses about the nature of experience—for example, in defense of a particular account of imagery or emotion. They are, at best, merely suggestive.

I regard this as a moderate view, and the course I would chart for consciousness studies in light of it is a cautious and pluralistic one—neither a wholesale rejection of Russ's experience sampling, nor the elevation of it over previous approaches. The field is for now, I think, in the unenviable position of possessing a stable of suggestive but unreliable (or at least unproven) methods, to none of which we can harness full scientific confidence.

10.1   We Have Not Established the Validity of Russ's Interview Method

Russ rejects my cautious pluralism because he believes his approach to the study of conscious (or "inner") experience gives substantially more faithful access to experience than does any other contemporary scientific approach. He believes, if I understand him correctly, that we should largely disregard the accounts of experience given by other contemporary scientific methods because he thinks they don't adequately manage the methodological problems DES is designed to avoid. Of course, as we mentioned in the opening chapters, many philosophers and psychologists over the centuries have claimed they possessed singularly trustworthy methods of studying consciousness. The contradictory results arising from this diversity of methods show that many such claims must be false. The burden of proof is squarely on Russ to show that his method, unlike the others, does in fact merit our trust. In my view, Russ has not shown this.

Russ has emphasized the advantages of obtaining an arbitrary, brief sample of experience, reflected on immediately after it occurs. He has emphasized the advantages of not forcing that experience into a pre-conceived structure and of restraining the interviewee from making general claims or claims about causation. He has shown in the interview chapters that he is capable of soliciting reports without palpable bias. Melanie, for her part, makes interesting assertions about her experience, assertions that are not obviously self-contradictory and don't crumble into an uninterpretable mess when she is asked to elaborate. This is all good. But it still falls a considerable distance short of showing that we should, as a general matter, accept the deliverances of Russ's method. We need, in addition, some sort of *external corroboration*. That is, we need to find evidence *not grounded solely in interviews of this sort* that sheds light on the accuracy or inaccuracy of Melanie's reports. And this book, of course, presents nothing of the sort. It records an exploration, not a verification.

A measurement technique may require external corroboration at the outset without remaining forever hostage to, and judged inferior to, the sources of evidence that first help establish its validity. A scientist intends to create an extraordinarily precise thermometer, let's say. She has good theoretical reason to anticipate outstanding accuracy. Yet she will not accept its deliverances immediately. She compares its measurements with the measurements of other, cruder, thermometers she already trusts to some extent. If it's too far off, she has cause for concern. She puts the thermometer in a situation where she would expect, theoretically, a very slight rise in temperature—a rise perhaps unmeasurable by earlier thermometers—and hopes her new device registers it. If her device passes enough such tests, she may go back and use it to correct or displace her older thermometers or to revise some of the theories she initially used in testing it. Corroboration doesn't imply subservience. It is no objection to the demand for corroboration that the method in question will likely prove superior to the prior methods (and theories grounded in those methods) to be used in corroborating it. In science, few methods command trust without independent corroboration, at least at first.

Consequently, even if we had excellent reason to think Russ's method superior to all prior methods, prudence dictates that we compare its results to the results of those other methods (as the measurements of the new thermometer were compared to the measurements of old thermometers) and that we check its results against what can be theoretically predicted or retrodicted (as the thermometer was checked to see if it recorded the predicted slight rise in temperature). Direct verification of the first sort is beyond the scope of this book: We employ no independent means of measuring Melanie's experience. Russ does offer some corroboration of the second sort in chapter 2 when he discusses features of Fran's behavior that seem to support her unusual introspective reports. (I find the case of Robert less compelling, for reasons described in box 2.6.) Russ and I have also contemplated the possibility of a study correlating experience while reading with cognitively measurable differences in reading comprehension. [See box 5.3.] None of this, however, pertains directly to Melanie or to the transcripts at the center of this book. We have no videotape, say, of Melanie's behavior at the sampled moments, against which we could check her reports, no cognitive tests that might shed (tentative) light on matters such as whether she really is more self-conscious than others or particularly prone to detailed imagery.

Perhaps we wouldn't need such external support if Russ's method had no flaws, left no sizable space for error to enter, was indisputably massively superior to all the preceding methods that have produced uneven (but sometimes interesting) results. However, as I'm sure Russ would agree, his method is not as resplendent as that. Even if, in the end, we decide it is better than all preceding methods, granting exemption from the general requirement of external corroboration is extreme.

Russ will dispute with me the extent to which his method leaves room for distortions due to experimenter bias and situational pressures, even with a skilled interviewer (more on this later). However, I think he cannot reasonably dispute that his method (like many others) leaves considerable room for *errors of memory and communication* and for distortions due to the *preconceptions and reconstructions of the subject.* Even if we assume (optimistically) that there is no significant memory issue in the minute or so after the beep when the subject is first reflecting on her sampled experience), the interview itself is conducted up to 24 hours later. The interviews touch on many details the subject did not explicitly record, or possibly even reflect on, immediately after the beep. Surely, there is substantial room for error here.

The interviewer exhorts the subject to set aside preconceptions, to be fully receptive to her experience regardless of how surprising it may be, not to confabulate or reconstruct on the basis of theory, to express uncertainty where it seems appropriate, to be absolutely frank. But of course exhortation alone, though it may be helpful, can't guarantee that the subject actually attains all these desirable (?) goals. Nor can we be assured that the *appearance* of frankness, of open-mindedness, of atheoreticity, indicates their actual presence. Indeed, I doubt it's humanly possible to attain some of these goals even approximately. What would it be to be completely open-minded, atheoretical, unreconstructive in one's memory and reports? Would that be mere infancy? Don't we need pre-existing frameworks, categories, theories, causal maps to remember, even to perceive, anything at all—to have anything other than unreportable, immemorable, "blooming, buzzing confusion," as William James (1890/1981) puts it? Melanie's biases and preconceptions *can't but* inform her reports. Risks to her accuracy ensue, which may be impossible to disentangle from the benefits.

Let's contrast Russ's method with the archetypal method of introspective psychology as practiced by Titchener and others a century ago. The latter method generally involved setting up a controlled situation with precisely measurable stimuli (color plates, in constant lighting conditions, for example, viewed at a constant distance and angle). Practiced introspective observers reported on their experience as it occurred or immediately afterward, and in cases of uncertainty, or for verification, the stimuli could be repeated. This method has some of the same virtues as Russ's method, including that it targets specific, brief episodes after only a short (or no) delay. Like Russ, Titchener and other introspective psychologists exhorted their observers to set aside their presuppositions. Also like Russ, they generally attempted to reduce or disarm their own expectations. Experiences weren't sampled arbitrarily from everyday life, however, and Titchener's observers were surely affected by the experimental set-up, by the expectation of experiences of a certain sort (e.g., visual experiences of varying hue), and by the potentially distracting or distorting knowledge that they would shortly be reporting on those experiences. On the other hand, conditions were better controlled and the observers' reports more easily allowed for certain sorts of verification (e.g., checks for consistency with what's theoretically predicted; see Titchener 1901–1905, Schwitzgebel 2004, and Schwitzgebel 2005). Perhaps most important, the memory demands in Titchener's studies were not nearly as great as in Russ's. Titchener generally asked his observers only to report one aspect of their experience, very swiftly. He didn't ask them to reflect on the experience as a whole. Thus, observers didn't require several minutes to generate their reports, as Russ's subjects often do. (Nor were Titchener's observers interrupted by the task of turning off a beeper, retrieving pen and paper, etc.) They could focus on making an instant judgment about a single thing. And of course, Titchener's observers generated their final reports on the spot, not after an interview the next day. Titchener also emphasized his preference for *trained* observers, with considerable introspective experience. One might object that trained observers have more theoretical commitments and bias than do observers who enter untrained—but it's not clear that this is so. Titchener stressed that untrained observers too usually have preconceptions and theories about their experiences and often leap to generalizations quickly after one or a few trials (Titchener 1899, 1901–1905, 1912).

Or consider the armchair phenomenological investigations of contemporary philosophers such as Charles Siewert (1998, 2006) and Terry Horgan (Horgan and Tienson 2002; Horgan, Tienson, and Graham 2003). Siewert (2007, forthcoming) is particularly explicit about his method, which he calls "plain phenomenology." He urges phenomenologists to reflect repeatedly and patiently on both their ordinary lived experience and on particular types of invoked experience. He asks them to take special care in drawing conceptual distinctions, to bear in mind the theoretical implications, and to consider a variety of related and nearby cases before reaching their final judgment. For example, Siewert (1998, chapter 8) invites the reader to reflect on the difference, if any, between the experience of imagining an "M" tilted on its side and the experience of imagining the Greek letter sigma. Are these imagery experiences the same or different, and in what respects? Must there be a difference in imagined shape for a difference in imagery experience? To what extent does it seem that such imagery experiences vary with, and depend on, one's intentions and concepts? Maybe Siewert's approach risks, more than Russ's approach, importing the theories of observers invested in particular answers. On the other hand, careful theoretical reflection and the consideration of nearby contrasting cases may also help forestall confusion. The method runs comparatively greater risks than does DES of unrepresentative selection, and of potentially severe and undetectable distortion of the experience by the act of introspectively reflecting on it as it occurs. But on the other hand, wise selection may help us better appreciate subtle contrasts and discern issues of theoretical import. Furthermore, concurrent introspective reflection reduces or eliminates problems of memory inherent in reflecting on experiences already past, and it may allow us to slow down and focus better on detail.

It is by no means clear *a priori* whether Titchener's introspective methodology and contemporary philosophical armchair phenomenological reflection, which Russ rebuke, contain more potential for error than Russ's own methodology. Each has its apparent strengths and shortcomings. *Maybe* Russ's method will find compelling external corroboration that warrants its elevation over other introspective approaches, but absent such corroboration, I see no reason to regard DES as vastly superior to other methods, with their flawed and divergent results.

10.2 Should We Credit Melanie's Reports at All?

We might, then, put every introspective method, Russ's, Titchener's, Siewert's, and all others, on an equal footing: prone to obvious sources of error, inconsistent in their results, relatively uncorroborated, unworthy of scientific credence. Proper scientific caution, we might think, demands that we discard everything Melanie says, pending positive and robust evidence that we're on firm ground.

The problem with this approach is that no swift and decisive corroboration or disconfirmation is in the cards for *any* method of studying experience. Insisting on firm ground thus means abandoning the theoretical exploration of consciousness. Of course, we should at least *try*, more than we do, to find external corroborations of subjective descriptions of experience and to illuminate the conditions under which such descriptions are credible. But the results of any such attempts will inevitably be controversial and difficult to interpret for some time to come. As I mentioned in discussing Russ's disagreement with Flavell about how to interpret his children's denial of the experience of thinking (section 3.2), there's just too much room to posit whatever experience best supports our theory or conforms to our favorite reports.

I see no reason to think the task Russ sets Melanie is absolutely impossible. People must have at least some inkling of what's going on in their own present and immediately past conscious experience. That inkling is, I think, surprisingly poor and unstable (as I have argued in other work), but it would be a radical skepticism indeed to suppose that we have no clue whatsoever about the ongoing flow of our experience. Asking people about their present or immediately past experience is not *entirely* pointless. Suppose someone judges himself to have just been (consciously) thinking about his plans for Saturday. Suppose also the usual sources of error in judgment are minimal, as far as we can tell. It seems churlish not to give him at least tentative credit.

Russ's method builds on that fundamental credibility. Although the interview isn't conducted until hours later, basic features of the experience are explicitly noted within a short time. I see no reason to think that such basic features couldn't, in general, be accurately recalled in the later interview, especially with a notepad as a cue. Russ allows the subject to approach the task in her own terms, solicits a report without overt pressure toward any particular outcome, discourages mere hypothesizing. It again seems churlish, a mere stance, to give her no credit whatsoever, absent some specific reason for skepticism. Minimally, let's say, it seems in most cases more likely than not that the basic topics of thought or reflection that Melanie reports (e.g., her chair in beep 1.1, scuba diving in beep 4.1, her appointment in beep 5.1) were indeed in consciousness somewhere around the time of the beep. Maybe also (more questionably perhaps) those topics were present in roughly the modes she describes (inner speech or hearing in beep 1.1 [but for cautions about this case in particular, see Russ's comments in the next chapter], bodily imagery or feeling in beep 4.1, visual imagery in beep 5.1).

Given the uncertain state of consciousness studies and the lack of any well-established general methods, to endorse a blanket skepticism about such matters exhibits a misguided and crippling purism. However, I do think a blanket skepticism may be in order regarding the *details* of Melanie's reports, unless we find further corroboration of them—corroboration either of those reports in particular or of the validity of Russ's experience sampling method in general. I'll develop this idea in section 10.4 and beyond. But first I'll describe an experiment of my own. Perhaps this experiment—an awkward experiment, I confess—can in an imperfect way illustrate some of the untapped potential in experience sampling.

10.3   Adapting Russ's Methodology to Explore the Richness of Experience

The experiment addresses the "richness" of experience—the extent to which we have constant experience in a variety of modalities. According to the *rich* view, we have constant visual experience (at least when our eyes are open, maybe also when they're closed), constant tactile experience (e.g., of our clothes against skin), constant auditory experience, maybe constant emotional experience, conscious thought, imagery, etc.—all simultaneously. [See box 4.8.] According to the *thin* view, experience or consciousness is limited to one or a few modalities or topics at a time. For example, maybe when I'm wholly absorbed in writing, the background noise of traffic plays no part in my conscious experience at the moment. (I may, of course, still non-consciously process auditory input, so that if the sound suddenly changes or stops, the change or cessation may capture my attention and enter my consciousness.) Most of the day, my shirt rubs against my shoulders. On the rich view, I have a constant, peripheral—maybe quite faint—tactile experience of this. On the thin view, I have no experience of it whatsoever, not even in a faint and peripheral way, most of the time, unless I'm actually focally attending to or thinking about my shirt. I have found ordinary people to report divergent intuitions regarding the relative richness or thinness of experience, even when I make my best effort to guard against variation in the use of terms. Some people (but few theoreticians of consciousness) also endorse a moderate view, between rich and thin, on which experience outruns focal attention to some considerable degree but isn't the constant plenum envisioned by the rich view.

What I called the "refrigerator light phenomenon" in box 4.18 frustrates any attempt to study the richness of experience using concurrent introspection of experience as it transpires. Surely, when I think about whether I'm having visual experience, I have it. When I think about whether I'm having tactile experience, I have that, too. But I shouldn't thereby conclude that I have constant visual and tactile experience. We can't rule out the possibility that my inquiry itself creates the experiences in these cases, lifting the relevant sensory processing into consciousness. The proper question to ask is whether visual and tactile experience are present when I'm *not* thinking about them. You can see why it would be appealing to employ a beeper to get at this issue.

I divided 21 subjects (11 philosophy graduate students and 10 non-philosophers) into five roughly balanced groups. (For more methodological detail, as well as considerable self-critique, see Schwitzgebel 2007a.) With one group, I did something like Russ's DES procedure (less expertly, I'm sure), but with a few modifications: First, I avoided the phrase "inner experience," which I worried might be interpreted as emphasizing imagery, thoughts, emotions, and the like over ("outer"?) sensory experience. Second, I spent some time explaining what's meant by "consciousness" or "experience" or "phenomenology," citing examples of conscious processes (vivid emotions, focal sensory experiences, inner speech) and non-conscious ones (subliminal perception, immune system response). I invited discussion of this topic. Third, in discussing the first sample, once the participant was done reporting the most salient aspects of her experience, I explicitly asked whether there were also other aspects of her experience, giving examples like feelings of hunger or tiredness; visual, auditory, tactile, or olfactory experiences; emotions; visual imagery; conscious thoughts; etc., repeating this question with arbitrary examples of potential experiences until the subject denied recalling anything more. Fourth, generally in discussing the first sample, and always on the first interview day, I mentioned the debate between the rich and the thin view, citing arguments on either side and expressing neutrality on the question. However, I did not particularly emphasize that issue. I encouraged theoretical and methodological discussion on a variety of topics, generally recommending cautious restraint in such matters. Broad and open theoretical discussion was encouraged throughout four days of sampling and interview.

Participants in the other four conditions, unlike those in the first condition, were told explicitly that the purpose of the research was to explore the richness or thinness of experience. They were given an explanation of the debate and some arguments and intuitive examples on both sides of the question, and they were asked for their own initial impressions. Like the first group, they were mostly beeped over four days and invited to reflect on the theoretical and methodological issues pertinent to their reports. Each was asked about one aspect of sensory experience. One group was asked simply to report if they were having visual experience at the time of the beep, and if so what that experience was. Another group was similarly asked about experience in the far right visual field, another group about tactile experience, another about tactile experience in the left foot. They collected their samples with these types of experiences in mind, instructed to make a first judgment of "yes, I had such an experience" or "no, I didn't" (or "maybe" or "sort of") as quickly as possible after each beep. Participants were repeatedly assured that it was fine if they had no experiences of the sort in question—that that would be nice evidence for the thin view—and conversely that it would be fine, and good evidence for the rich view, if they found such experiences in every single sample. Participants who leaned toward one view were periodically reminded of the viability of the other view. Occasionally, a participant who claimed to have had an experience of the sort under study was pressed about whether there really was such an experience, or whether she was just reporting some external object in the visual or tactile environment. Conversely, participants who claimed to be having no experience of the sort under study were occasionally pressed about whether they really thought there was *no* experience, as opposed to merely vague or secondary or peripheral experience.

Every participant in the full experience condition (resembling DES) and the two visual experience conditions reported some sort of visual experience in most samples—even those initially inclined toward a thin view, with no obvious difference or trend between the three conditions.

A majority (8 out of 13) reported visual experience in *every single sample*. In contrast, participants in the full experience and full tactile experience conditions reported tactile experience in only about half to three-quarters of all samples (depending on how liberally one interprets "tactile"—e.g., whether pain and proprioceptive experiences count). Somewhat lower rates of experience were reported in the far right visual field and the tactile left foot conditions—though even the "thinnest" participant in the tactile left foot condition confidently reported tactile left foot experience in 2 of her 19 samples. How exactly to interpret these results is a complicated and uncertain matter that I can only partially explore here. However, *if* we credit the participants' reports, overall they seem more supportive of a moderate view than either a rich or a thin view.

Russ will surely say that in conducting the interviews as I did, I allowed my own biases and presuppositions to inform the results. I acutely feel the merits of this objection. Here are a few not entirely sufficient responses to that concern: (1) At the end of my time with each participant, I asked her to guess whether I personally leaned toward the rich or the thin view. Subjects were divided on this question, generally saying they felt I was even-handed. (2) The asymmetry of response between the visual and tactile conditions suggests that situational pressures creating a general bias toward reporting sensory experience can't fully explain the results. (3) Explicitly discussing the theoretical possibilities and explaining some of the appeal of both sides of an issue may actually be preferable to allowing such issues to pass undiscussed, since it may serve as something of a check on participants' initial suppositions.

Since the experiment (except in the DES-like, full experience condition) centers around a single yes/no/maybe question, the memory demands are considerably less severe than in the standard DES format. There's no several minutes of recalling and describing the experience, no great likelihood of forgetting the key piece of data between the after-beep scribble and the next-day interview.

In our discussion of beep 1.1, Melanie explicitly denies having visual experience at the moment of the beep, and in general she denies having any more than 2 or 3 types of experience at any one moment. She doesn't usually include visual sensory experience in her reports. In these respects, she is typical of Russ's subjects and different from mine. This difference could, of course, be due entirely to design flaws in my experiment or to my deficiencies as an interviewer, or it could point to an insurmountable instability in beep-and-interview methods.

Another possibility is that the difference turns on linguistic or theoretical issues. Russ uses a variety of terms and phrases to talk about what he's trying to get at, all somewhat interchangeably, including "inner experience" (with its hint of favoring "inner" processes over sensory ones), "attention," and "awareness." [For his justification of this practice, see box 2.1.] Unfortunately, the use of "attention" as equivalent to the others seems to invite the thin view. On the rich view, of course, many things outside of the fairly narrow band of focal attention are nonetheless experienced, so "in attention" and "experienced" are decidedly *not* interchangeable. Notice how Russ asks the relevant question of Melanie on the first day:

Russ: So is there anything else going on at this particular moment? You're seeing the white parchmenty paper . . .

Melanie: Um hm.

Russ: And does that seem to be in your awareness, or is it . . .

Melanie: No it's not. I'm not aware of how my body is positioned or of what I'm holding. It's very much just in my head.

Russ: You're paying much more attention to your thought process here, about "isn't it strange . . . ?" "isn't it funny?" You're obviously seeing the parchment, because that's what started this process, but it's not in your awareness.

Melanie: Yes, exactly.

By using "attention" and "awareness" interchangeably here to mean "experience," Russ implicitly suggests that something outside attention is outside experience, in direct contravention of the rich view. Melanie might thus be forgiven for interpreting Russ's questions as about what she is attentionally focused on or centrally aware of, rather than about a wider panoply of peripheral experience that may or may not exist. Though Russ's first use of the word "attention" in the recorded dialogues is only after Melanie's first denial of experience above, its use here conveys an implicit assumption that may already more subtly have been communicated to Melanie—or even explicitly communicated in Russ's initial interview with her, in which he gave instructions about how to use the beeper. The difficulty may be further compounded by what I regard as Russ's frequent blurring of the epistemic (having to do with knowledge) and phenomenal (having to do with the stream of experience) senses of "awareness." [See boxes 8.6 and 9.4.] If Russ's subjects interpret "in awareness" to mean (epistemically) something like "a matter of explicit knowledgeable reflection" *and also* (phenomenally) something like "part of the stream of experience," that also could lead to overly thin reports, if the rich view is correct that the contents of the stream of experience considerably outrun the matters to which we are devoting explicit focal attention.

Since Russ avoids general theoretical and terminological discussions, it is difficult to know exactly how his subjects understand him on such matters. By the time I have the opportunity to raise the question in my own way, Melanie has already committed herself to denying visual experience. (If you think it problematic that Melanie would both deny visual experience and not object to Russ's statement that she was "obviously seeing," you probably lean toward the rich view.) After her exchange with me, Melanie's denial of visual experience becomes more qualified—not absolute, but relative, expressed in words like "primarily" and "much more." Such a relative claim is of course consistent with the rich view, which generally assumes a focal center of experience and a periphery that is in some way vaguer or less vivid.

Russ's subjects may disregard peripheral aspects of their experience for other reasons, including these: (1) Subjects will naturally tend, after the beep, to focus first on what was central in their experience. By the time they start to think about whether they were also having (say) visual experience—if they ever think about that—it may be several minutes after the beep, and their memory may have faded too much for accurate recall. (2) Subjects will have collected six to eight samples per interview session. Given the details of Russ's questions, if there is any hope of getting through a substantial portion of those samples, peripheral aspects of experience must be excluded. (3) Russ himself explicitly declares a lack of interest in peripheral aspects of experience, which he thinks probably can't be reported accurately. [See box 4.8.] I fully support Russ in wanting that limit on inquiry in standard (unadapted) DES interviews—but that means we are on shaky ground using the reports of subjects like Melanie to undermine the rich view.

I regard the experiment described in this section as preliminary and exploratory. I don't entirely trust my own subjects' reports, and I certainly don't mean to suggest that the reader should accept that in fact people do have visual experience most of the time and tactile experience about half the time. The results require interpretation and are at best only suggestive. (In Schwitzgebel 2007a, I discuss a variety of concerns about the data, suggesting ways in which the results can be reconciled with thinner or, especially, richer views of experience.) However, the debate about the richness of experience has thus far been conducted largely impressionistically, or in terms of questionable general theories of consciousness (e.g., James, 1890/1981; Jaynes 1976; Dennett 1991; Searle 1992; Siewert 1998). A version of the beep-and-interview method gives us the opportunity to explore the question in a different and maybe better way—a way beyond even what Russ himself envisions. If future researchers discover still other means of exploring this question, and if the results of the various researches appear to converge, then perhaps we will have some solid basis for a scientific opinion.

10.4   Memory in Introspective and Eyewitness Testimony

Let me return now to my case for skepticism about the details of Melanie's reports. I propose a *blanket* skepticism about all but the grossest features of her reported experience. I simply don't trust Melanie accurately to remember the details.

Actually, I don't really *trust* Melanie's descriptions of the grosser features of her experience either, though I'm willing tentatively to accept them. So let me put the point a bit differently. When Melanie reports the details of an experience—for example when she describes the details of an image or attempts to specify her degree of self-consciousness in feeling an emotion—her reports *may* accurately reflect the content of the original experience; but I think it just as likely that the imputed details are erroneous inventions, arising from her theories and preconceptions about experience, from situational pressures, from accidents of language, from distorted and unrepresentative reconstructions formed either shortly after the beep or during the course of the interview, etc. I'm willing to accept that in most cases Melanie preserves some rudimentary memory of her experience as it transpired shortly before the beep, but how that trace is articulated and described in the course of the interview, the specifics in which it's dressed, seems to me very likely to depend as much on factors only tenuously associated, or unassociated, or even negatively associated, with accuracy, as on genuinely remembered particulars.

I could be wrong about this. If Russ or others are able consistently to corroborate reports like Melanie's down to a fine level of detail, then we may be justified in accepting all or most of what Melanie says. Of course, as the field stands now, even the most basic aspects of DES reports remain uncorroborated and will require considerable effort and ingenuity to corroborate. Judgments about how far to believe Melanie can only be speculative.

Melanie's task in these interviews invites comparison to the task of reporting the details of an outwardly witnessed event. Although Melanie isn't literally an "eyewitness" of her experience—we see *things*, of course, not our *experiences* of those things—her task bears an important resemblance to the task of an eyewitness asked to report some specific event, such as a crime. Like an eyewitness, Melanie is expected to report details of specific, unique events that she was (presumably!) in good position to record, as the result of a relatively swift and unmediated process beginning with those events. A comparison between Melanie's reports and eyewitness testimony is inviting because although the literature on the accuracy of reports of conscious experience is spotty and controversial, the accuracy of eyewitness testimony has been extensively examined, with some relatively robust findings. Chief among them: Eyewitness reports contain what most people find to be a surprising degree of error.

Two passages in Elizabeth Loftus's classic book on the topic (Loftus 1979) give the flavor:

Two female students entered a train station, one of them leaving her large bag on a bench while both walked away to check the train schedules. While they were gone, a male student lurked over to the bag, reached in, and pretended to pull out an object and stuff it under his coat. He then walked away quickly. When the women returned, the older one noticed that her bag had been tampered with, and began to cry, "Oh my God, my tape recorder is missing!" She went on to lament that her boss had loaned it to her for a special reason, that it was very expensive, and so on. The two women began to talk to the real eyewitnesses who were in the vicinity. Most were extremely cooperative in offering sympathy and whatever details could be recalled. The older woman asked these witnesses for their telephone numbers "in case I need it for insurance purposes." Most people gladly gave their number.

One week later an "insurance agent" called the eyewitnesses as part of a routine investigation of the theft. All were asked for whatever details they could remember, and finally, they were asked, "Did you see the tape recorder?" Although there was in fact no tape recorder, over half the eyewitnesses "remembered" seeing it, and nearly all of those could describe it in reasonably good detail. Their descriptions were quite different from one another: some said it was gray and others said black; some said it was in a case, others said it was not; some said it had an antenna, others claimed it did not. Their descriptions indicated a rather vivid "memory" for a tape recorder that was never seen. (pp. 61–62)

Subjects viewed a film of a traffic accident and then answered questions about the accident. Some subjects were asked, "About how fast were the cars going when they smashed into each other?" whereas others were asked, "About how fast were the cars going when they hit each other?" The former question elicited a much higher estimate of speed. One week later the subjects returned and, without viewing the film again, they answered a series of questions about the accident. The critical question was, "Did you see any broken glass?" There was no broken glass in the accident, but because broken glass usually results from accidents occurring at high speed, it seemed likely that the subjects who had been asked the question with the word "smashed" might more often say yes to this critical question. And that is what we found. (pp. 77–78)

Distortive influences on eyewitness testimony include information or suggestions built into the wording of questions, the expectations or theories of the witness, the expectations of the interviewer, stress, the solidification of guesses or conjectures into confident assertions as they are repeated over time ("confidence inflation"), and the confusion of what is imagined with what is remembered, to name a few. (See, e.g., Loftus 1979; Narby, Cutler, and Penrod 1996; Wells and Loftus 2003.)

It's not surprising, of course, that eyewitness testimony is subject to distortion. We don't need a raft of journal articles to tell us that. What is striking, however, and repeatedly confirmed, is the *extent* of the distortion. Most people just don't expect witnesses to be as badly mistaken or as easily influenced as they often are. They don't expect a *majority* of eyewitnesses to invent, and describe in detail, a tape recorder they have never seen. They don't expect subtle differences in the phrasing of questions to have the profound effects they often have on witnesses' reports.

Since the earliest days of eyewitness research, instructors have been fond of classroom demonstrations of eyewitness inaccuracy. Münsterberg describes one typical classroom demonstration: A shouting match breaks out between two students; one draws a weapon; the professor intervenes. Immediately afterward, the professor tells the class that the episode was staged and asks them for a written account of the events. (In the case Münsterberg describes, some students recounted the events only later.) Inevitably in such demonstrations, the students' reports are rife with error. Münsterberg writes:

Words were put into the mouths of men who had been silent spectators during the whole short episode; actions were attributed to the chief participants of which not the slightest trace existed; and essential parts of the tragi-comedy were completely eliminated from the memory of a number of witnesses. (1908/1927, pp. 50–51)

The students witnessing such demonstrations are generally quite surprised at the results, shocked that they and their peers could diverge so widely in their descriptions of the perpetrators' height, race, hair color, and clothing, in their characterization of key events, in almost every feature of the evaporated scene. This surprise is a crucial pedagogical tool in undermining students' misplaced faith in the accuracy of eyewitness testimony (Charlton 1999; Gee and Dyck 2000).

Psychologists have also more formally tested the degree to which people tend to overestimate eyewitness accuracy. Researchers have, for example, asked undergraduates and ordinary citizens to read through descriptions of eyewitness testimony experiments and then to predict the outcome of the experiments. Subjects in such studies often severely overestimate the accuracy of other subjects' eyewitness performance. (For reviews, see Leippe 1995; Devenport, Penrod, and Cutler 1997). In another series of studies, Wells and colleagues (Wells, Lindsay, and Ferguson 1979; Lindsay, Wells, and O'Connor 1989) staged crimes before subject-witnesses. The witnesses were asked to identify the perpetrator from a photo lineup, then testify and undergo cross-examination. Subject-jurors who viewed the testimony and cross-examination generally overestimated the witnesses' accuracy, judging not only the accurate witnesses to be accurate, but also the inaccurate ones. In the study by Wells, Lindsay, and Ferguson (1979), subjects judged not only 76–84 percent of the accurate witnesses to be accurate (depending on condition) but also 73–86 percent of the *inaccurate* eyewitnesses. Needless to say, the subjects were not especially good at distinguishing accurate from inaccurate eyewitnesses on the basis of their testimony.

Indeed, generally speaking, people seem to be fairly poor at distinguishing accurate from inaccurate eyewitness testimony, except in extreme cases, such as when a witness is blatantly self-contradictory or explicitly avows uncertainty (Leippe, Manion, and Romanczyk 1992; Leippe 1995; Devenport, Penrod, and Cutler 1997). Our poor judgment on this front may spring from a variety of factors. For example, psychological research suggests that people tend especially to believe *confident* eyewitnesses, but that confidence correlates only weakly with accuracy, or correlates well only in special conditions. (See, e.g., Wells, Lindsay, and Ferguson 1979; Wells and Murray 1984; Bothwell, Deffenbacher, and Brigham 1987; Sporer, Penrod, Read, and Cutler 1995; Kassin, Tubb, Hosch, and Memon 2001; Brewer and Burke 2002; Weber and Brewer 2004.)

Are we to think Melanie better than a typical eyewitness? What we asked her to observe was in some sense closer to her than any outward event—but is that sort of proximity an advantage? In vision, certainly, one can get too close. Things nearby and essential may nonetheless be only poorly seen and rarely reflected on—such as one's eyeglasses. I may talk more coherently about, and reach more accurate judgments about, the road I'm driving on than the steering wheel I use to drive on it. (I know that the road curves 90 degrees, but can I say how far I need to rotate the steering wheel to make that turn?) Likewise, even if sensory phenomenology is in some sense essential to sensory judgment, we may know it only very poorly. As I pointed out in chapter 3 (along with a variety of other reasons to doubt the accuracy of our introspective judgments), we normally observe, attend to, think about, and describe *outward* events, not inner ones.

The task we set Melanie was an alien one—one that strikes many subjects at first as strange and difficult. Though Melanie gained some practice over the course of the interviews, it seems unlikely to me that her comfort with the task in the end should justifiably exceed the ordinary eyewitness's comfort in reporting nearby outward events. Immediately after each beep, Melanie knew that she would need to remember and report the experience in question, but at least some criminal eyewitnesses (not to mention subjects in eyewitness experiments) are in a similar position, realizing either immediately after a crime occurs, or even as it is occurring, that they should remember details for later report. Russ and I gave Melanie some feedback about her reports, but that feedback consisted mainly in exhortations to be open-minded, to resist generalizations, and to attend closely to the beeped moment, coupled with Russ's general willingness to accept confidently asserted declarations about specific episodes and my varying degrees of theory-laden skepticism. Although our feedback may have had some limited value, I certainly risked affecting Melanie with my theories and Russ may have encouraged a kind of blasé confidence by his readiness to accept confident reports, almost regardless of content. The events Melanie reported were mostly fleeting—momentary images, passing thoughts. Opportunities abounded for theory-laden reconstruction, for unintentional confabulation. No external check or second witness existed to keep Melanie careful and modest.

Here's a further point of difference between eyewitness testimony and introspective report: Normally, when someone witnesses a robbery or car accident, she'll have some sort of schema or sense of the world into which they fit. Such events may be surprising in a certain way, perhaps undermining our expectations and stereotypes, but they rarely impugn our sense of the *possible*. In experience sampling, however, our most basic conceptualizations are often undermined: We simply must be wrong in much of what we believe about our stream of experience—if for no other reason than that the massive diversity of opinion about basic structural features of human experience considerably exceeds the likely diversity in the experiences themselves (box 7.4). Much of what is true of experience is going to strike at least some people as, if not inconceivable, at least rather strange.

Consequently, in introspecting we must frequently encounter events that fit our concepts poorly. Such events, especially if they are fleeting and we are not practiced in reflecting upon them, may be difficult to report accurately and particularly susceptible to theory-based reconstructive distortion. In the relatively rare cases when externally witnessed events challenge our sense of the possible—for example, when the final position of the cars doesn't seem to make sense given the trajectories we seem to recall—our memories, theory-laden and reconstruction-based as they are, appear to be undermined. I'm judging here only from personal experience: I know of no research directly on that issue in the eyewitness literature. However, a number of studies inspired by the work of Schacter, Cooper, and Delaney (1990) suggest that memory is poorer for line drawings of "impossible" objects than for (novel) possible ones. On a more introspective note, Gopnik (1993a,b) argues persuasively that children's memory for past false beliefs is severely hampered when children accept a theory that allows no room for false belief in general. Likewise, surely, what is alien (a cricket match) will generally be harder to remember and report than what is comfortable and familiar (a baseball game). The merely *unusual* may vanish in reconstruction, or it may be better remembered because it is striking and salient; but events so foreign to our ordinary conceptions that we lack easy schemata or categories for them—events, if Russ and I are right, that we are quite likely to encounter in introspection—should, it seems, be hard to retain.

People asked to imagine events often confuse those events with events actually experienced. (For a review, see Johnson, Hashtroudi, and Lindsay 1993. For connections with eyewitness testimony, see Lindsay 1994.) I've spent half an hour looking for my keys. Suddenly, I picture them on the kitchen ledge. But am I having a genuine memory of having seen them there, or does the image of them on the ledge seem familiar only because I imagined the keys there before, earlier in my search? After the crime, I imagine the perpetrator with a moustache; later I'm confused about whether I actually saw him that way, or only imagined it. What about events in the stream of experience? Once again, I'm forced to conjecture: I know of no research that looks directly at whether we can conflate "inner experiences" we actually had with those only imagined later. However, it seems likely the rate of conflation would be comparatively high. If Melanie has a visual image of a shed at the moment of beep 1.3, then reconstructs that image shortly afterward in taking note of that experience, then reconstructs it again when she is reviewing her notes before to the interview, then again finally (as she admits) during the interview itself, she runs a considerable risk, I think, of misattributing features of one image to the other. If the information available to me as I entertain that image of my keys on the ledge marks only poorly whether the source of that representation is a past imagination or a past perception, mustn't it even more poorly mark one past imagination from another?

The literature on eyewitness testimony calls into question the very project of this book as Russ and to a lesser extent I conceive it. The reader is invited, as I was invited, to listen to Melanie and reach his own more or less intuitive judgment about how believable she is. But if people tend greatly to overestimate the trustworthiness of eyewitness reports, and if we have only mediocre skills in discerning accurate from inaccurate eyewitness testimony, and if our standards for assessing accuracy arise principally from our experience with what seems to me the comparatively easy and familiar matter of reporting on outward events and judging the accuracy of such reports, then maybe we've been invited into a trap. Melanie's testimony may well be considerably less accurate, and we may be considerably poorer judges of where it is accurate, than most of us are initially inclined to think.

The point here is not that Russ's method introduces some special source of distortion into Melanie's testimony. The point is that we should be wary of trusting our intuitive judgments about how accurately she is reporting. Melanie's preconceptions, Russ's and my subtly (or not so subtly) communicated expectations, Melanie's potential confusion of the remembered with the merely imagined, the changeable and elusive nature of the events to be described, the universal human investment in being right in what one has said in the past—all these and their kin have larger effects than most of us naively expect. Melanie's testimony may *seem* trustworthy and yet be surprisingly full of error. Given the novelty of the task and the methodology, we can only speculate how far such error may go, but my sense is that it likely penetrates quite far. If an eyewitness can invent a tape recorder, replete with convincing detail, then much more easily, I think, can Melanie invent a feeling of lightness in her chest, or confuse inner speech with unsymbolized thinking, or be mistaken about the degree of detail in a visual image.

10.5 Pressures of the Interview Situation and Experimenter Expectations

A large and compelling body of evidence in social psychology (reviewed in Ross and Nisbett 1991) has demonstrated that subtle features of a situation can have a striking impact on behavior. An oft-cited example (from Isen and Levin 1972) is the following: People who had used a phone booth in a suburban shopping plaza saw another person (a confederate of the experimenter) spill a folder of papers in their path. The situation had been arranged in advance so that some callers had found a dime in the phone's coin-return slot immediately before witnessing the mishap and others had not. Of the 25 who had not found a dime, only one helped to gather the papers. Of the 16 who had found a dime, 14 helped. Apparently, what we might have thought to be principally determined by durable character traits—how considerate and helpful someone is—can be largely decided by a minor feature of the situation. Hundreds of experiments, using a variety of methods and venues, show similar results.

It is well known that such subtle situational pressures can greatly compromise a psychological study, through their effects on both experimenters and subjects. Expectations conveyed by or to experimenters, in particular (which we might think of as part of the social situation surrounding the experiment), can have a surprisingly large influence on the outcome of research (e.g., Rosenthal 1976). In one famous study (Rosenthal and Fode 1963), undergraduates acted as experimenters, running supposedly "bright" or "dull" rats in a maze (the rats were actually from the same population). The "bright" rats performed considerably better than the "dull" rats, and continued to improve over the course of the experiment. Presumably, they were better encouraged, better treated, and given the benefit of the doubt in multiple difficult-to-track ways. Similar effects have been found, disturbingly, with children in the classroom, even with only minimal experimenter contact (Rosenthal and Jacobson 1968/1992).

Closer to the present topic of study, Intons-Peterson (1983), using advanced undergraduates, has shown substantial experimenter expectation effects on subjects' reports of their imagery experiences and on imagery-related tasks, even when many of the most overt sources of potential experimenter influence are eliminated. For example, undergraduate experimenters gave subjects a mental rotation task, requiring the subjects to judge quickly whether a visually presented outline of a hand was a left hand or a right hand (as seen from the back). Hands were presented at different angles of rotation (always from the back), and prior to each presentation the subject either received a "perceptual prime" (a left or a right hand in canonical upright position, presented for comparison with the target hand) or was asked to imagine visually such a comparison hand. All presentations and time recordings were done by computer. When experimenters expected better performance in the perceptual prime condition than in the imagination condition, the computer recorded performance times in accord with that expectation. Conversely, when the experiment was conducted by experimenters with the opposite expectation, the opposite result was found. Outside observers brought in to check for subtle sources of experimenter influence (e.g., in voice modulations and facial expressions) had difficulty discerning any such differences between the two groups; Intons-Peterson did, however, find substantial differences in the experimenters' pauses while reading the instructions.

Situational and experimenter-effect influences tend to be stronger than most people (or at least most Westerners) expect (Ross and Nisbett 1991; Choi, Nisbett, and Norenzayan 1999). Thus, we must be cautious in relying on our intuitive sense about the extent to which Russ's and my expectations, and the pressures of the interview situation, may have influenced Melanie's reports. Here, as with eyewitness testimony, an untutored sense of Melanie's believability may lead us astray: She may be considerably more swayed by us than the reader would naively expect. In fact, Melanie later wrote: "I struggled during the first set of samples, and, I will admit, for most of the experiment, with a desire to gloss over what I was really experiencing and try to say what I thought was expected of me." (personal communication, September 2004) This later statement, if it is to be believed, supports my impression that Melanie felt potentially distortive pressure from what she took to be our expectations.

The open structure of Russ's interviews allows plenty of opportunity for experimenter expectations to some into play, especially if such subtle factors as the length of a pause are considered relevant. So I don't think we're safe inferring from the lack of *palpable* bias on Russ's part that his expectations had only negligible distortive effect. I myself, of course, made much less effort to hide my biases, and in one case at least I'm inclined to think they had a discernible effect: in Melanie's move from reporting very detailed imagery with almost no indeterminacies to her reporting more indeterminate imagery. [See box 5.11.]

One situational pressure that may be easily missed is the pressure on Melanie to provide some kind of fairly specific description of her experience. She has worn a device for exactly that purpose; to confess ignorance would be a defeat; other subjects apparently can do this; two professors await her report with interest. Intuitively, one might think it nonetheless quite open to Melanie—especially given Russ's and my verbal endorsements of caution—regularly to say she doesn't recall very well, for her to provide only a very rough sketch and then stop, to open the door to uncertainty. Such restraint would probably better reflect her (and most of our) actual capacities. If the general picture that Ross and Nisbett draw is right, such situational pressures toward specific and confident reports may be substantially more compelling than they seem to untutored intuition. Furthermore, Russ's persistence in asking for details, while in many ways laudable, may amplify this pressure (for example, in beep 4.1, where Melanie struggles to describe the experience of craving to go scuba diving). Inaccuracies of memory may thus conspire with subtle situational pressures—pressures both to conform to our (perceived) expectations and to confidently produce details of some sort or other—to create substantial inaccuracies in Melanie's reports. And the vaguer the memory, the more ineffable and elusive the targeted experience, the more room for such factors to operate. If the task is intrinsically very difficult—if we are simply not capable of accurately reporting that kind of detail—confabulation, or simply taking one's best stab, without much sensitivity to whether confidence is justified, may almost be forced.

Let me mention also that situational pressures doubtless affect the *interviewer*, as well as the interviewee. In particular, I'd like to emphasize one pressure that I think may run pretty deep in the DES situation: the pressure to accept what the subject says, especially when she's reporting confidently on a moment of experience conscientiously sampled and carefully scrutinized in the interview. For the interviewer to remain unsatisfied in such a condition undermines the apparent basis of the activity. The subject has been asked to describe her experience and no flaws have been found in her report. What more could the interviewer want? If the interviewer consistently remains skeptical, the subject may legitimately wonder if she has been lured into a winless task. I'm quite familiar, from numerous informal interviews, with the awkward tension that arises when I ask someone her opinion about some aspect of her experience and then express a disinclination to believe the resulting statement. It feels much more natural and comfortable to come on board, agree, be collaborative rather than judgmental.

In his 1990 book, Russ explicitly states that the subject and interviewer should try to reach agreement. Indeed, Russ had his subjects examine and criticize the interviewer's final descriptions of their experiences. Russ's highly collaborative method no doubt vividly conveys a respect for the subject and a concern for deeply scrutinizing what the subject might antecedently have thought to be irrelevant details. The interview may benefit enormously from conveying these impressions. However, it may also become difficult for the interviewer to achieve the distance and detachment necessary to view the subjects' reports in a sufficiently skeptical light.

10.6 Further Concerns Particular to Reporting Conscious Experience, and "Bracketing Presuppositions"

I have recommended a general skepticism about the details of Melanie's reports. In light of these concerns, should we still, at least tentatively, accept the gross features of her reports, as I suggested in section 10.2? Should we accept that Melanie experienced, at or around the time of beep 1.1, a thought in inner speech or hearing about the peculiarity of having to plan the inheritance of her new chair, as well as an experience, perhaps visual ("rosy-yellow"?), of the humorousness of that thought—never mind details about the pacing and vocal characteristics of the speech, the location and exact tint of the glow? Should we accept that Melanie experienced, at beep 5.1, a visual image of some sort, of an intersection, and some kind of feeling or knowledge of anxiety? Such gross features seem much more likely than the details to have been reflected upon and written down immediately after the beep, and thus to have been accurately ascertained and preserved in memory, relatively unchanged, from the moment of experience to the moment of report. One might also suspect that gross features would be less subject to revision or confabulation under situational pressures than a nuance or detail.

But how likely *are* we to get it right about the gross features of our conscious experience in the first moment of introspective reflection? Let's set aside questions of long-term memory for the moment and consider short-term memory or even concurrent introspection. Returning to the eyewitness analogy: How likely is Melanie to have "seen" things correctly in the first place? Except in unusual circumstances of visual illusion or magic shows, we're generally unlikely to misperceive the gross features of nearby events witnessed in good conditions. We might misperceive the thief's hair color in the sun, but we wouldn't misperceive his blue getaway car as red or see him as driving down the hill when he is actually driving up the hill—much as we might, surprisingly often, misremember such matters later. An eyewitness who *immediately* (within a few seconds) explicitly notes such easily perceptible features of the event, and who keeps her notes for consultation, is considerably less likely to misremember those features later than one who waits a few minutes or hours. If Melanie's immediate knowledge of the gross features of her own experience is as good as an eyewitness's knowledge of large, nearby events, we might likewise be justified in accepting the first thing or two she notes in each sample.

However, I would argue that our introspective and immediately retrospective knowledge of our own experience is generally *not* as good as our knowledge of the most easily perceptible outward events in our vicinity. This is the reversal of Cartesianism that I advocated in chapter 3. Preconception, expectation, lack of practice, weak linguistic and conceptual tools, the instability and skittishness of experience (combined, perhaps, with its complexity), conspire to produce introspective judgments that are often grossly false, even regarding the most basic features of current or immediately past experience. As I suggested in chapter 3, there's little reason to think we get it right, even in the most careful reflection, about such things as the basic structural features of our imagery (regarding, for example, how detailed it is in the periphery and whether it arrives instantly or is built up a piece at a time) and emotional experience (regarding, for example, whether it is experienced as entirely bodily or whether there's some non-bodily cognitive component) and the clarity of peripheral vision (as I argue in box 4.18). (For further development of these points, see Schwitzgebel 2002a, 2006, and in preparation.) Philosophers, psychologists, and ordinary folk persistently disagree about such matters, and it seems indolent utopianism to suppose that everyone is simply right about their own experiences and wrong about everyone else's—especially given the lack of evidence for cognitive differences between people corresponding to their different experiential reports.

We can even neglect and invent whole modalities of experience, as I've argued in the case of echolocation (the ability to hear the location and properties of silent objects through attunement to how they reflect and alter environmental sounds). Many people—even, historically, many blind people who've actively used echolocation in navigating around walls and obstacles (and also, famously, Nagel 1974)—deny any auditory experience of or capacity for echolocation; yet most can be brought to change their minds with a few introspective experiments. (Close your eyes and say "shhhh" while a friend moves her hand around in front of your face; you can *hear* where her hand is. For more examples, see Schwitzgebel and Gordon 2000.) Likewise, there is a lively controversy about whether there's a distinctive experience of thinking over and above the experience of imagery and inner speech. (For a brief review, see Schwitzgebel, in preparation. See also Russ's discussion of "unsymbolized thinking" in subsection 11.1.7.4.)

I won't argue these points further here, but I draw the following conclusion: Even at the first instant of reflection about her experience, Melanie might be quite badly mistaken about it. Introspection is more difficult than ordinary perception. Convincing or reminding ourselves of this difficulty is crucial in our evaluation of Melanie's accuracy. Thus, I think we must add to the concerns discussed in the previous two sections another major source of error, one that undermines even the first and most basic aspects of Melanie's reports: the intrinsic difficulty of the observation. Although Russ has done good work in trying to reduce certain sources of error (as discussed in chapter 2), the fundamental difficulty of the observation remains.

Of course, with our current knowledge about experience in general and about Melanie in particular we cannot *prove* gross error in any of Melanie's reports. However, let me list some of the relatively gross claims about which I'm most suspicious: that Melanie literally visually experienced a "rosy-yellow glow" in beep 1.1 [see box 4.7]; that she was as consistently and robustly self-conscious as she claims in beeps 5.1, 6.1, and 6.2 [see boxes 8.9 and 9.3]; that her imagery was as detailed as she says in beeps 1.3, 2.1, 2.2, and 5.1 [see boxes 4.18 and 5.4]; that she literally imagined individual overlapping echoes of "nice long time" in beep 6.4. In some sense, such matters are details. They are not the sort of thing an untrained reporter would probably first notice about her experience—and maybe, indeed, Melanie did not reflect on such matters swiftly after the beep (without her notes—see box 4.15—we have no way of knowing). At the same time, these are the kind of basic structural facts about experience that should interest a researcher in consciousness studies. Furthermore, in general, I think it quite possible that Melanie is missing whole modalities of experience that are difficult to discern and report—such as perhaps imageless or "unsymbolized" thinking, if it exists, or unattended visual experience—focusing on and remembering, instead, only those aspects that happen to come to mind first or are easiest to parse.

Why, you might ask, am I more skeptical of *these* particular reports—the ones described at the beginning of the previous paragraph—than others? I have no reasons internal to the interviews. I can detect no tell-tale signs of error in Melanie's patterns of speech, for example, or any special hesitation, uncertainty, or inconsistency on Melanie's part in making these reports (though I confess that I may have a tin ear for such things). My reasons are entirely external: Melanie's reports here poorly match my pre-existing impressions about what is common in experience, based on my understanding of my own experience and my reading of the psychological and philosophical literature. Now Russ will surely object here that in so evaluating Melanie's reports, I have failed to "bracket pre-suppositions," and thus am not giving his method a fair shake in its own terms. Russ and I have been through this dialogue multiple times (e.g., box 9.9). Let me add a few thoughts to it.

First, I acknowledge the appeal of "bracketing presuppositions" for the purpose of conducting a friendly, relatively unbiased interview. Surely an interviewer can err through too lively a commitment to seeing the subject a particular way; perhaps indeed this is the error most to be avoided. But it's one thing to bracket presuppositions (insofar as possible or desirable; see section 10.1) as part of an interview technique, and quite a different thing to discard all prior (non-DES) evidence about experience in one's *later evaluation* of that interview. I don't know whether Russ really means to recommend the latter course; but sometimes it seems to me he comes across that way, for example in his reference to earlier methods as "failures" and in his tendency to disregard previous literature in interpreting his results. This point is central to understanding the role Russ envisions for DES in relation to other methods. So let me re-emphasize here that one could only justifiably take the extreme position of disregarding *all* prior evidence in one's evaluation of Melanie's assertions if it were somehow already established that Russ's experience sampling method was so superior to all other sources of evidence as to automatically trump anything contrary. As I argued in section 10.1, I don't think that has been established. Unless we've decided to accept DES as our sole guide to the truth about conscious experience, it makes no sense entirely to forgo our previous inclinations—whether the fruit of other methods or general plausibility arguments—in reaching our final judgments about how far to believe Melanie's reports.

Second, although I said in the first section of this concluding essay that we have no means of comparing Russ's picture of Melanie's experience with the picture that other methods would have produced, that may not be quite true. No *direct* comparison between methods is possible here, but maybe we can make indirect comparisons. If Russ's picture of Melanie generally comports with what we would expect based on other methods, that provides a kind of support for it; if not, that may raise concerns. It seems to me that the above-cited claims comport worse with my sense of prior research, and my own experience, than other of Melanie's claims. In particular, all those claims strike me as relatively *unusual.* I think I am, then, justified in being somewhat more suspicious of them. [For further development of this point, see box 9.9.] Of course, we don't want to rule out *a priori* that DES interviews could reveal anything undiscovered by previous approaches. I am not saying that Melanie *must* be wrong, just that I'm worried.

Third, I acknowledge that my own sense of plausibility and likelihood differs from others'. This is problematic. I claim no unusual introspective expertise. I have read widely on consciousness and reflected somewhat on my own experience, but no more than others who disagree with me about various substantive issues. The phenomena are elusive, the literatures complex, contradictory, and confused. So I can't say that I feel myself to be on any especially solid ground when I am inclined to accept one piece of Melanie's testimony more than another based on prior impressions.

Reflecting in this way, I begin to feel near total darkness about experience. Can I really make any good judgments about the better and worse in Melanie's reports? When I consider my own poor antecedent knowledge about conscious experience, my self-assurance begins to fail. I was inclined to mistrust Melanie's reports of detailed imagery because I have a general impression that visual imagery is sketchier, less determinate in its details, especially when quickly generated, than many people suppose. But on the basis of what have I arrived at this opinion? I have already said that there is no single, dependable method for studying consciousness. Maybe, then, I believe what I do about imagery because there's a consensus among researchers applying a variety of methods, individually weak but jointly persuasive? No, there is no such consensus. I must admit by my own lights, then, that I could easily be quite wrong in my opinions about imagery. Indeed, it was my genuine dissatisfaction with my own (and the field's) condition on such matters that led me to Russ in the first place, looking for something better, or at least something additional.

So maybe Melanie is quite right about her imagery (her rosy-yellow glow, her self-consciousness, her echoes), and I am wrong.

Conversely, however, maybe in other cases I should mistrust Melanie more than I do. When she reports a feeling of conviction in beep 6.1, or a lightness in her chest in beep 6.2, or some degree of visual imagery in beeps 1.3, 2.1, 2.2, and 5.1, I feel no particular suspicion. But if the state of the field, and my own epistemic state, is as much a mess as I think—and if I am right in insisting that gross introspective errors are generally quite possible—perhaps I'm too easily taken in by what seems to me the plausibility of these reports. Can conviction really carry some sort of positive phenomenology, a "feeling" of conviction? Or is conviction just a state of reaching a definite judgment, perhaps accompanied by general arousal or specific imagery, but without any distinctive experiential element of its own? Is "lightness in the chest" a misleading metaphor (but one that, for some reason, ensnares me more than "seeing rosy-yellow" [box 4.7] or "hearing echoes" of inner speech [beep 6.4])? Could Melanie's imagery all be invented after the fact? I feel I'm losing my grip on what good reasons there are for thinking Melanie hasn't gone astray in these ways.

In his talk of "bracketing presuppositions" and of the need to reject "armchair" speculations and earlier failed methods, Russ conveys doubt about the value of people's—including my—prior (non-DES) sense of what is credible or relatively less credible in Melanie's reports. Perhaps I should join Russ here and mistrust myself. However, I can't afterward bring myself to the next move Russ recommends: trusting his interview techniques instead. Melanie's internal consistency, her evident conscientiousness, her happy confidence alone, I've argued, can't justify our credence, even if Russ has succeeded in producing an admirably neutral context for reporting. But now it seems only a short step to radical uncertainty about Melanie's reports. I have no idea where to doubt and where to believe, so I am left only doubting. And worse: Since I have no reason to think myself any better an introspector than Melanie, my own introspective judgments come under skeptical threat as well. In any reflection I could very easily be wrong, and my prior sense of plausibility is too ill-founded to be of much help.

But utter uncertainty (about anything sufficiently broad: the external world, other minds, the future) is philosophical madness, isn't it? And few philosophers even among the radical skeptics have said we have no knowledge whatsoever of our own ongoing conscious experience. How could we be totally in the dark about *that*? I just experienced some "auditory imagery" or "inner speech" or "inner hearing" (if I try to be too precise here, I might lose hold of it): I heard or spoke, silently, the sentence I was about to type. I can't seem to bring myself sincerely to doubt that claim or to assign it any but the very smallest probability of being false, despite all the reflections that have led me here. And if Melanie seems to be reporting something similar in her own experience—well, there we have a beginning!

So maybe it's only modesty and caution I should recommend, and not utter skeptical uncertainty. For what is nearer to hand and riper for discovery than our own experience? Yet even the meekest and most tentative reflections about experience are bound soon to conflict with what others have said, so widespread and fundamental are the disagreements in consciousness studies.

At the most general level, I suppose I haven't moved far from where I began before meeting Russ—tempted by radical skepticism, suspicious of every method, doubtful about the future of the field. At the same time, this temptation, suspicion, and doubt, this kind of half-convinced pessimism, is *not* a deep conviction that introspective science must fail. In fact, in the long run I feel hopeful that we will make some sort of progress, simply by virtue of applying our good minds to it hard enough and long enough in enough different ways. And Russ *has* convinced me that beep-and-interview methods deserve as large a role, for now, as anything else.

11 Russ's Reflections

Russ Hurlburt

We have traversed a crooked path over the course of this book, following randomly selected concrete instances of Melanie's experience into whatever thickets they happened to lead. Now it is time to straighten things out, for me to say what I thought happened here and why the path was worth the effort. I do so in two parts. In section 11.1, I discuss my own observations. In section 11.2, I reply to Eric's observations in chapter 10.

First, however, I wish to emphasize how much I respect Eric's participation in this project. Despite his skepticism, he was willing first to try out Descriptive Experience Sampling for himself, then to recognize the conflict of serving as his own subject and to agree that we should find a more neutral subject (ultimately Melanie), and then to participate in the making public of this interchange that took place in an arena where I was far more experienced than was he. That is the heart of good science: as much as possible to subject one's own views to the scrutiny of reasonable but not-necessarily-like-minded others. In passing, let me say that over the years I have made similar would-you-like-to-participate-in-DES offers to many other philosophers and psychologists, nearly always with the same result: their retreats make Roadrunner look like he is dragging an anchor.

I think Eric and I did a good job of avoiding a "My theory is better than your theory" interchange. Instead, we have brought our quite different views into a candid collaboration/confrontation where both of us expected to be altered and would have been happy to be proven partly or entirely wrong.

Also at the outset I emphasize that I agree with Eric that skepticism about introspective reports is highly desirable; that the base rate of successful introspections is small; and that Melanie's sincerity and conscientiousness and my carefulness and even-handedness does not in any way guarantee that my conclusions about Melanie's experience are correct. It is the size and extent of the skepticism, not its desirability, that is at issue here.

11.1   Russ's Views

11.1.1   About Melanie

We discussed 17 samples with Melanie. On that slim basis we learned quite a bit about her, I think. We discovered that she engaged in an active self-monitoring of her own actions: observing her mouth closing while speaking in beep 1.3, observing being bent over the sink in beep 2.4, observing the fogginess of her experience in beep 3.2, observing her forgetfulness of the parking brake in beep 3.3, observing that her eyes were looking straight ahead while talking in beep 6.1, observing the bodily aspects of feeling happy in beep 6.2, observing her brow furrowed in concentrating and the positioning of her feet in beep 6.3.

We discovered that she paid thematic attention to the sensory aspects of her environment: the green color of the TV screen in beep 1.4, the coldness in her toes in beep 2.3, the coldness and gooiness of the toothpaste in beep 2.4, the bodily bobbing up and down in her imagination in beep 4.1. These awarenesses are not merely paying attention to the *objects* in her environment, but paying particular attention to the *sensory aspects* of those objects.

We discovered that she had detailed visual images: of the soldier on a dirt road in beep 2.1, of Stukas in beep 2.2, of a shopping-list pad in beep 2.3, of the Bicycle card joker in beep 4.2, of an intersection with apartment buildings in beep 5.1; and we discovered that she created those details even in the absence of the correct knowledge of what those details should look like: the Stukas were F-18s in beep 2.2, the joker was incorrectly imagined in beep 4.2.

We discovered that she had feelings, sometimes expressed bodily: of sadness/dread pressing on her chest in beep 2.2, of yearning in beep 4.1, of conviction that she was correct in beep 6.1, of happiness (a lightweight feeling in her lungs) in beep 6.2, of concentrating in beep 6.3. But we also discovered that sometimes her feelings were apparently ongoing in her body but were not directly experienced: of being exasperated but not experiencing it directly in beep 3.3, of concern and resentment not being directly experienced in beep 4.2, of anxiety about being late not being experienced in her body but being thought about in beep 5.1.

Melanie, by her own retrospective report, was surprised by some aspect of all these characteristics. She had apparently no knowledge at all of the fact that she was as absorbed by the sensory aspects as she was; she knew she had visual images but was surprised by the incorrectness of their detail; she was unaware of the emotional processes ongoing outside of her awareness.

11.1.2   How Far Does Russ Believe Melanie?

I believe, pretty much as Eric does, that there is reason to accept at least in broad strokes the veridicality of Melanie's reports. Certainly there is reason to quibble about some things: as we have seen, her reports on the first sampling day or so might reflect more her presuppositions than her actual experience; her images may be incorrect in some of their details because the interview took place the next day; and so on. But none of these quibbles is enough to overturn the overall accuracy of the observations. If we were particularly concerned about the first few sampling days, we could discard those beeps and sample with Melanie for a few more days. If we were particularly concerned about the forgetting or confabulating of image details, we could give Melanie a tape recorder and ask her to dictate the image details immediately following the beep rather than rely on written notes. Thus I believe that Melanie's accounts are pretty darn good; we could incrementally but not dramatically improve on them if we wished.

I have sampled with several hundreds of subjects at the same or greater level of detail and skepticism as we applied with Melanie. I am convinced that the general statements that we made about Melanie (that she engaged in active self-monitoring of her own actions, that she paid thematic attention to the sensory aspects of her environment, and so on) do not apply to all subjects or even to most subjects. I do not wish to claim that we discovered Melanie's essential uniqueness, but I do believe that, for example, most of my subjects do not engage in the kind of active self-monitoring that Melanie did. Whether observed differences reflect actual phenomenological differences or merely expressional differences is of fundamental importance. I assure the reader that for 30 years I have interrogated subjects in what most would say is excruciating detail on this particular issue, and during that time I held no particular position on the desirability of one outcome or the other. Those observations have forced me to conclude that people's experience actually differs from one person to the next—that these differences are not merely differences in reporting style. I would have been just as happy if the universe had turned out otherwise, but it didn't.

11.1.2.1 Raw vs. Exposed Reports

In evaluating Melanie's accuracy, we need to make a distinction between what I call "raw reports" and "exposed reports." A raw report is what a subject unaidedly reports about her inner experience; an exposed report is the result of the DES expositional interview, the result of clarifying to the extent possible the subject's inner experience. As we have seen, I think that Melanie's raw reports contained much that was believable and much that was not to be believed (particularly early in her participation in this process). Melanie was, I think, a typical subject in this regard. I was skeptical of her early raw reports, for example, of her inner thought voice of beep 1.1. [See boxes 4.1, 4.8, and 9.10. Also see my discussion of faux generalities below.] However, I found much less to be skeptical about in her raw reports from the final few sampling days.

I think our exposed reports of Melanie's experience, the understanding of her experience that Melanie and I (and to some extent Eric) shared at the end of each interview about her experience, contained very much that was believable and very little that was not to be believed. Thus, for example, I do believe Melanie's reports about the detailed nature of the images of the soldier on the road (beep 2.1) and that the Stukas really looked like F-18s (beep 2.2). I am perfectly willing to accept that a few of the details in those images may have been confabulated or otherwise mistaken—Melanie and we are not infallible—but I see no reason to believe that Melanie confabulated all or most of the details. Stukas as F-18s (box 5.9) is a good example. If one denies the existence of details in images, where did the F-18ness come from? What would have motivated Melanie, in telling us about her experience, to say that these Stukas looked like F-18s? It is hard to believe she was simply trying to please us by giving such an outlandish report. The more plausible explanation is that she was somehow seeing in inner experience something that looked like an F-18. I can accept the possibility that the F-18ness was not a part of the image at the moment of the beep, but was created only in the telling about the beep, but then one has to explain why an image at the moment of the beep *can't* have details when an image at the time of the report *can* be detailed. That is of course possible, but I can see no reason to force such a complicated explanation in the absence of any direct evidence.

I accept the fact that the exposed reports so obtained may not be a *complete* account of Melanie's momentary experience. (See subsection 11.2.2.) However, in general I agree with Eric's limited approval: I do think that "what [our interviews of Melanie] deliver is probably about as good as can reasonably be expected from open interviews about sampled experiences."

11.1.2.2 Faux Generalization

When Melanie uses the terms "all the time" and "whenever" (for example, in beep 1.1: "It's my inner thought voice, so it's the one I recognize and hear *all of the time whenever* I'm thinking"), she shows that she is making what I have called a faux generalization. [See box 5.17.] Her statement has the appearance of a truly inductive generalization, as if she had observed a series of instances of thought voices, noted that they all have the same characteristics, and reported that generalization. But it is highly unlikely that her statement is actually the result of such a truly inductive process. That statement is much more likely the result of the cognitive heuristics such as availability, recency, salience, accessibility that Kahneman and Tversky (and others) have described.

DES has shown that such self-characterizations are often not true and occasionally dramatically not true. I have had seemingly normal graduate students say they experience frequent images, but sampling produced none. I have had other seemingly normal graduate students say they have no visual images, but sampling produced many. Now it is certainly possible that some faux generalizations are true—Melanie may well have the kind of inner voice she described—but by and large they cannot be trusted. That's why part of the DES strategy is to discourage faux generalizations, to encourage subjects to suspend their belief in their own self-characterizations, to focus on the actually occurring instants on which true generalizations can be built.

Subjects typically understand this quite readily. If I say something like "Well, your self-characterization might or might not be true; let's try not to be influenced by it one way or the other and see what emerges in the samples," most subjects are not offended and recognize the value of such an approach. As a result, most of the time, the expression of faux generalizations gradually disappears during sampling. One might argue that I punish the expression, so the expression disappears while the belief lingers on. I don't think that's true; most subjects would convincingly say that it's not true. Melanie was a quite typical subject in this regard. I believe she came to see that her faux generalizations interfered with her ability to observe her experience accurately and that she gradually developed the skill of suspending them. As a result, her raw reports became more accurate, and it became easier for us to filter out remaining inaccuracies and do a better job of creating accurate exposed reports.

11.1.3   Inner Speech

It is useful to comment on Melanie's lack of inner speech because many theorists hold that all thinking is inner speech and that inner speech should therefore be ubiquitous across all DES subjects. Bernard Baars, for example, claims that "human beings talk to themselves every moment of the waking day" (2003, p. 106).

It is usually very easy for DES subjects to report inner speech and very easy for investigators to recognize it. Subjects who have frequent inner speech (and there are many such subjects) make for generally the easiest, least ambiguous sampling studies. Inner speech often involves full sentences, naturally inflected, with the same kind of pauses, stutters, voice pitch and rate, emotional tone, and so on as external speech.

Melanie was not like that. First of all, she had *no* clear-cut examples of inner speech. She reported inner speech twice out of the four samples on the first sampling day, but those reports are dismissible, I think. It is often the case that DES subjects, like Melanie, frequently report talking to themselves on the first sampling day and rarely make such reports later in sampling. I take that to be the result of the subjects' initial presupposition that thinking is inner speech. The questioning of the first day is designed to bracket all presuppositions including that one. If subjects later report no inner speech, then I attribute the early reports to the presupposition and the later lack of report to the successful bracketing of that presupposition.

The closest Melanie got to inner speech was sample 3.1, where she was thinking "peri-, peri-," to herself, the first part of the word "periodontist" that she was trying to remember. But questioning revealed that she wasn't really sure whether she was saying "peri-" or experiencing it in some other way. I take no position on whether this "peri-, peri-" experience was or was not (vaguely or faintly experienced) inner speech; I think trying to force such a conclusion is a mistake. (See subsection 11.2.2.) Certainly Melanie did not have the kind of clear and frequent inner speaking phenomenon that is common among many DES subjects.

At sample 3.3, Melanie experienced her own voice saying the first part of the sentence "Why can't I remember about the parking brake." Melanie, like most DES subjects, apparently made the discrimination between inner speech and inner hearing confidently and experienced this sample to be inner hearing. Inner speech, the more common phenomenon across subjects, is experienced to be "going away," "produced by," "under the control of" the subject, "just like speaking aloud except no sound." Inner hearing, by contrast, is the experience of a sound "coming toward," "experienced by" rather than produced by, "listened to" rather than spoken, "just like listening to a CD." Typical subjects are not confused between inner speech and inner hearing any more than they are confused between speaking aloud and hearing a tape recording of themselves speaking.

11.1.4 Why the Personal Is Important

In one sense, this book is entirely about Melanie; in another sense, it is not about Melanie at all. Clearly our main intent was to find out something about inner experience, about interviews, about the difficulties of apprehending another's conscious experience; our major aim was *not* to find out something about Melanie as a particular individual. Melanie herself, really, means little to the reader.

So why do we have to spend so much time with Melanie? Couldn't Eric and I just juxtapose our theoretical positions like semiprecious stones in a tumbler and turn on the critiquing process? I think not. Melanie's moments are, to stretch the metaphor, the carbide grit in the tumbler. It's not merely that our theories grind on each other as the tumbler rotates, but that our theories grind on the facticity of Melanie's reports in which both Eric's and my views are bathed. We need Melanie to keep us in the concrete, to prevent us from flying away to the abstract.

In *The Stranger*, Camus has Meursault say to the priest "And yet none of his certainties was worth one strand of a woman's hair." I take that as an artistic critique of theory, formal knowledge, science, philosophy, psychology, abstract ideas in general. Perhaps to overdraw the point somewhat, the more one is involved in theoretical/formal/scientific/abstract knowledge, the less one confronts, contacts, encounters, is impacted by, touches real people. It's not merely that a person has a limited capacity, as if time spent in theory reduces the time spent encountering real people. It's not merely personal idiosyncrasy, as if some personalities incline to theory while others incline to people. On the contrary, theory (or formal knowledge in general) tends to hide real people, to split one away from real people, to create the illusion (I might better say "delusion") that it approaches real people while at the same time eliminating the knowledge that real people are actually being lost in the process.

I don't think that theory *must* hide real people, only that it over-whelmingly *has*. A science of people might well be built up one hair (with apologies to Camus) at a time; a few (Oliver Sacks comes to mind) have pointed in the right direction. Eventually, perhaps, many hairs might be braided into a beautiful and secure scientific coiffure. But at this time, it seems to me, psychological science and philosophical analysis has for the most part maintained that we can do the coif without paying attention to the individual hairs, a view I think is fundamentally mistaken.

I think an interest in theory and in formal knowledge in general tends actively to *interfere with* an interest in personal truths. Interests, includ-ing interest in theory, are sets of skills, involving real bodies/minds engaged in real activities, strengthening this muscle, building that coor-dination, and so on. A proper theoretical interest involves the skills of standing still while the surroundings change and of suppressing the indi-viduality of the theorist. A good theory is one that is independent of the person stating it—you would be critical of a theory if it held when you state it but didn't when I state it. And the best theory is the one that is most independent of the characteristics of the target as well—the more universally true the better. Universal truth doesn't care whether we are talking about Eric or me or Melanie. So the best theory (or best formal knowledge in general) is the one that is the *least* interested in real people, least interested in the theorist or in the subject.

Thus one of the main aspects of the general/theoretical skill is to suspend the personal, to act as if the personal didn't exist or wasn't important, so that the general/theoretical speaking can take place inde-pendent of the speaker and independent of any particular person spoken about. If one exercises that skill, gets good at it, one usually develops the skill of ignoring the personal, of holding the personal at bay.

The problem is that formal knowledge can create the illusion that it approaches real people when in reality it turns its back on real people. Psychology (philosophy too, probably) graduate programs emphasize formal knowledge and as a result spend little time teaching how to observe people accurately. It's a striking omission, so ubiquitous it is rarely noticed. To observe people accurately (or even to *try* to observe people accurately, or even to observe one's *failure* to observe people accurately) is in many ways incompatible with (even antagonistic to) modern psychology.

In some ways the situation is similar to the distinction between the classical and the jazz musician. Classical performance is a skill that involves suppressing many of the bendings and other licenses that are the hallmark of jazz performance. Classical performers get good at such suppression; that's why opera singers who sing popular tunes or symphony orchestras that play jazz almost always sound stilted and awkward. But there are a few exceptions (Wynton Marsalis comes to mind), performers who can advance both the classical and the jazz mediums.

I do not in any way wish to contend that the personal is more important than the general/theoretical. The ideal psychological scientists, in my view, would be at home in both worlds, Marsalis-like. I do contend that the corrective that currently needs to be applied is to push strongly in the direction of the personal. That's why we involved Melanie, to keep us focused on at least one flesh-and-blood person while we discussed general issues.

11.1.4.1 Personal Truth

So I think we want a "hairy" science, one that starts with personal truths and builds toward the general/theoretical. By "personal truths" I mean that which is both personally true and truly personal. Suppose we know that Melanie's femur is 16 inches long. That is a true fact about Melanie as a particular person—we can say that feature is *personally true* of her. But it is not *truly personal*—it does not reveal much about what Melanie is really like. Certainly it says *something* about Melanie as a person— she's of about average height—and that fact is indeed important to such things as her promise as a volleyball player. But that fact is not truly personal. By contrast, our general observation of Melanie's samples that she frequently makes self-reflective, self-monitoring observations is truly personal. This observation allows Melanie to emerge *as Melanie really is*, of herself, by herself, for herself, not as a member of one of my favored theoretically created groups, not by comparison to some standardization group in a psychological test such as the MMPI, not as an instance of some universal truth, but as Melanie revealed to herself on her own terms one moment of lived experience at a time. Out of the nearly infinite welter of experiential phenomena that *might* present themselves to Melanie, self-analytical phenomena *do* present themselves to her repeatedly.

We have looked at only 17 moments of Melanie's existence. That's obviously a very small sample, but even so a substantial pattern emerges. Clearly we need to observe more samples to be confident of any general statement and its limitations and range of convenience, and we should do so. Then psychological science, if it is to be efficacious, can start with a true understanding of what Melanie is really like, and similarly of what John and Jane and Maria and Sam and Julio are really like and how they are the same and/or different from Melanie and each other.

Thus I think good theory is possible but rare. It would be truly personal—it would acknowledge and start with the messy, tangled idiosyncrasy of the objective reality with which we are dealing. DES is an attempt to create a personal starting point. One may dispute whether the attempt is successful, but at least it is an attempt. One might be able to advance different, perhaps more effective attempts; that would be terrific, from my point of view.

11.1.4.2 Developing a Taste for Specific Moments

It seems to me that psychological science must develop a taste for the exploration and accurate reporting of concrete moments of experience. One might argue that this taste is perhaps the result of my many years of creating such reports using DES, but I think it is the other way around. DES is at least as much the result of the taste for accurately described concrete moments as the cause of the cultivation of that taste.

I do think the cultivation of that taste is possible, and the first step is to accept that that cultivation might be valuable.

11.1.5 Discovery vs. Confirmation

Modern psychological science is very impatient, it seems to me; for the most part, its practitioners can see little value in wading through the details of randomly selected moments in hopes that some substantial personal truth might emerge. But if there is to be any significant discovery in the science of psychology, it will have to be built up out of real generalizations (as thoroughly distinct from faux generalizations) about personal truths (as thoroughly distinct from valid measures).

There are two related but separable dimensions to this impatience, the personal-vs.-impersonal and the discovery-vs.-confirmation dimensions. I have just discussed the personal-vs.-impersonal dimension and made the case that science needs more emphasis on the personal end of that dimension. Now I make the case that science needs more emphasis on the discovery end of the discovery-vs.-confirmation dimension.

Psychological science typically proceeds by making a generalization (often called a hypothesis) before it collects its data and then seeking to validate that generalization (test the hypothesis) afterward. There is nothing inherently wrong with that procedure; good science would be at a substantial loss without it. However, the creation of the to-be-validated generalization is an important part (arguably the most important part) of the validation process, because a validation study is quite fully constrained by the original generalization. An experiment, for example, lays out its possible results at the time of its design, before the data are collected; the interpretation of an experiment is mostly a selection from among the possibilities laid out in advance (including the possibility that the generalization is false).

Unfortunately, in my view, modern psychological science pays inadequate attention to the creation of hypotheses in its impatient rush to validate them. I don't think that that sequence can be effective in the long run, because (among other reasons) it elevates the status of presuppositions rather than diminishes it: A hypothesis is entirely (or almost entirely) shaped by the presuppositions behind it. Psychological research should spend much of its time carefully observing personal truths, advancing tentative real generalizations, making more observations, and revising the real generalizations, and only then advancing hypotheses that might explain those generalizations. It is through that process that discoveries will be made, which can later be validated by standard psychological science.

Thus the *order* of generalization-making is a fundamental structural issue for the field. A validation study states the generalization at the outset and tests that generalization. Eric's rich-vs.-thin investigation is of this type: his generalization that all or most subjects have visual experience all or most of the time shaped the very structure of his entire experiment. By contrast, our investigation of Melanie is a discovery study, which collected the data first and made generalizations only later. We did not set out, before interviewing Melanie, to determine whether Melanie had frequent self-monitoring experience. On the contrary, we observed Melanie the way Melanie was, with as many of our presuppositions held at bay as possible. On the basis of that series of observations, we arrived at the emergent real generalization that Melanie had frequent self-monitoring experience. Subsequently, after the observation of Melanie and many others, we might advance hypotheses such as that people who have frequent self-monitoring also X. Then it would be appropriate to validate that hypothesis.

I am entirely in favor of validation studies—I've written a book about how to do that process (Hurlburt 2006). My criticism is only that psychological science expends far too much of its energy far too soon on validation, and expends far too little energy perfecting the careful observation skills that can lead to genuine discovery.

11.1.6 On the Science of Inner Experience

As we have said all along, we are not here particularly interested in Melanie; our main interest is in the science of inner experience and what our discussions of Melanie have to say about it. The main question for me, then, is that if we accept the characterization of Melanie's sampling presented above, and if we accept that the same characterization applies to many if not most subjects, are the data obtained from DES good enough on which to build a science of inner experience? I think the answer is Yes, at least in an engineering sort of way. The engineer knows about a variety of building materials: steel girders, wood two-by-fours, etc. He also knows that he should *not* have absolute confidence in any particular steel or wood beam due to imperfection in materials, inconsistency in processes, incorrect installation, etc. Instead, he accounts for his lack of single-beam confidence by incorporating the margin of error and redundancy that his science has found desirable. The science of engineering is thus not to specify exactly how a particular object will perform, but to understand the materials available and the tasks at hand, to try to match them appropriately, and to design for expectable flaws.

I think it likely that a science of experience can be constructed in a similar fashion. We can accept the fact that we don't believe *all* confidently-asserted-and-robustly-vetted reports; however, at the same time we can have confidence in a science of experience built out of a redundant set of independent reports, as long as the independent reports are pretty good. What we need is a science that, at least approximately, credits apprehensions of experience to the extent that they are creditable, and discredits apprehensions to the extent that they should be discredited, and uses reports in appropriate venues. We don't have to be perfect in this regard; we need enough redundancy that we can continue to support the science even if an occasional subject is mistaken, or doesn't understand, or lies, etc.

11.1.7 Bracketing Presuppositions

Many if not most of Eric's and my points of disagreement have in some way to do with whether or not or to what extent we should bracket presuppositions. The bracketing of presuppositions is a central or at least major peripheral issue in: the problematic of retrospective and armchair introspection (boxes 4.2, 4.11, 5.6, 5.7, 5.17, 8.5, 8.7); inner vision has the same characteristics (angle of field, etc.) as exterior vision (box 4.6); visual experience always occurs (box 5.7, etc.); visual experience is sketchy (box 8.2); imagery should parallel external seeing (box 8.3);

accepting more easily things that seem plausible (boxes 5.7, 8.5); the issue of auditory imagery vs. inner speech (box 5.7); people are mostly alike (boxes 7.4, 8.5); the cultural impact on reports of thinking (boxes 7.12, 7.13); the situational impact on reports of inner experience (box 8.1); emotionality does not involve color (box 4.7); that the laws of physics and time apply to inner experience (box 9.8 and the surrounding discussion); the standard of evidence (box 9.9); and so on. I now take this opportunity to expand my views on the bracketing of presuppositions, an essential feature of what I would call a good science of inner experience.

My quarrels with Eric about the bracketing of presuppositions have not been mere cavils; on the contrary, they have reflected the fact that I believe that the bracketing of presuppositions is, at least at the present time, the central issue of consciousness studies and psychological science. Get the bracketing of presuppositions adequately right and consciousness studies can advance; don't get it right, no advance.

The concept of the bracketing of presuppositions is not, of course, my invention; Husserl and other phenomenologists have discussed the "bracketing," the "setting aside," the "putting out of play" of presuppositions as part of the reductions that occur in a phenomenological analysis. I have adopted the same terminology, although we should note that my use of the term "bracketing presuppositions" is somewhat different from that of Husserl. Husserl's intention by bracketing presuppositions is to arrive at pure ego, pure consciousness, the differentiation of the perfection of evidence, apodictically secure philosophy. My use of the term "bracketing presuppositions" is quite pedestrian by contrast, because my goal is adequacy, not purity, perfection, or apodicticity. I want investigators to bracket presuppositions to enable them to move from being substantially blind to being "pretty darn good" at conducting an expositional interview. That's a substantial move, but less than Husserl advocated.

11.1.7.1 Bracketing Presuppositions Is Necessary

I have explored the inner experience of several hundred people at the same or better level of detail and skepticism as we did with Melanie. Furthermore, I have observed and/or participated in the training of a few dozen investigators. On the basis of those explorations, I am convinced that most subjects misrepresent their own experiences to a greater or lesser degree, usually as the result of incorrect presuppositions about the characteristics of their own experiences. I am also convinced that most psychologists, philosophers, and laypersons (including those who are attracted to methods like DES) misrepresent their subjects' experiences, usually as the result of incorrect presuppositions about the characteristics of experience.

The common denominator in both misrepresentations is the failure by subject and/or investigator to bracket presuppositions. Both the subject and the investigator should set aside or put out of play the notions that distort the reports about experience.

The adequate bracketing of presuppositions is a necessary condition for the "independent" requirement of my summary "we can have confidence in a science of experience built out of a redundant set of independent reports." A presupposition, whether conscious or unconscious, known or unknown, forces all observations into alignment, forces all observations to have the same flaw, thereby ruling out independence from one report to the next. That is just as destructive to the science of experience as it would be to the engineer who used beams that all had the same flaw—when the conditions are just right, all the flaws work in concert and the structure collapses.

The main skills of the investigator's task are to bracket the investigator's own presuppositions and to help the subject bracket the subject's own presuppositions. There is nothing fundamentally complex about that, but in practice it is quite difficult. Presuppositions run deep, and people (subjects and investigators) are blind to their own most important presuppositions.

11.1.7.2 Helping the Subject Bracket Presuppositions

I want to help the subject bracket whatever presuppositions about inner experience she may have. As an example, I want to help Melanie bracket her presupposition of talking to herself, which we discussed in subsection 11.1.3. On her first sampling day, Melanie described herself as talking to herself, apparently on the presuppositional belief (with Baars and most of the Western tradition) that *all* thinking involves talking to oneself. The bracketing task in such situations is neither to accept Melanie's talking-to-herself reports as being accurate nor to reject them as being false. Instead, I want somehow to convey to Melanie the desirability of suspending judgment (bracketing) about whether talking to herself is an accurate description of her experience. I want to convey to Melanie that it is okay with us either way: if she does in fact talk to herself, we want to hear about it in her reports. If, on the other hand, she does not talk to herself, we want to hear about whatever phenomenon is present other than such talking.

11.1.7.3 Bracketing the Investigator's Presuppositions

Melanie's inner speech is an example of helping the subject bracket her presuppositions. DES also asks its investigators to bracket their own presuppositions. We have discussed at length several of Eric's presuppositions, for example that he believes that people do not experience plentiful detail in their visual imagery. [See boxes 4.18, 4.19, 5.1, 5.4, 5.11, 7.8, 8.2, and 8.3.] That view of images doubtless is the product of some combination of armchair introspection (Eric's own imagery is perhaps not detailed), his reading of the imagery literature, his informal questioning of others about their imagery, and other influences. DES asks Eric to bracket that presupposition (among all others) when exploring the experience of any individual subject such as Melanie. Bracketing presuppositions in this instance means being sensitively open to the possibility that Melanie has detailed imagery, but being equally open to the possibility that Melanie does not have detailed imagery. That is, the task is to be open to Melanie's visual phenomena as they unfold themselves to Melanie and through her to Eric and me. Bracketing means that we should structure a level-playing-field situation for Melanie, that we should not let our own (or Melanie's) presuppositions knowingly or unknowingly bias us (or her) in favor of one outcome or in opposition to another. Bracketing does *not* mean that Eric should pretend that his own experience or his reading of the imagery literature doesn't exist. Presumably he has profited to some degree from his self-observation and from that reading, has a greater understanding of the traps, pitfalls, successes, and blind alleys that that literature includes. On the basis of that understanding he should feel free to ask skillful questions that assist Melanie to distinguish between this aspect and that, to make as sure as possible that Melanie understands what is being asked in known-to-be-problematic areas, and so on. But he should not, it seems to me, prejudge the answers to those questions. Melanie maintained that she has detailed imagery despite Eric's probing (in some cases leading) questions. That should count against his presupposition that all imagery is not detailed.

I have conducted many DES investigations where subjects provide detailed imagery reports that were at least as convincing as Melanie's. I have tried to keep those studies independent in the sense that I have worked hard at bracketing presuppositions about such things as detailed imagery. As a result, I have discovered to my satisfaction that there is a range of detail in visual imagery. Some subjects have no visual imagery whatsoever; some have visual imagery that is not detailed, some subjects have much visual imagery, some of which is detailed and some of which is not; some subjects have much visual imagery, all of it detailed. It's harder for me than for Eric to discount all those results because I have seen them all first hand and can vouch for their thorough examination because I was there. The existence of a range of imagery detail across subjects in my opinion provides evidence that I have bracketed whatever presuppositions I might have in this regard.

11.1.7.4   An Example
In the early 1980s, before DES existed as a relatively formal method, I was giving subjects beepers and asking what was going on with them at the moment of the beep. Occasionally, usually on about the third day of such sampling, subjects would say they wanted to quit; that they weren't any good at sampling; that they didn't wish to waste my time; they couldn't observe their own thinking; that I should get someone who could perform the sampling task better than they could. I typically said something to the effect of, Why don't we discuss today's samples and see what the problems are, and after that if you want to quit, okay. At the end of such early interviews, I myself would agree with the difficulties the subject was reporting—sampling did seem impossible for us.

But eventually I noticed that similar sequences were happening across several subjects; not all subjects, to be sure, but enough to provide a pattern. I therefore worked harder to understand what was happening. It turned out that these subjects were having frequent (what I came to call) unsymbolized thinking—thoughts that have clear, differentiated content but no discernible features that "carry" that content: no images, no words, no other kinds of symbols. For example, a subject might be thinking, at the moment of the beep, something that if expressed in words would be "I think I'll make a ham sandwich—no, I'll have a hot dog." But there were no words (no "ham sandwich," no "hot dog," no "no") and no images (of a sandwich or a hot dog), and no other discernible symbols. The subject was clearly thinking, clearly thinking specifically of a ham sandwich and specifically a hot dog, and clearly changing his mind from one to the other, but there was no way to describe *how* that thought appeared, other than to say it *did* appear.

The problem was that my subjects and I all shared the (commonly held) presupposition that, of course, thinking *had to be* in words or in some other kind of symbols. It never would have occurred to us to suspect the existence of thinking without words or symbols. The subjects were distressed—they were pretty sure about what they were thinking but they were totally unable to report it in a way that was acceptable to them. Even more distressing, as they got better at paying attention to what was happening at the moment of the beep, as naturally happened in a few sampling days, they seemed to get *worse* at reporting it—they now were beginning to observe themselves thinking without words or symbols, which they *knew* was impossible. Therefore, they saw themselves as bad subjects and wanted to quit. I was of little help because our presuppositions colluded, and we were stuck.

What eventually got us through this impasse was my willingness to bracket presuppositions, even those presuppositions that were so basic, so ingrained, so taken for granted, so unquestioned, as that thinking was in words or symbols. I wasn't particularly skillful at that bracketing, but I had read enough phenomenology and Eastern meditative traditions to open myself to its possibilities. Once the presupposition that thinking had to be in words or symbols was successfully bracketed, it was relatively easy to recognize the pattern and to talk about that kind of thinking from then on.

This example illustrates the interplay of the presuppositional points we have been discussing. The subjects and I happened to share a presupposition about the nature of thinking. That made it difficult for me to ask evenhanded questions, for the subjects to give accurate answers, and for me to interpret what was being said and not said. When I finally could bracket my presupposition, it made it much easier for me to help the subjects bracket theirs, and the knot was untied. This example also illustrates the insidiousness of presuppositions: we didn't know, at that time, of the very existence of the presuppositions that needed to be bracketed. *Of course* we thought that thinking was in words or symbols; how could it be otherwise? It didn't (at the outset) occur to us to bracket that presupposition any more than it would occur to us to bracket the fact that we need air to breathe. *Of course* we need air to breathe. The presuppositions that are the hardest, and also the most important, to bracket are those which exist prior to any understanding that they should be bracketed.

To bring this example to a close, let me add one additional anecdote. During the past 25 years, I have declined to participate myself as a DES subject on the logic that I, like other investigators, am fallible. I recognized that investigators are likely to favor (value, etc.) their own characteristics, so it seemed prudent to me that if I was to be an evenhanded observer of the characteristics of the inner experience of others, I should avoid being captured by the particular idiosyncratic characteristics of my own experience. One way to facilitate that was simply not to know what were the idiosyncratic characteristics of my own experience. Therefore I declined to sample myself.

Last year, the students in my sampling lab, understandably curious about what my own sampled experience might look like, prevailed on me to let them sample me. I agreed, on the logic that now, after 25 years of practice, I was probably pretty secure in my ability to bracket my own personal characteristics. So I wore the beeper and reported back to the lab for a joint sampling interview. At the outset I somewhat apologetically reported that I wasn't a very good subject; I said that probably as a result of my years of sampling I had lost the ability to pay attention to my own experience, that sampling with me wasn't likely to be very useful, that they should probably find a better subject, but they could go ahead and ask about my experiences. It turned out that my own samples contained much unsymbolized thinking but that I hadn't recognized that in myself despite 25 years of recognizing it in others! I had said to my student interviewers exactly the same kinds of things that my subjects had been saying to me for 25 years, but I didn't recognize it.

Presuppositions die hard.

11.1.7.5   The Beep as the First Bracketing Step

The first step of an exploration of inner experience should be to apprehend that experience as it is in its occurrence, to get to the experience itself.

I believe that the reflective task is made substantially easier by the DES beep, which provides a substantial head start in the bracketing of presuppositions by selecting the precise experience to be reflected upon (Hurlburt and Heavey 2004). It makes that selection at, or at least very nearly at, the moment that the experience is occurring and signals the subject to consider this particular experience, not one a few seconds, hours, or days earlier. Without the beep (or some other equally or more effective means of selecting a particular experience) the subject has to work her way back to the target experience, and that retrospection is subject to a host of pressures. Without the beep, a substantial bracketing of presuppositions is therefore required to get retrospectively to the experience itself, unadulterated by similar events that occurred at different times, different events that occurred at about the same time, fantasized events that never occurred at all, and so on. The beep simplifies the bracketing task. Certainly the beep does not guarantee that we will get to the experience itself—effective bracketing of presuppositions is still required—but it makes it very much easier.

11.1.7.6   Random Sampling as a Second Step in Bracketing Presuppositions

The randomness of the DES beep is an extremely effective bracketing-presuppositions tool because the unexpected nature of the random beep catches the subject off guard, thus outsmarting the mind's habitual pre-suppositional activity, and because the experiences to be investigated are chosen randomly, not to match some presupposition or to avoid some presupposition, not because an experience is thought to be important or thought to correspond to some theory. The random nature of the beep slices through all those presuppositions and produces an even-handed collection of non-presupposition-driven experiences; then those experiences can be examined to determine whatever characteristics emerge from them. For example, we did not at the outset of sampling with Melanie presume that inner speech is important, nor did we presume that it is unimportant. On the contrary, we randomly sampled Melanie's experience and if inner speech *turned out to be* important, fine; if not, fine. Data, as free of presuppositions as possible, drove conceptualizations such as that inner speech was not a major aspect of Melanie's experience.

Part of Eric's critique of DES from the point of view of classical intro-spection is that the classical introspectionists controlled their experimental conditions better than does DES. However, from the standpoint of bracketing presuppositions, the controlling of conditions is a liability rather than an asset, because the controlling of conditions is in fact a substantial concretization of presuppositions. Control presupposes that the experimenter knows before the data are collected what is and what is not important. There is a time when such control is desirable, but that is not until the phenomena are clearly understood as they naturally occur.

11.1.7.7   Armchair Introspection as a Failure to Bracket Presuppositions

I have railed against armchair introspection frequently during the course of this book because I think consciousness studies has relied far to heavily on the armchair and its failure to bracket presuppositions. Above I used Bernard Baars, a prominent researcher in consciousness studies who claimed that "human beings talk to themselves every moment of the waking day" (Baars 2003, p. 106), as an example of failed armchair intro-spection, because one of the most robust findings of DES is that there are many people who, apparently like Melanie, talk to themselves only rarely if at all. I suspect that Baars's position comes from armchair intro-spection buttressed by analysis; I suspect that Eric's view that people are mostly the same and his doubt that Melanie's images are richly detailed come from similar procedures.

In box 4.5, Eric reported his own armchair introspective investigation of Melanie's report of speeded up but not compressed or rushed inner speech. He observed, correctly as I recall, that his own inner speech, when he wore the DES beeper, was at about the same rate as his external speech; that is what most (but not all) DES subjects report about inner speech. Then he, armchairwise,

walk[ed] across campus deliberately producing inner speech and attempting to observe its pace as I did so. I found myself getting tangled up, feeling like I often produced the speech twice, once in forming the intention to produce a specific instance of inner speech and then again in carrying out that intention (as though I didn't realize the intention was already executed in the forming of it). I also found myself unsure of the pacing especially of the first of these two acts of inner speech—indeed, unsure even of whether the first was in fact an act of inner speech at all.

It is simply not adequate, I think, to support or discount a position because it happens to agree disagree with one's own armchair. Eric's tangle comes from the inadequate armchair method, not from some fundamental difficulty or impossibility of introspection.

It appears that Eric used his armchair introspection to discredit his own DES experience. At box 4.5, he stated that, apparently as a result of observing the tangles in his armchair introspection, "In my own earlier sampling, in fact, I believe I reported that my inner speech was paced at roughly the same rate as my external speech, but now I find myself wondering if I was correct in that observation." It seems to me that, when observed contemporaneously, he wasn't as tangled when responding to the DES beep as he was in his armchair introspection. That strikes me as straightforward evidence that DES is in some important ways better than his armchair. There are other potential explanations (I pressured him in the DES situation, we weren't careful enough in the DES situation, and so on) but those seem quite convoluted by comparison.

Eric might respond that perhaps his cross-campus-walk observation was just a particularly bad armchair introspection and a bad application doesn't invalidate the general armchair process. I would agree with the logic but I don't think that evades the criticism. There is no way that I can see to discern whether his observation is good or bad short of a series of validation studies, and as I have said above, resting validation studies on inadequately grounded hypotheses is not in my view a productive way for science to proceed.

11.1.7.8 Bracketing Presuppositions in Experiments: Flavell

Eric sometimes rankles when I suggest that his resistance to accepting Melanie's reports is due to his armchair introspections, saying that his views are the result of not just his armchair introspections but also of his reading of the various literatures. I accept that; the problem is that the same presuppositions that drive his armchair may also drive the literature he reviews.

For example, in section 3.2 Eric described the "vast mistakes" that children make when describing their thinking, basing his observations on his review of studies of 5-year-olds by Flavell and his colleagues. I believe it likely that Eric has some of the same presuppositions as does Flavell, and as a result both may be substantially mistaken about the thinking of 5-year-olds. (I greatly respect the Flavells, who have tried to understand inner experience when such work was eschewed; nonetheless, it seems to me that their conclusions may not reflect their own data.)

Here are the instructions that a typical Flavell experiment puts to children. The child is seated on a carpet, and the experimenter says

I'm going to ask you a question, but I don't want you to say the answer out loud. Keep the answer a secret, OK? Most people in the world have toothbrushes in their houses. They put their toothbrushes in a special room. Now don't say anything out loud. Keep it a secret. Which room in your house has your toothbrush in it? (Flavell, Green, and Flavell 1995, p. 57)

The experimenter then moves the child to a table and asks the child if she had been thinking while seated on the carpet, and if so, about what. Most older children (and adults) say that indeed they were thinking, that they were saying to themselves "bathroom" or seeing an image of their bathroom, or the like. However, the majority of 5-year-olds deny the existence of such thinking while seated on the carpet; if they acknowledge they were thinking, they typically report themselves to have been thinking about something other than the bathroom. As a result, Flavell and his colleagues conclude that 5-year-olds lack the ability to observe the thinking that was taking place: "children lack the disposition and the ability to introspect. Lacking introspective skills, they would be unlikely spontaneously to notice and reflect on their own mental experiences and, consequently, unlikely to attribute such experiences to others" (Flavell, Green, and Flavell 1995, p. 52).

It seems to me that a much more straightforward conclusion might be that 5-year-olds don't experience thinking. It appears that Flavell and his colleagues don't reach this conclusion because they don't take seriously enough the possibility that children's thinking may be different from adults' and older children's:

We can imagine a number of possible reasons why … 5-year-olds tend to perform poorly on introspection tasks. (1) The 5-year-olds had no thoughts of any kind …, and therefore had nothing to report. *This explanation seems implausible on its face. It is tantamount to saying that, unlike older people, young children do not have a continuous or near-continuous stream of consciousness when in a conscious state.* There is also empirical evidence against it. … Flavell et al. (1995) found in several studies that 5-year-olds would often deny having had thoughts even when it was not just likely, *but virtually certain*, that they had just had some (e.g., about which room they keep their toothbrush in). (Flavell, Green, and Flavell 2000, p. 108, emphasis added)

It seems to me that the "virtual certainty" that thinking was ongoing is the result of the Flavells' presuppositions about thinking. They cannot accept that "young children do not have a continuous or near-continuous stream of consciousness when in a conscious state" even though their own 5-year-old subjects consistently deny it, no matter how hard the Flavells work at setting up situations where 5-year-olds might report that stream. The Flavells don't accept their own subjects' reports because that would be "implausible on its face," which seems to me to be a presupposition trumping a whole series of observations. That is, I think, a large mistake.

I think it is simply not true that it is "virtually certain" that 5-year-olds were thinking in that situation. By "thinking" Flavell and his colleagues (and most others, including me) apparently mean some kind of conscious introspectible process (like talking to yourself, or seeing an image of the bathroom, or the like); part of a Flavell instruction to children is that "our brain or mind is sort of like a flashlight. It shines on just a few things at a time, and while it shines on some things, it can't shine on others" (Flavell, Green, and Flavell 1995, p. 61).

So the question is as follows: Is it possible to be confronted with the "Which room in your house has your toothbrush in it?" situation without thinking about the bathroom while seated on the carpet? I think the answer is Yes, and I will advance four reasons.

First, what I call the "subtractive" logic: My DES studies show that if I were to beep adults in the pause of this situation, some would report inner speech (such as "In the bathroom"), some would report images (such as seeing the toothbrush holder in the bathroom), and some would report unsymbolized thinking. Because inner speech is present only some but not all of the time, it follows that inner speech is not necessary to correctly answer, aloud, "In the bathroom." For the same reason, neither images nor unsymbolized thinking is necessary to give a correct answer. It therefore seems plausible, by subtraction as it were, that since none of the forms of inner experience are necessary, that it might be possible to say "In the bathroom" aloud without having had any form of inner experience present to awareness. I acknowledge that *it is common* that people employ one or the other (or several) forms of inner experience in this situation, but I see no reason to believe that *it is necessary to* employ one or another of these forms.

Second, I have sampled with some adults who, in my conclusion, did not have inner experience. I have written about that with respect to schizophrenia (Hurlburt 1990), but some non-schizophrenic people also apparently have no inner experience on some occasions (Hurlburt and Heavey 2006, chapter 2). In the Eastern tradition, adept meditators report having no inner experience.

Third, the (scanty) DES evidence from children. I described in box 5.8 the image a 9-year-old boy described of a hole he had dug in his backyard. The image was incomplete, he said; if I had beeped him a few minutes later, he would have had time to put his toys into the image. If, as is plausible, image-making is a skill that is acquired gradually, we should extrapolate from adults' (or older children's) to 5-year-olds' thinking with caution.

Fourth, I think it quite reasonable to suppose that children learn inner speech long after (possibly years after) they learn to have external speech (Vygotsky 1962).

Thus, I think it quite plausible that 5-year-olds have not developed the skills of image making or of inner speech. By analogy, I think it quite plausible that they have not developed any skills which an adult or older child would call "thinking." Therefore I think it quite plausible that 5-year-olds are being straightforwardly descriptively correct when they deny that thinking was ongoing in Flavell's tasks. Finding that to be "implausible on its face" is a substantial failure to bracket presuppositions, a substantial, unwarranted over-reliance on what seems familiar to an adult.

I am not arguing that 5-year-olds haven't developed those skills; in fact, I do not consider myself an expert on children's thinking. I'm arguing that *it is plausible* that they have not developed those skills, and that it is highly *un*desirable to dismiss that possibility on its presuppositional face. In fact, I believe that the best evidence we have on children's thinking comes from the Flavells' studies, but it seems reasonable to me (but not to the Flavells or Eric) to interpret those studies as showing that

5-year-olds do *not* have a stream of consciousness similar to that of adults.

My antipathy toward armchair introspection is that what seems natural or familiar in the armchair may then infect subsequent interpretations of the literature and experiment, leading (for example) Eric to use the phrase "*vastly* mistaken" when describing Flavell's 5-year-old's failure to report thinking. The core problem is the failure to bracket presuppositions; if presuppositions were bracketed adequately then I would have no objection whatsoever to armchair introspection. (The Buddha comes to mind.) However, I fear that Eric's and the Flavells' armchair *enhances* presuppositions rather than *brackets* them. It's hard to imagine a more consistent set of results than those provided by Flavell's 5-year-olds, and yet, apparently, neither the Flavells nor Eric are listening. I blame the armchair. Perhaps I should blame the presuppositions, not the armchair. However, presuppositions become accepted, reified, entrenched in the armchair, as if the armchair provides some independent evidence. The armchair is a dangerous place for consciousness studies.

For a similarly skeptical view of children's dreaming, grounded in careful sampling and interview techniques that seem to point against the armchair assumption of similarity between children's and adults' experience, see Foulkes 1999. Here is Foulkes's summary of his findings about the dreams of 3–5-year-olds:

> The single most amazing finding . . . was how puny the dream process turned out to be. However rich and detailed preschoolers' dream "reports" may be when they are elicited at some delay by parents, clinicians, or other credulous interviewers, when children are awakened during REM sleep periods and asked, on the spot, if and what they were dreaming, the most common response by far is that they were not dreaming anything at all. (Foulkes 1999, p. 56)

11.1.8 The Desirability but Difficulty of Objective Observations

Eric has stated frequently that he would more readily believe reports about inner experience such as Melanie's if they were confirmed by objective (experimental) results. I have agreed that objective results would be desirable, but so far, no one has undertaken studies that I think would be adequate.

I would make a rough distinction between theory-driven and experiential-phenomenon-driven objective studies. All of the objective studies that Eric has considered are theory-driven; those that I would find adequate are experiential-phenomenon-driven.

For example, the mental rotation studies that are used to explore imagery are theory-driven. In an early such study, Cooper (1975) presented subjects with two random forms and asked them to decide whether the second form was reflected or rotated from the first. Cooper found that the greater the angle of rotation, the greater was the time necessary to perform this task, and therefore concluded that subjects were rotating mental images at some constant rate in the performance of this task.

The Cooper (1975) study and those that it spawned attempt to discover the characteristics of imagery without examining the experiential phenomena of imagery. However, as we have seen, DES studies show that people are quite different in their image experience: some have clear, detailed images all or nearly all the time; some have images not at all or hardly ever. It seems quite reasonable to wonder whether people who engage in detailed imagery nearly every waking moment would approach an imagery task in a substantially different way from that of people who rarely if ever engage in visual imagery in their everyday lives. Furthermore, mental rotation tasks may be quite irrelevant to the way people actually use imagery in their everyday lives.

I think it is possible to create tasks that would objectively explore images but that are based on the actual experiential phenomenology of images. Here are two examples.

DES observations of reading show that some people produce images as they read while others speak the read text in inner speech. [See box 5.3.] It seems reasonable to conjecture that there should be objective differences between those two groups—imagers may read faster, for example, than those whose reading is time-locked to the rhythm of external speech; imagers may make comprehension errors related to the inaccuracy of their images; and so on.

The second example follows from the DES observation that a minority of subjects have frequent what we call visual sensory awareness: they pay attention not so much to the objects of their environment but the sensory aspects of those objects: the color of the 7-Up can, the roughness of the stucco on the house, the particular way the skin folds around a smile, and so on. I have observed that one such person also finds it impossible to fuse random-dot stereograms. I further notice that the three-dimensional figures that emerge from fused random-dot stereograms have a substantially different phenomenology for me (who can fuse them easily) than do the stereograms themselves. The stereogram itself, before it is fused, seems real, whereas the staircase that emerges from the fused stereogram, while absolutely compelling in its three-dimensionality, seems derived, or constructed, or created, rather than perceptually real. All that leads me to speculate that people who habitually pay attention to the real sensory details of perception will have difficulty fusing stereograms because they have to leave those real sensory details behind in order to allow the more imaginary three-dimensional figure to emerge.

I don't know whether that speculation about sensory awareness and stereograms is true, but the example highlights the features of the experiential-phenomenology-driven objective studies that I would find compelling. First, a careful observation of the phenomenology of experience needs to be conducted. As the result of many DES studies, I know that most subjects who have frequent sensory awareness don't recognize that about themselves until sampling demonstrates it to them, and many people who believe they have frequent sensory awareness become convinced by sampling that they were mistaken. Thus it is *not* adequate merely to ask people about their experience, and it matters little whether that asking is done orally or by questionnaire. Second, subjects will have to be selected on the basis of careful examination of phenomena—it is not adequate to lump all subjects together. Third, such studies are conceptually easy (create two groups, one with much sensory awareness and one with little, and explore their stereogram abilities) but labor intensive (sensory awareness is relatively rare, and to determine its presence requires something like several days of DES exploration).

As far as I know, no study that differentiates readers on their *experience of reading*, or that differentiates stereogram fusers on their experience of visual sensory awareness, or any other such study that differentiates on the basis of carefully examined experiential phenomenon, has been performed. The closest study that I know of examined the inner experience of two groups, one whose subjects were objectively measured rapid talkers and one whose subjects spoke at more average rates (Hurlburt, Koch, and Heavey 2002). They found that fast talkers have richer, more complex experience than normal-rate talkers.

Thus, I agree with Eric on the desirability of objective investigations, but only if they are properly performed. I believe that objective studies that are sensitively tied to carefully explored experiential phenomena can be done, and that their results will likely be illuminating.

11.2 Replies to Eric's Reflections

11.2.1 On Eric's Rich-vs.-Thin Study

Eric's adaptation of DES to explore the richness of experience is in many ways an admirable study. First, I think he is correct in his analysis that the beeper method is better than concurrent introspection in this situation. Second, the study he describes is quite ambitious: 21 subjects is a lot for a descriptive sampling study. Third, I have listened to some of the tapes of Eric's interviews, and I can attest that he does in fact give his subjects a quite balanced introduction to the concepts "rich" and "thin."

Eric's subjects, despite his efforts, reported tactile experience in only half of samples, and tactile experience in the left foot in less than that. Thus out of the welter of possible facets of consciousness *only some few* are apparently manifested to Eric's subjects. Eric and I might disagree about the number of facets that are manifested; but whether that number is one or three or seven or "a lot" isn't nearly as important as the recognition that, at least as reported by his subjects and mine, experience does not include a broad array of many simultaneous experiences (that is, is not rich).

I think it may be a mistake to try to determine precisely how many facets are manifested because that determination depends far too closely on the details of the definitions like "attention," "faint," "peripheral," "experience," and so on. I might think that Eric too-heavy-handedly leads his subjects to describe visual experiences, but that leading probably adds only about 1 to the number of features his subject reports, perhaps increasing it from 2 to 3 or from 4 to 5. Eric might think that I too cavalierly disregard subjects' peripheral experience, but that disregard probably subtracts only about 1 from the subject's number of experiences. Thus, at a plus-or-minus-one-or-so level, Eric and I agree that our subjects can accurately identify only some limited number of facets as being experienced at any moment.

I think that to try to go further than that plus-or-minus-one-or-so level would be to fall into a trap that contributed greatly to the demise of classical introspection a century ago. As is well known, Titchener and the introspectors at Würzburg disagreed about the existence of imageless thought. Titchener held that all thoughts had imaginal cores. The Würzburgers, in opposition, maintained that they had discovered "imageless thought," occurrences of thinking that had no perceptible images whatsoever. Titchener retorted that all thoughts indeed had

imaginal cores, but some of these cores were so faint as to be impercep-
tible to all but the most highly skilled introspectors. Thousands of introspective hours were spent on both sides trying, without success, to resolve
the issue. The failure of introspection to agree about such a fundamentally important issue was seen as highlighting the inadequacy of introspection as a method, and, partially as a result (certainly there were other
important factors; see Danziger 1981), introspection was discredited for
the ensuing century.

However, Monson and Hurlburt (1993) showed that the introspecting
subjects in both Titchener's and the Würzburg labs gave highly similar
if not identical descriptions of the phenomena that the Würzburgers
called imageless thought; the disagreement came not in the descriptions
of the phenomena but in the interpretation of those descriptions.
Titchener and the Würzburgers were so focused on their differing
views of the fundamental building blocks of thinking that they failed
to appreciate how similar were their observations and descriptions of
phenomena.

Any attempt to use DES or any other phenomenological method to
determine the exact number of phenomena existing simultaneously in
experience is likely to fall into the same trap that snared Titchener and
the Würzburgers when they attempted to use classical introspection to
settle the imageless-thought debate. In both situations, investigators on
both sides observed similar phenomena. In both situations, the things
being investigated were (often) exceedingly faint. In both situations,
much depended on the fine points of definition.

Two further comments on Eric's rich-vs.-thin commentary:

First, he concludes that "we are on shaky ground using the reports of
subjects like Melanie to undermine the rich view," and by that apparently means that experience, despite the thin-to-moderate reports of
Melanie and his own subjects, may actually be radically rich. I agree that
it is entirely possible that experience is radically rich, but I also think
that the evaluation of that possibility is beyond the reach of phenomenological investigation. Eric's study is pretty good, and I think there is
not going to be a phenomenological study that is fundamentally better
(in a plus-or-minus-one sense) than his. Thus I think phenomenological
studies are going to incline toward some moderate position in the thin-
rich continuum. It is still possible to claim that experience *really* is radically rich and that all phenomenological studies miss that richness, but
(a) that claim has to be supported on some other basis and (b) it's
not fair to use that claim as an argument against phenomenological
investigations.

Second, when Eric asks subjects about visual experience in the far right visual field or about tactile experience in the left foot, he is asking them to ignore the most important aspects of experience (except in those rare cases where experience happens to be focused on the far right visual field or the left foot). In essence, he is asking his subjects to perform tasks that are almost impossible (unless you accept the strong form of the rich position) while at the same time avoiding the tasks that are centrally easy. I think that is highly problematic. Eric's interest in whether consciousness is rich or thin causes him to put more and more stress on things that are less and less clearly available to consciousness. DES is the opposite: it puts less and less stress on things that are less and less clearly available.

11.2.2 DES and Titchener's Introspection

Eric compares DES to Titchener's introspection and concludes: "It is by no means clear *a priori* whether Titchener's introspective methodology, which Russ rebukes, contains more potential for error than Russ's own methodology. Both have their apparent strengths and shortcomings." In reaching this conclusion, Eric points out that Titchener controlled conditions better than DES, but as we have seen in subsection 11.1.7.6, I think that is often a liability rather than an asset because control reifies presuppositions. Eric also points out that Titchener's studies typically have fewer memory demands; I will return to that issue in subsection 11.2.3, where I will conclude that it is not a severe problem.

At the same time, I believe that classical introspection made two major mistakes that DES avoids (three mistakes counting the experimental control issue), and I wish the reader to balance them against the criticisms of DES. First, the classical introspectionists failed to bracket presuppositions adequately and as a result failed to notice that their observations were quite consistent. I discussed that mistake in subsection 11.2.1, where I showed how DES avoids that mistake. Second, Titchener often emphasized the subtle at the expense of the obvious (Hurlburt and Heavey 2004). Titchener was primarily interested in fundamental mental processes and what we might call the psychophysical aspects of consciousness. His laboratory conducted experiments like comparing the relative brightness of two different colors; discerning a very low tone sensation from a sensation of atonal noise; making the quantitative assessment that two sensations are each an equal distance, in different directions, from a third; distinguishing difference (or combination) tones; reporting the characteristics of the "flight of colors" (complex afterimages); and perceiving non-obvious visual illusions. All those are obscure, although (according to Titchener) fundamental processes.

DES seeks to describe obvious incidental occurrences, not fundamental processes. If inner speech happens to be present at the moment of the beep, DES describes that speech; if an image happens to be present, DES describes that image; and so on. DES is *not* interested in obscure or the hard to detect processes, theoretically fundamental or not.

As a result, Titchener and DES come at phenomena from opposing directions. Titchener had to train his introspectors to *suppress* the very things that DES seeks to *discover*—whatever happens to be passing through awareness at any given moment—whereas DES trains subjects to ignore any interest in fundamental processes and simply pay attention to the details of whatever incidental occurrence happens to be ongoing. The DES task is substantially easier than that of Titchener's introspection, and this accounts for the large differences in training time required.

I use the difference tone studies as an example because they are rather typical of Titchener's introspection, because Eric has provided a very useful discussion and example of Titchener's difference-tone training procedure at http://www.faculty.ucr.edu/~eschwitz, and because they illustrate the introspectionists' (and Eric's) overconcern with small effects.

A difference tone (sometimes called a combination tone) is a lower tone that is heard when two higher notes are played loudly together. For example, suppose you hear two trumpets playing loud tones, one at 800 hertz and the other at 1,000 hertz. You may also hear a third, quieter tone whose frequency is 200 hertz, the difference between 800 and 1,000 (thus the name "difference tone"), as if three instruments were playing instead of two.

Difference tones are well-known musical effects, but they are quite subtle in comparison to the actually played notes: the two original notes are loud while the difference tone is soft. Eric goes to great lengths to ensure that visitors to his website can detect the difference tones, telling them to increase the volume so that it is "unpleasant but not painfully loud," to get better audio speakers, to practice with remedial stimuli, to take breaks to "cleanse the palate," and so on. Difference tones are thus soft sounds audible only when two other voices are very loud, and are therefore by no means the most salient feature of the experiential world. Surely, then, we must accept that the difference-tone demonstration is asking subjects to do difficult things.

The difference-tone demonstration shows that subjects have difficulty noticing and/or identifying phenomena that are known to exist, an important observation that justifiably should give rise to some skepticism about introspective reports. However, it is important to keep that skepticism targeted at the subtle or difficult introspections and not to overgeneralize, as has sometimes been done, to all introspection tasks. I would go one step further: If subjects have difficulty making difficult introspections, then until the science of experience matures substantially, we shouldn't ask that of them. Instead, we should prefer to ask them to make the relatively easy introspections that have been overlooked for at least 100 years.

11.2.3 Does DES Have the Same Defects as Eyewitness Testimony?

Eric believes that the eyewitness testimony literature calls into question the veridicality of DES reports, noting that people tend greatly to overestimate the trustworthiness of eyewitness reports. He further maintains that it is *comparatively easy* to report outward events, so Melanie's testimony about inner experience may well be considerably less accurate than typical eyewitness testimony.

I think Eric is correct to characterize eyewitness reports as being largely untrustworthy. I agree that eyewitnesses can be influenced by the specifics of the questioning. I agree that most people substantially overestimate the accuracy of eyewitness testimony. However, I see two main reasons that Melanie's reports are likely to be considerably *more* accurate than eyewitness testimony.

First, I created DES in full knowledge of the eyewitness testimony literature and designed it specifically to minimize eyewitness-type errors. For example, the eyewitness literature suggests that it is better to have witnesses tell their stories initially in their own words and in their own manner before external questioning begins. We ask DES subjects to do that. Eyewitness testimony suggests that words such as "smashed" can have substantial impact by comparison to words such as "hit." DES explicitly tries to be neutral in its word choice, usually using the subject's own words. The eyewitness literature suggests that the less retrospective the report, the better; DES minimizes retrospection. And so on. Eric, having observed my interviewing at close range, has identified few or no specific areas where when we sampled with Melanie we failed to follow the principles that the eyewitness literature (and other literatures) suggest would be desirable. Thus, Eric's argument apparently is that even though I (or Eric and I) have conducted these interviews with a very high level of skill and with substantial sophistication about the problematics of eyewitness testimony, there is still the possibility that our interviews fall prey to the same kinds of errors that plague eyewitnesses. I agree that that is possible, but it seems likely that because we (I think quite successfully) substantially reduced, if not eliminated, precisely those influences that the eyewitness literature finds important, what eyewitness pressures that remain are likely to be orders of magnitude more subtle than the kinds of factors explored by the eyewitness literature. Therefore I think that it is not fair to apply the criticisms that justifiably apply to eyewitness testimony to skillfully implemented DES.

Second, the eyewitness paradigm differs from DES in that the eyewitness observations are always one-shot, no-preparation, no-training events, usually in emotion-arousing situations, whereas DES involves substantial training, support, clarification, and practice. To apply an eyewitness-testimony study's results to DES, the study would have to have approximately the following instructions:

As you go about your everyday activities for about three hours this afternoon, you will encounter six incidents of potential petty theft. Each instance will be identified immediately afterward by a clear, unambiguous signal. Furthermore, these events will be arranged so that they always take place directly in your view—for example, you will not need to turn around and look to see the event.

Within 24 hours of seeing these six events, an insurance agent will call you and ask you to report what you have seen; therefore we ask that immediately following each event, you take whatever notes you think might be relevant so that they might remind you of the details of the event. That agent will not be interested in what happened before or what happened after the petty theft, but only what was happening at the moment of the signal.

During the course of the interview, the insurance agent (who, by the way, is extremely highly skilled) will help you to understand what is meant by "at the moment of the signal," help you to refine your observational skills, help you to clarify what you should have been paying attention to and what not, help you to clarify what might be useful to record in your initial notes, and so on.

Then the next day, you will observe another six potential petty thefts, following which the skilled insurance agent will again help you to improve your skills. That will be repeated for a half dozen or so days, perhaps 36 potential petty thefts in all. We may largely ignore your observations of the first 6 or so petty thefts, because you will be mastering the skill of theft-observation.

Furthermore, the agent will work for neither the prosecution nor the defense, and is genuinely interested only in discovering what you saw, not what is best for his/her client nor indeed in what actually happened.

I don't think there any eyewitness testimony studies that are in the same universe as that. And I don't think that that vignette overdraws the situation; in fact, I think that that minimizes the skill-of-the-insurance-agent part of the situation. The thought experiment to be undertaken is, Would the eyewitness in such a study learn to be an accurate reporter of petty theft details? I think so. A highly accurate reporter? I think so. A perfect reporter? I think not.

Eric makes two additional eyewitness points. The first is that what we asked Melanie to observe was closer than any outward event, and that the observation of such close-up characteristics is "strange and difficult" by comparison to the attending to outward events. Eric acknowledges that Melanie improved in this regard, and I think adequately. But if he thinks Melanie's improvement was not adequate, then we should be able to minimize this difficulty by sampling over more days. Furthermore, observing an outward event is not as easy as Eric implies: Usually eyewitnesses are *not* looking at the event at its outset and must orient themselves to it and thereby usually don't see the important initial details; furthermore, eyewitnesses are not always in a good position (too far away, obscured by darkness or a tree, etc.) to see the event. The second additional eyewitness point is that Eric thinks that introspectors are in a worse position than are eyewitnesses because introspectors often find themselves reporting experiences they would have thought were impossible (unsymbolized thinking, for example), whereas eyewitnesses often find themselves reporting events that they would find merely surprising, not impossible. I think that is a justifiable criticism of one-shot introspection but not of DES: the explicitly iterative, acquire-this-skill-over-several-days feature of the DES procedure is specifically designed to mitigate that criticism. The typical subject who eventually will report unsymbolized thinking finds that phenomenon unthinkable on the first sampling day, threatening but perhaps possible on the second day, open-mindedly possible on the third day, and obviously occurring on the fourth. It is the art of the interviewer to open up possibilities gradually while at the same time maintaining a dispassionate even-handedness about actualities.

Eric's point is that overcoming perceived impossibility is more difficult than overcoming perceived unlikelihood, but I disagree with that. Some presuppositions are more difficult to overcome than others, but that has little to do with whether impossibility or merely unlikelihood is at issue. If a robbery witness holds the presupposition (more often called the prejudice) that most robberies are committed by blacks, his testimony is likely to be distorted even though he would easily recognize the possibility that a robber could be white. That presupposition/prejudice is false, just as false as is the presupposition against unsymbolized thinking. But I think overcoming the robbery prejudice is more difficult (for a variety of shameful reasons) than overcoming the presupposition against unsymbolized thinking, even though the person might at the outset think unsymbolized thinking is impossible.

Thus, an important difference between DES and eyewitness testimony is that DES explicitly and repeatedly tries to identify and bracket such presuppositions before the observations are made, and that is simply not possible in eyewitness events.

The eyewitness testimony literature is important because it points out some of the things that can be problematic in reports. It is highly useful in that it can be and has been mined for suggestions about how to avoid errors in reports. Eric and I agree that DES does avoid some of those potential errors, and we agree that DES can*not* be said to have avoided *all* of the potential errors. Eric and I disagree on the extent to which DES may have been successful in reducing the influence of the theories and expectations of the witness and interviewer; I think he may not have seen enough good DES interviews and he thinks I may be captured by the overconfidence of the witness. Because there are substantial differences between DES and eyewitness testimony, I think it is unfair simply to extrapolate eyewitness criticisms to DES. However, I do think it is fair to be wary and to seek ways to evaluate DES informed by the failures of eyewitness testimony. I look forward to those studies.

11.2.4   Does DES Rely Too Heavily on Memory?

Eric is concerned that errors of memory may lead Melanie to confabulate, if not in the minute or so after the beep when the subject is first reflecting on her sampled experience, then in the interview itself up to 24 hours later. I agree with Eric as a matter of principle that any human science researcher must be concerned about the veridicality of memory, and in fact, have spent much of my career criticizing retrospective measures.

However, the historical fact is that my colleagues and I have explored the data collection aspect of DES investigations in a variety of informal ways. We have followed subjects into their natural environments and conducted expositional interviews on the spot, and we have arranged situations where subjects sampled in my presence. Those efforts minimize the problems of retrospection but increase the experimenter's intrusiveness. I have positioned myself "on the edge" of the subject's environment, for example, by sitting in my car parked outside a subject's house, and asked the subject to come to me immediately after being beeped. That's a compromise between minimizing retrospection and increasing intrusiveness. We have conducted the "standard" DES except that we have insisted that the expositional interview take place on the same day as the sampling, thus reducing the retrospectiveness (from about 24 hours to about 4 hours) and eliminating whatever distortions might be caused by the intervening sleep. We have allowed longer-than-24-hour delays between sampling and interview. We have asked subjects to take long notes and short notes. We have asked subjects to tape record responses rather than write them, on the probability that more detail would be provided in the recorded statement.

The result of all these explorations is that, as far as I can tell, it doesn't make much difference how the initial recording is made or when the interview is performed as long as it's within about 24 hours of the sampling. Certainly I agree that the shorter the retrospection the better, but only up to the point that the shortness of the interval causes experimenter intrusiveness. Certainly I agree that the longer the retrospection, the more likely that some details will be confabulated. However, I have granted all along that some details are confabulated, and I don't see a small increase in confabulation as overly serious. I do not think that a trained subject will confabulate the main characteristics as the result of a less-than-24-hour delay.

I grant that most of these explorations have been informal and all of the resulting observations were made by one group, namely me and my colleagues. But at the same time, I believe we were serious and committed observers, willing to alter the DES procedure in whatever way we thought was necessary to obtain what I thought were accurate reports. My sense is that the length of the delay is more crucial early in the training of a DES subject, and that the interval can probably be relaxed somewhat with a subject who, because of DES experience, knows what is being asked and what is at stake.

I can easily imagine that future, more formal studies might show that 24 hours is too long for some purposes. If that happens, then I of course would recommend shortening the interval between obtaining the sample and discussing it.

11.2.5   Do Subtle Interview Pressures Have Large Effects?

Eric believes that the large and compelling body of evidence in social psychology (reviewed, for example, in Ross and Nisbett 1991) has demonstrated that subtle features of a situation can have a striking impact on behavior. I agree that situations have important influences on behavior. I agree that most people substantially underestimate the importance of the situation. However, Eric seems to use that literature as a strong argument against our believing Melanie, and I disagree with that conclusion for much the same reason that I disagreed with his use of the eyewitness testimony literature against our understanding of Melanie.

There are two main points here.

First, the effects of subtle features on behavior have been substantially overstated, in my view, by the situationism literature in general and Eric in particular. Eric refers to the situational manipulations repeatedly as being "subtle," and in this regard he follows in the path of Ross and Nisbett (1991) and many others. For example, Ross and Nisbett introduce their section titled "Social Influence and Group Processes" as follows:

This chapter's review of classic studies of social influence and situational control will emphasize two themes: first, that social pressures and other situational factors exert effects on behavior that are more potent than we generally recognize, and second, that to understand the impact of a given social situation, we often need to attend to its subtle details. (Ross and Nisbett 1991, p. 28)

However, most of the manipulation examples that Ross and Nisbett cite are not at all subtle. Here are their lead-off topics: Sherif's (1937) confederate consistently and substantially misrepresents his "autokinetic effect" estimates, giving "estimates that were either *consistently much higher or consistently much lower* than those typically made by subjects left to make judgments on their own" (Ross and Nisbett 1991, p. 29; emphasis added). Asch (1951, 1952, 1955, 1956) had ten "subjects" in a room, of which nine were actually confederates who substantially misrepresented their length estimates, "with no hesitation or expression of indecision, *offered a patently wrong answer*" (Ross and Nisbett 1991, p. 30; emphasis added). Newcomb (1943) found that "young women from predominantly upper-middle-class families entered Bennington College between 1935 and 1939, sharing the generally conservative Republican political views and voting preferences of their parents. Within a couple of years, after having been exposed to the Bennington milieu, the students' views and preferences had shifted far to the left of those of their family members and of most other Americans of their social class" (Ross and Nisbett 1991, p. 35). The several-year influence of roommates, friends, professors, activities, and so can hardly be called subtle; neither should "much higher" or "patently wrong" untrue verbalizations. Ross and Nisbett's summary illustration—in its own section, titled "Putting It All Together" (1991, pp. 52–58)—was Milgram's shock-administration study, which may be as instructive for us as it was for Ross and Nisbett. Two people appear at the laboratory to become subjects in an experiment. In plain view of both subjects, slips are drawn, and one subject becomes the "teacher" and the other becomes the "learner." The experimenter instructs the teacher to administer ever-increasing doses of electric shock to the learner, saying things like "the experiment requires you to continue; *you have no choice*" (Ross and Nisbett 1991, p. 57, emphasis added). (Unknown to the "teacher," the "learner" is actually a confederate of the experimenter, and no shocks are actually administered.) This experimental manipulation was not subtle; "you have no choice" is subtlety's diametric opposite. Thus, Ross and Nisbett's chapter leads the reader to believe that subtle influences have dramatic effects, but their primary and most dramatic examples are not at all subtle. Certainly there are studies where subtle influences do have somewhat large effects—I would probably call Isen and Levin's (1972) dime-in-the-phone and Intons-Peterson's (1983) hand-position priming studies that Eric cites "subtle." However, the results of those studies are usually substantially less dramatic than the than the ones Ross and Nisbett emphasize. Thus I agree that Ross and Nisbett, and many others, have convincingly demonstrated that the situation is indeed important in determining behavior. However, Ross and Nisbett, and many others often overemphasize the subtlety of these situational determinants and the strikingness of their effects.

Second, one of Ross and Nisbett's main conclusions is that the situational influences that they identify can be effectively mitigated by "opening up the channel factor." Ross and Nisbett define "channel factor" as follows:

When we find an apparently small situational circumstance producing a big behavioral effect, we are justified in suspecting we have identified a channel factor, that is, a stimulus or a response pathway that serves to elicit or sustain behavioral intentions with particular intensity or stability. (1991, p. 46)

According to Ross and Nisbett, as a result of this channel factor, Milgram's "teachers" administer extremely high doses of electric shock to the learners. However, Ross and Nisbett believed that undermining one, some, or all of the features of the channel factors in Milgram's study would have dramatically weakened the effectiveness of the communication:

Suppose that the experimenter [Milgram] had announced at the beginning of the session that, if at any time the teacher wished to terminate his participation in the experiment, he could indicate his desire to do so by pressing a button on the table in from of him. We trust the reader agrees with us that if this channel factor had been opened up, the obedience rate would have been a fraction of what it was. (ibid., p. 57)

Thus, Ross and Nisbett themselves recognized that the obedience-engendering characteristics of situations can be substantially mitigated. Merely giving the subject the explicit right to terminate participation, Ross and Nisbett apparently thought, was enough to wipe out or at least dramatically reduce Milgram's situational influence.

DES was created in full recognition of the situational influences that Nisbett, Ross, and many others have observed on communications. DES incorporates clear, unequivocal, multiple "channel-opening" instructions to forestall such influences. For example, we explicitly and repeatedly conveyed to Melanie that she could withdraw at any time; that saying "I don't know" or "I don't remember" was a perfectly legitimate response, that we valued her best effort over any predetermined expectation; that it was quite possible that things wouldn't be clear and that that was okay; that the task was perhaps impossible; that we would learn as much or more from her inability to perform a task as we would from her ability to perform it easily; that we much preferred her unexaggerated candor to any attempt to figure out what we wanted to hear; and so on. Not only did we say such things repeatedly, but we meant them sincerely; and not only did we mean them sincerely, I think Melanie recognized that we meant them sincerely. Therefore, by Ross and Nisbett's own argument, we, I think, successfully undermined the channel effect and therefore should *not* expect large obedience effects.

I have quibbled with Ross and Nisbett's and Eric's use of the word "subtle" not for merely pedantic reasons, but because the "subtle" pressures that might be applied by us to Melanie are not the same as the "subtle" pressures Ross and Nisbett reviewed. I fully accept that a justified claim of subtle pressure might still be made by saying that despite our repeated, explicit instructions to the contrary; and despite the fact that an avowed skeptic, knowledgeable about the situationism literature, watched the procedure every step of the way and could not identify any explicit pressure communications; we still somehow subtly conveyed to Melanie, by word, deed, or situation, that she must give responses that went far beyond what she could remember. However, we should recognize that that would truly be a very subtle pressure, far more subtle than most if not all of the situations examined in the situationism literature. It therefore seems unfair broadly to invoke Ross and Nisbett against our DES interview of Melanie.

I have no reason to deny categorically the existence of such a subtle pressure in general, nor its existence in our interaction with Melanie, but it does seem more unlikely than likely that such subtle pressures as we may have applied had a large effect.

11.3 About the Form of this Book

As we described in chapter 1, our collaboration, including Melanie's participation therein, was originally intended to be a private conversation between Eric and me. Once we decided to shape this ongoing conversation into a publicly available book, we were faced with the problem of how to continue our frank and private, tentative and exploratory conversations alongside our public ones, and so we developed the following scheme. We agreed that with respect to any given topic, we would initially communicate with each other in what we called the Personal-Russ-Eric (or PRE) mode. Either of us could initiate a PRE communication. If I wrote in the PRE mode, I would try to say exactly what I really thought, without undue need for documentation or undue concern for Eric's feelings or sensitivities. My PRE comment invited a reply by Eric in the same PRE mode: He could give his view on the same issue; he could agree or disagree with what I had said; he could ask me for clarification or simply supply his own clarification; etc. Once we felt we both understood what was really going on in the conversation, we trimmed and simplified the exchanges, or discarded them as being irrelevant now that issues had been clarified. Consequently, much of what follows each of the "Russ:" icons in this book is actually my point of view as clarified, corrected, expanded, contracted, and otherwise adjusted by Eric; similarly the "Eric:" comments have been shaped by me. A few of the Russ: comments were actually originally written by Eric, and vice versa.

There are two reasons that I think this mode of collaboration is worthy of comment.

First, it was a genuinely engaged collaboration. There is no talking past one another in this book—we tried as best we could to clarify with/for each other exactly what was meant at every sentence in this book. This is not an essay in favor followed by an essay in opposition that leaves neither party unchanged (or, worse, hardened). On the contrary, this is teamwork by two trusting but differing individuals that leaves both (and hopefully the reader) bettered by the process. I now find myself thinking about things and saying things in ways that Eric would think and speak, and Eric finds himself voicing my thoughts as well.

Second, Eric's and my collaborative process seems directly in the spirit of the DES values. In the PRE mode, Eric and I tried to be as direct with each other as possible about specific, concrete issues (to what extent did Russ believe what Melanie said at 24:05 in transcript 4, for example); we accepted those communications as being preliminary attempts that were aimed at some particular thing but not necessarily reported in high fidelity; we helped the other to clarify what was thought and what was said; we improved those skills over time; and so on. That process of trying to be as clear as possible with each other about specific concrete issues is very similar if not exactly the same as our trying to be as clear as possible with Melanie about her specific, concrete experiences. Everything in this project was tied to specific, concrete instances. I think that's rare; we found it to be quite valuable.

11.4   Conclusion

This study has left me quite optimistic about the future of the science of inner experience. I'm confident that it is possible to fashion introspective methods that keep most of the risks that we have discussed at bay, that we should not tar all methods of exploration of inner experience with the broad brush that tarred introspection. I'm confident that there is much of importance to be learned about inner experience, and that it is possible to explore it with accuracy. Much hinges on science's ability to learn and teach observational skills, including, very importantly, the skill of bracketing presuppositions. It *can* be done; whether it *will* be done only time will tell.

I would have said all that before embarking on this project with Eric. In that light it might seem that I have been unmoved by our interaction, but that is substantially untrue. On the contrary, my thinking about all the issues raised in this book has been clarified, deepened, disexaggerated, amplified, corrected. That has been so thoroughgoing a process that it is now impossible to remember a time when I wasn't so clarified, deepened, and so on.

The question, I guess, is whether this clarification is of value to the reader. I hope so. I think the issues that Eric and I have debated are important. I do believe that the care that Eric and I have taken to "get it right" with and for each other is evidenced in every box and every discussion in this book, with the result that the issues are left pretty well exposed without too many (implied or assumed or taken for granted) distracting excesses—he has trimmed mine away, and I his. We may not have resolved those issues, but I trust that this project has provided a step in the right direction.

And as my last word, thanks again to Melanie.

12   Eric's Response to Russ, and Some Parting Thoughts

Eric Schwitzgebel

12.1 Response to Russ's Reflections

At a certain level of description, Russ and I believe the same thing. Both of us are inclined to accept the grosser aspects of Melanie's reports and to treat the details cautiously. We both think that beep-and-interview methods of the sort described in this book are an important tool for studying consciousness. Yet in a way this appearance of common ground is misleading: We diverge considerably in our assessment of the virtues of the present method relative to other existing and prior methods, such as the methods of early introspective psychology (e.g., Titchener) and philosophical armchair reflection (e.g., Siewert). We differ substantially in *how far* to trust the gross features of Melanie's reports—that is, her "exposed" reports as [see subsection 11.1.2.1] brought out by Russ: I trust only tentatively, while Russ is pretty confident. And we differ in what counts as a detail small enough not to warrant even tentative acceptance: I recommend skepticism about all but the general topic and main content while Russ is willing to accept a considerably finer level of detail.

Our interaction has, as both Russ and I think, substantially deepened our thinking without—perhaps predictably—moving us very much from our original positions. For my part, though, I have become convinced that interviews of this sort are as trustworthy as any other method of studying consciousness—which is to say, not very trustworthy at all, but better than nothing. I have begun to envision potentially suggestive experiments turning on developments of the method, which in conjunction with a variety of other methods and considerations might begin to show something.

I am in sympathy with much of what Russ says in section 11.1—especially regarding faux generalizations, inner speech, the desirability and difficulty of objective observations, and the importance of the personal.

I like his personal stories about failing to bracket presuppositions, and I find his treatment of Flavell interesting. His points against me in section 11.2 have some merit, too, though in the end I am not persuaded.

Our different assessments of Flavell reflect and illustrate, I think, two fundamental disagreements between us that may underwrite our different summary assessments of Melanie's trustworthiness: First, Russ is more optimistic than I about the accuracy of immediate retrospection (given certain precautions). Second, Russ is readier than I to see radical differences in people's inner lives. He isn't put off by seeming strangeness or by the fact that people's reports diverge widely.

Such broad differences of perspective aren't easily rebutted in a short space. I can only repeat some general considerations I have touched on throughout this book: the fundamental physiological and behavioral similarity between people; the general lack of behavioral differences corresponding to differences in experiential report (e.g., in the literature on imagery); the instability of our claims about experience, even when conscientiously introspected or immediately retrospected (e.g., people's tendency to change their opinions about peripheral visual experience and echolocatory experience in conversation with me; see box 4.18, Schwitzgebel and Gordon 2000, and Schwitzgebel, in preparation); the history of divergent and changing views in philosophy and psychology; the fleeting and (probably) complex nature of experience; the novelty of the task; the room for reconstruction, bias, theory-driven distortion, and capture by metaphor; the difficulty of conceptualizing experience and articulating it verbally. All this together suggests, to me, that when people differ in how they describe the basic structure of their experiences, even when their reports are collected as carefully as Russ collects them, these differences may often fail accurately to reflect real differences in the experiences themselves. At a basic, structural level, we may be fairly similar inside, though we answer questions about our experience differently.

Russ's charming story about failing to recognize his own unsymbolized thinking (subsection 11.1.7.4) prompts further reflections along these lines. Maybe unsymbolized thinking, if it exists, is particularly difficult to conceptualize and articulate, so that at first some people will misreport it as something else or miss it entirely. Russ has suggested (subsection 11.1.3) that people tend especially to overreport inner speech on the first interview day, due to a preconception that inner speech is a typical mode of thought; some shift later to reporting more unsymbolized thinking. I wonder then whether a subject reports unsymbolized thinking or not may depend at least as much on her personality or approach to the task as on her underlying experience. Surely some people are better at changing their minds and recognizing the unexpected than others. Some will be more willing to appear uncertain and inexpert, to go through the awkwardness Russ characterizes as typical of the first report of unsymbolized thinking. Some might tend to ignore "unsymbolized" aspects of their experience, if any, in favor of more easily reportable visual imagery and the like. Some might be less conscientious about whether their thoughts really do involve inner speech or not, if reports of inner speech meet with the approval of the interviewer. Maybe, for example, it is in Russ's personality to be willing to say "I'm a bad subject, I don't have any idea what to say about this sample" and less in Melanie's personality, and it is this characterological difference that underlies their difference in reporting, rather than a real difference in underlying experience.

Russ suggests I might grow less skeptical if I were exposed to as many subjects as he has been, each interviewed as carefully as we have interviewed Melanie. He may be right. However, conversely, Russ's judgment may be as colored and distorted by his long dedication to the method, and the social and emotional commitments that flow from that, as mine is impoverished by limited exposure. I see no ideal standpoint.

Russ's particular criticisms of me in section 11.2—expressing our different stands on what can and should be "bracketed," our different sense of the impact of subtle social pressures, our different assessments of the comparison to eyewitness testimony—these issues also seem mostly to turn on broad matters of perspective and judgment in the face of conflicting evidence. I will not repeat my reasons for relative pessimism here. I don't think Russ has proven me wrong. Rather, he has articulated a different interpretation of the mass of difficult and discordant data. I acknowledge that his perspective is a reasonable and attractive one, arising from a long career of careful study. Reading his chapter, I almost believe it. I would *like* to believe it. I hope the next few decades will shed more light on the matter.

12.2 What Should We Want From These Interviews?

I may also be more dissatisfied with these interviews for another reason: Whereas Russ is principally interested in the central, most easily reported aspects of Melanie's experience and in the particular, idiographic picture of Melanie that emerges, I have wanted mainly to explore general, structural issues in consciousness. The questions I focus on seem often to be particularly difficult to answer, requiring subtle discernment or conceptual sophistication or an accurate recollection of details not salient to Melanie in the moments after the beep. Consider for example my questions about whether Melanie's experience is rich or thin (beep 1.1), whether her emotional experience is exhausted by bodily sensations (e.g., beep 2.2), how broad the range of clarity is in her visual experience (beep 1.3). Presumably, Melanie might more easily go wrong in such matters than about, say, whether she had an image of airplanes in beep 2.2 or was feeling confident in beep 6.1. Thus, Russ and I hope for different things from these interviews, not equally easy to achieve. Russ wants a mostly accurate view of central features of Melanie's experience, and he thinks we've attained that. I want insight into some of the big structural and theoretical questions about consciousness, and I'm not sure we have attained that.

Have we achieved what Russ wants? I don't know. I find something to hesitate over in each major portion of Russ's summary of Melanie's idiosyncrasies. Russ says Melanie is especially self-observational; but I wonder whether that sense might derive simply from Melanie's having fallen into different ways of *expressing* what is essentially similar between people, given the inherent difficulty conceptualizing and communicating about self-consciousness. [See box 9.5.] Russ says Melanie tends to pay attention to sensory aspects of her environment—not just to the objects themselves but to the sensations they produce in her; but I'm concerned about the difficulty of distinguishing memory of external objects from memory of the sensory experiences those external objects produce in us. [See beep 2.4.] Russ says Melanie has detailed visual imagery; but I worry that that detail may be created in the reconstruction of those images without having been present in the original imagery. [See box 5.4.] Russ accepts the basic characteristics of Melanie's reports of her emotional experience; but I remain concerned about the difficulty of accurately reporting the structural aspects of emotion. [See beep 2.2 and boxes 5.14 and 5.15.] Still, despite these worries, I can't help but feel that we do have at least *some* tentative sense of Melanie's experience and how it might differ from the experiences of others. Maybe she inclines more toward visual imagery, for example. We might profitably contrast our data about Melanie with similarly obtained data from other subjects, or we might attempt to associate Melanie's measurable abilities and behavioral patterns with her reports. Acquiring *any* usable data is already no mean accomplishment, as Russ emphasizes in his conclusion.

But should we want more? Or better, can we *reasonably hope* for more—something more general, more theoretical, more foundational? Or am I, in wanting insight already into general, structural questions about consciousness, displaying the "impatience" (subsection 11.1.5) or the "asking too much" (subsection 11.2.2) that Russ rebukes? Should we restrain ourselves, start only with the rough approximation of particular individuals, and postpone the grand theoretical questions? That, at least, would be highly unusual in the history of science. From the beginning, every science I know of has sought answers to broad, theoretical questions in tandem with the accurate portrayal of particular details.

At a minimum, Russ has convinced me that candidly facing a subject whose reports about experience seem (to the interviewer!) strange and surprising—whether that subject is ultimately correct and trustworthy or not—opens up avenues for inquiry and argument that may previously have remained unnoticed. Does inner speech or hearing really have to elapse over time (beep 6.4)? Could emotional experience literally possess color for many people (box 4.7)? People diverge more than most of us tend to assume in what they find obvious or plausible about conscious experience, and frank interview is one way to cast light on those divergences.

Furthermore, even if Melanie's answers by themselves aren't entirely convincing, it's possible that a *pattern* of answers from a variety of subjects may nonetheless illuminate even subtle and difficult structural issues—especially if that pattern is corroborated by data from other methods. For example, I find Russ's encounter with unsymbolized thinking suggestive. And surely this is a deep, structural question about conscious experience if anything is. (See, e.g., Carruthers 1996; Siewert 1998; Horgan and Tienson 2002; Wilson 2003; Pitt 2004; Robinson 2005.)

12.3   The Future of Consciousness Studies

If the study of consciousness is to thrive, researchers must face up to, and not minimize, the serious methodological problems at the heart of the discipline. Our everyday, intuitive impressions about inner experience are divergent, unstable, and ill informed. Philosophers can't simply reflect from the armchair and expect to find the truth within easy reach. Psychologists and neuroscientists can't simply ask their subjects about inner experience and expect accurate, trustworthy reports representative of how experience transpires in everyday contexts. Common sense and modern philosophy are badly mistaken if they suggest that ordinary people, reflecting in ordinary ways, have a good and ready grasp of their stream of experience. Introspective methodologies that build uncritically on that supposed grasp will inevitably fail.

Nonetheless, most researchers in consciousness still depend on some combination of unsystematic armchair reflection and naive report; and attempts to systematize and regulate, to sort the good from the bad, garner very little agreement between laboratories (or armchairs). Chaos and dissension reign, even about the apparently simplest facts and methods, undermining the basic data of the field. In every science, of course, there is *some* dispute about what data to credit and dismiss, but in consciousness studies the dissent and divergence are so extreme as practically to cripple the enterprise. Until this situation is resolved, the field will remain a pandemonium of theories with little common ground. Consciousness studies is not yet a mature or progressing science.

Russ and I disagree to what extent careful interview can overcome these difficulties. Russ is optimistic; I am less so. We can't claim to have resolved this question in this book. What have we done, then? Maybe we have helped illuminate the issue by casting our different, and conflicting, lights upon it? I'm not sure I'm ready to endorse even that characterization. Our lights play tricks on us. I don't know if this book is in any way an advance. I will say this, at least: We have offered this interchange in the spirit of friendly conflict and in faith in Socrates's (and Mill's, and Habermas's, and Feyerabend's) precept that open dialogue will eventually show a way forward.

Appendix A: Lists of Boxes and Threads

Boxes

2.1 A note about terminology: "inner experience" or "conscious experience"?

2.2 Summary of sampling methods

2.3 The truth, the whole truth, and nothing but the truth

2.4 Open-beginninged questions

2.5 Nisbett and Wilson's critique exempted DES, and indeed (contrary to myth) consciousness generally.

2.6 How compelling is the Case of Robert?

3.1 Churchland's thought experiments

3.2 Dennett on introspection of current conscious experience

3.3 How should we interpret Flavell's children?

3.4 On experience while reading

4.1 What is "thinking"?

4.2 Doubts about Melanie's "inner thought" voice

4.3 Present tense or past tense?

4.4 Fast or normally paced speech?

4.5 Evidence that Melanie is careful. The pace of inner speech, continued.

4.6 Bracketing the known characteristics of the outside world

4.7 Color in emotional experience

4.8 The periphery of experience

4.9 Should we believe Melanie's report of her first sample?

4.10 Focusing on a single moment and the dynamics of experience

9.4 More on Russ's use of "awareness"

9.5 Consolidating Melanie's sense that she is self-analytical

9.6 Melanie's carefulness

9.7 Melanie's experience of activity

9.8 Mozart's claim to hear a symphony instantaneously

9.9 Should unusual reports be held to a higher standard of evidence?

9.10 Do people know when they are being metaphorical?

9.11 Is DES an example of irreducibly "first-person" science?

Threads

Bracketing presuppositions: boxes 2.6, 3.3, 4.6, 4.10, 5.7, 7.4, 7.13, 8.3, 8.5, 9.9; section 10.6; subsection 11.1.7

Emotion: boxes 4.7, 5.13, 5.15, 6.2, 6.3, 7.4, 7.9, 8.5, 8.8, 8.9

Human similarity and difference: boxes 2.6, 3.3, 4.1, 4.7, 4.18, 4.20, 5.3, 7.4, 7.12, 8.8, 8.9, 9.9; section 12.1

Influence of metaphors: boxes 4.7, 5.2, 9.10

Inner speech and hearing: boxes 4.2, 4.4, 4.5, 4.11, 5.7, 6.5; subsection 11.1.7.7

Interview techniques: 2.3, 2.4, 4.3, 4.6, 4.15, 4.17, 4.19, 5.10, 5.12, 5.17, 7.3, 8.6; section 2.2

Limits of DES: 4.10, 5.14, 9.2, 9.10; subsections 11.2.1, 12.2

Loose language: 2.1, 4.1, 5.16, 7.9, 8.6, 8.9, 9.4; section 3.3

Melanie's Trustworthiness: Attunement to distinctions: boxes 4.5, 6.4, 7.8, 8.9, 9.6

Melanie's Trustworthiness: Details: boxes 4.13, 5.14, 7.3, 8.1, 8.2, 9.6; section 10.4; section 10.5; subsection 11.2.1; section 12.2

Melanie's Trustworthiness: General: boxes 4.9, 5.7, 5.16, 7.15, 7.16; chapters 10 and 11, *passim*

Melanie's Trustworthiness: Influence of generalizations: boxes 4.2, 4.11, 4.14, 4.18, 7.1, 7.14, 9.3; section 10.4

Melanie's Trustworthiness: Interview pressures: boxes 4.17, 5.1, 5.11, 5.12, 7.3, 8.1; subsection 2.3.1; section 10.5; subsection 11.2.5

Melanie's Trustworthiness: Memory: boxes 4.8, 5.4, 7.5, 7.6; section 10.4; subsection 11.2.4

Appendix B: Summaries of Beeps

These are summaries of Melanie's "exposed" reports, as the phrase is defined in subsection 11.1.2.1. We leave it to the reader to determine with how much skepticism they should be met.

Beep 1.1 (pp. 40–75)

Melanie was unpacking a chair and saying to herself "How funny it is that I just received the chair and now I have to plan who is to inherit." The experience was more like inner hearing than inner speech and proceeded at a fast pace without feeling rushed. She associated a rosy yellow glow, which seemed to completely surround her, with the humor of that thought. Although her eyes were aimed at parchment paper, Melanie had little or no experience of it at the moment of the beep.

Beep 1.2 (pp. 73–80)

Melanie was going from the hallway into the kitchen and saying to herself, this time more in inner speech than inner hearing, "You can think you're really busy but even during those busy times there are periods of empty time." She also had visual experience of the stove and the microwave.

Beep 1.3 (pp. 80–93)

Melanie was having dinner with her boyfriend and had just finished saying the sentence "I remember the shed now." She was aware of her mouth closing as she was finishing speaking. She had a fairly detailed visual image of the shed.

Beep 1.4 (p. 94)

Melanie was watching the MGM logo with the lion frozen in mid-snarl and the words "ARS GRATIA ARTIS" at the very beginning of a video-tape. Her boyfriend was saying to her "Didn't the lion used to *[beep]* roar?" She was hearing and comprehending what he was saying and at the same time paying attention to the green color of the screen.

Beep 2.1 (pp. 95–108)

Melanie was reading a book about World War II in Kefalonia, Greece. The main character was asking a British soldier when the British are coming to liberate the island during World War II. Melanie was not attending to the act of reading; instead, she was seeing an image of that scene, with lots of sunlight on a dirt road, with the green olive trees and shrubs, and a woman—the main character—speaking to a soldier.

Beep 2.2 (pp. 108–122)

Melanie was reading a book about World War II Stuka aircraft. She was seeing an image of a line of military planes against a blue-sky background with a couple of white clouds. The imaged planes looked like F-18s, but were understood to be Stukas. She had definite feeling of sadness/dread like a pressing on her chest.

Beep 2.3 (pp. 122–123)

Melanie was standing in the bathroom and looking around, trying to make up a shopping list. She was seeing an image of a white pad of paper and of her hand writing the word "conditioner" while also saying the word silently to herself. Also at the same time, she was aware that her toes were cold.

Beep 2.4 (pp. 123–130)

Melanie was brushing her teeth, aware of being slightly bent over the sink and aware of the rhythmic motion of her hand. She was also aware of the cold and gooiness of the toothpaste.

Beep 3.1 (p. 131)

Melanie's boyfriend was asking a question about insurance letters. Melanie's focus was not on what he was saying but on trying to remember the word "periodontist." She was thinking "peri-, peri-," to herself, with the sense that this was the beginning of the word she was searching for. She felt she knew the word and was "waiting for the word to come." Although she initially said that she heard "peri-" in her own voice, she later felt unsure whether the word fragment was actually experienced auditorially or whether it was instead "slightly visual."

Beep 3.2 (p. 131)

Melanie was walking to her car. She was dimly aware, at the moment of the beep, *that* she was walking toward the car. She had an indistinct visual experience of the car, its big black shape but not its details. At the center of her experience was a feeling of "fogginess" and worry. She described the feeling of fogginess as involving being unable to think with her accustomed speed and as feeling "out of synch." In addition, Melanie was in the act of *observing* this fogginess. Her worry was felt as being behind the eyes, involving a heaviness around the brow line.

Beep 3.3 (pp. 135–136)

Melanie was in her car, shifting from reverse to drive with the parking brake still on. At the moment of the beep she was feeling exasperated at herself, hearing, in her own voice, the phrase "Why can't I . . ." Melanie had the sense that the sentence, had it not been interrupted, would have concluded with a phrase something like "remember about the parking brake." This episode of inner hearing was distinctly located in her head, moving from the region near her right ear toward the region near her left ear.

Beep 4.1 (pp. 139–165)

Melanie's boyfriend was talking about life-threatening sports. Melanie was thinking about scuba diving, feeling an intense bodily yearning to go diving, like her body was going forward, and she was apparently also cognitively recognizing that yearning. She also experienced her body bobbing up and down as if in waves, though she was not actually moving.

Beep 4.2 (pp. 165–166)

Melanie was reading a book. She had an image of a playing card with a joker on it, dressed in a Harlequin costume with a jester hat and pointy shoes, a jumpsuit with colorful triangles on it, and a big bicycle wheel. Looking back after the beep, Melanie was aware of the emotions of concern and resentment ongoing in her body at that time, but they weren't experienced by her at the moment of the beep.

Beep 5.1 (pp. 167–189)

Melanie was considering the appointments she had later in the morning, particularly the time pressure of getting to her second appointment, which was across town from the first. She had a mental image of sitting in her car and being stopped at a red stop light at a generic intersection. She could see the stoplight and the road stretched out in front of her and her hands on the steering wheel. Melanie was also cognitively aware that she was anxious, but the feeling of anxiety was not in her awareness at the moment of the beep.

Beep 6.1 (pp. 191–200)

Melanie was having dinner with her boyfriend, talking about how they divide up the games in the World Series between the National League and American League fields. Melanie was saying "But that doesn't make any sense because that means that one stadium gets the World Series games five times [*beep*] if you play all seven games." Melanie was experiencing a mental feeling of conviction that what she was saying was correct, which included an awareness of her eyes looking straight ahead.

Beep 6.2 (pp. 200–205)

Melanie was playing a video game and had said to her opponent "You're crowding me" in a joking manner. At the moment of the beep she was feeling happy, experienced as lightness in her lungs. She also experienced a cognitive awareness of the bodily aspects of this feeling.

Beep 6.3 (pp. 205–206)

Melanie was still playing the arcade game, standing in front of the arcade machine with her arms crossed, concentrating on what was on the screen.

She was very aware of the fact that she was concentrating, and in particular she was noticing that her brow was furrowed, that she was chewing on her lower lip, and that she had her arms crossed. She was also aware of the way her feet were placed and the way she was standing. The content of the video screen was only about 20 percent of her awareness.

Beep 6.4 (pp. 206–217)

Melanie was picking flower petals out of the sink. Her experience was divided pretty evenly between the activity of picking up the petals and hearing overlapping "echoes" of the phrase "nice long time" from a recently completed (but no longer ongoing) episode of inner speech.

References

Armstrong, D. M. 1963. Is introspective knowledge incorrigible? *Philosophical Review* 72: 417–432.

Armstrong, D. M. 1980. *The Nature of Mind and Other Essays*. Cornell University Press.

Aronson, E., and Carlsmith, J. M. 1968. Experimentation in social psychology. In *Handbook of Social Psychology*, volume 2, ed. G. Lindzey and E. Aronson. Addison-Wesley.

Asch, S. E. 1951. Effects of group pressures upon the modification and distortion of judgment. In *Groups, Leadership, and Men*, ed. H. Guetzkow. Carnegie Press.

Asch, S. E. 1952. *Social Psychology*. Prentice-Hall.

Asch, S. E. 1955. Opinions and social pressure. *Scientific American*, November: 31–35.

Asch, S. E. 1956. Studies of independence and conformity: A minority of one against a unanimous majority. *Psychological Monographs* 70, no. 9, whole no. 416.

Audi, R. 1993. *The Structure of Justification*. Cambridge University Press.

Ayer, A. J. 1963. *The Concept of a Person*. St. Martin's Press.

Baars, B. J. 2003. How brain reveals mind: Neural studies support the fundamental role of conscious experience. *Journal of Consciousness Studies* 10, no. 9–10: 100–114.

Bacon, F. 1620/2000. *The New Organon*. Cambridge University Press.

Bartlett, F. C. 1932/1995. *Remembering*. Cambridge University Press.

Berkeley, G. 1710/1965. *Principles, Dialogues, and Philosophical Correspondence*. Macmillan.

Block, N. 1981. Introduction: What is the issue? In *Imagery*, ed. N. Block. MIT Press.

Borges, J. L. 1962. *Labyrinths*. New Directions.

Boring, E. G. 1921. The stimulus error. *American Journal of Psychology* 32: 449–471.

Bothwell, R. K., Deffenbacher, K.A., and Brigham, J. C. 1987. Correlation of eyewitness accuracy and confidence: Optimality hypothesis revisited. *Journal of Applied Psychology* 72: 691–695.

Bower, G. H. 1970. Organizational factors in memory. *Cognitive Psychology* 1: 18–46.

Brentano, F. 1911/1973. *Psychology from an Empirical Standpoint*. Routledge.

Brewer, N., and Burke, A. 2002. Effects of testimonial inconsistencies and eyewitness confidence on mock-juror judgments. *Law and Human Behavior* 26: 353–364.

Brunswick, E. 1949. *Systematic and Representative Design of Psychological Experiments*. University of California Press.

Campbell, D. T., and Stanley, J. C. 1963. *Experimental and Quasi-Experimental Designs For Research*. Rand McNally.

Carruthers, P. 1996. *Language, Thought and Consciousness*. Cambridge University Press.

Carruthers, P. 2005. *Consciousness*. Oxford University Press.

Chalmers, D. J. 2003. The content and epistemology of phenomenal belief. In *Consciousness*, ed. Q. Smith and A. Jokic. Oxford University Press.

Chalmers, D. J. 2004. How can we construct a science of consciousness? In *The Cognitive Neurosciences III*, ed. M. Gazzaniga. MIT Press.

Charlton, S. 1999. Do you see what I see? Examining eyewitness testimony. In *Activities Handbook for the Teaching of Psychology*, volume 4, ed. L. Benjamin and B. Nodine. American Psychological Association.

Choi, I., Nisbett, R. E., and Norenzayan, A. 1999. Causal attributions across cultures: Variation and universality. *Psychological Bulletin* 125: 47–63.

Churchland, P. M. 1985. Reduction, qualia, and the direct introspection of brain states. *Journal of Philosophy* 82: 8–28.

Churchland, P. M. 1988. *Matter and Consciousness*, revised edition. MIT Press.

Chwalisz, K., Diener, E., and Gallagher, D. 1988. Autonomic arousal feedback and emotional experience: Evidence from the spinal cord injured. *Journal of Personality and Social Psychology* 54: 820–828.

Comte, A. 1830. *Cours de philosophie positive*. Paris: Bachelier. [We don't recommend the English translation by Martineau. For a translation of the relevant passage, see James 1890/1981, pp. 187–188.]

Cooper, L. A. 1975. Mental rotation of random two-dimensional shapes. *Cognitive Psychology* 7: 20–43.

Damasio, A. R. 1999. *The Feeling of What Happens*. Harcourt Brace.

D'Andrade, R., and Egan, M. 1974. The colors of emotion. *American Ethnologist* 1: 49–63.

Danziger, K. 1980. The history of introspection reconsidered. *Journal of the History of the Behavioral Sciences* 16: 241–262.

Davison, G. C., Robins, C., and Johnson, M. K. 1983. Articulated thoughts during simulated situations: A paradigm for studying cognition in emotion and behavior. *Cognitive Therapy and Research* 7: 17–39.

Dennett, D. C. 1969. *Content and Consciousness*. Humanities Press.

Dennett, D. C. 1991. *Consciousness Explained*. Little, Brown.

Dennett, D. C. 2000. The case for rorts. In *Rorty and His Critics*, ed. R. Brandom. Blackwell.

Dennett, D. C. 2001. The fantasy of first-person science. At http://ase.tufts.edu/cogstud/papers/chalmersdeb3dft.htm (accessed June 2006).

Dennett, D. C. 2002. How could I be wrong? How wrong could I be? *Journal of Consciousness Studies* 9, no. 5–6: 13–16.

Descartes, R. 1641/1984. Meditations on first philosophy. In *The Philosophical Writings of Descartes*. Cambridge University Press.

Devenport, J. L., Penrod, S. D., and Cutler, B. L. 1997. Eyewitness identification evidence: Evaluating commonsense evaluations. *Psychology, Public Policy and Law* 3: 338–361.

Dretske, F. 1995. *Naturalizing the Mind*. MIT Press.

Ericsson, K. A., and Simon, H. A. 1984/1993. *Protocol Analysis: Verbal Reports as Data*. MIT Press.

Ewing, A. C. 1951. *The Fundamental Questions of Philosophy*. Routledge.

Farthing, G. W. 1992. *The Psychology of Consciousness*. Prentice-Hall.

Fechner, G. 1860/1966. *Elements of Psychophysics*. Holt, Rinehart, and Winston.

Flavell, J. H., and Flavell, E. R. 2004. Development of children's intuitions about thought-action relations. *Journal of Cognition and Development* 5: 451–460.

Flavell, J. H., Flavell, E. R., and Green, F. L. 2001. Development of children's understanding of connections between thinking and feeling. *Psychological Science* 12: 430–432.

Flavell, J. H., Green, F. L., and Flavell, E. R. 1993. Children's understanding of the stream of consciousness. *Child Development* 64: 387–398.

Flavell, J. H., Green, F. L., and Flavell, E. R. 1995. Young children's knowledge about thinking. *Monographs of the Society for Research in Child Development* 60, no. 1, serial no. 243.

Flavell, J. H., Green, F. L., and Flavell, E. R. 1998. The mind has a mind of its own: Developing knowledge about mental uncontrollability. *Cognitive Development* 13: 127–138.

Flavell, J. H., Green, F. L., and Flavell, E. R. 2000. Development of children's awareness of their own thoughts. *Journal of Cognition and Development* 1: 97–112.

Flavell, J. H., Green, F. L., Flavell, E. R., and Grossman, J. B. 1997. The development of children's knowledge about inner speech. *Child Development* 68: 39–47.

Fodor, J. A., Bever, T. G., and Garrett, M. F. 1974. *The Psychology of Language.* McGraw-Hill.

Foulkes, D. 1999. *Children's Dreaming and the Development of Consciousness.* Harvard University Press.

Gallagher, S., and Zahavi, D. 2005. Phenomenological approaches to self-consciousness. In Stanford Encyclopedia of Philosophy, spring edition.

Galton, F. 1880. Statistics of mental imagery. *Mind* 5: 301–318.

Galton, F. 1907. *Inquiries into Human Faculty and Its Development.* J. M. Dent.

Gawronski, B., and Bodenhausen, G. V. 2006. Associative and propositional processes in evaluation: An integrative review of implicit and explicit attitude change. *Psychological Bulletin* 132: 692–731.

Gee, N. R., and Dyck, J. L. 2000. Using a videotape clip to demonstrate the fallibility of eyewitness testimony. In *Handbook of Demonstrations and Activities in the Teaching of Psychology*, second edition, volume 2, ed. M. Ware and D. Johnson. Erlbaum.

Goldman, A. I. 1989. Interpretation psychologized. *Mind and Language* 4: 161–185.

Goldman, A. I. 1997. Science, publicity, and consciousness. *Philosophy of Science* 64: 525–545.

Goldman, A. I. 2001. Correspondence. Quoted in D. C. Dennett, The fantasy of first-person science, at http://ase.tufts.edu/cogstud/papers/chalmersdeb3dft.htm (accessed June 2006).

Goldman, A. I. 2006. *Simulating Minds: The Philosophy, Psychology, and Neuroscience of Mindreading.* Oxford University Press.

Gopnik, A. 1993a. How we know our own minds: The illusion of first-person knowledge of intentionality. *Behavioral and Brain Sciences* 16: 1–14.

Gopnik, A. 1993b. Psychopsychology. *Consciousness and Cognition* 2: 264–280.

Gordon, R. M. 1986. Folk psychology as simulation. *Mind and Language* 1: 158–171.

Gordon, R. M. 1992. The simulation theory: Objections and misconceptions. *Mind and Language* 7: 11–34.

Grandin, T. 1995. *Thinking in Pictures.* Doubleday.

Hill, C. S. 1991. *Sensations.* Cambridge University Press.

Hohmann, G. W. 1966. Some effects of spinal cord lesions on experienced emotional feelings. *Psychophysiology* 3: 143–156.

Holmes, E. 1979. *The Life of Mozart: Including His Correspondence.* Da Capo.

Horgan, T., and Tienson, J. 2002. The intentionality of phenomenology and the phenomenology of intentionality. In *Philosophy of Mind*, ed. D. Chalmers. Oxford University Press.

Horgan, T., Tienson, J., and Graham, G. 2003. The phenomenology of first-person agency. In *The Metaphysics of Mind and Action*, ed. S. Walter. Imprint Academic.

Hume, David. 1739/1978. *A Treatise of Human Nature.* Oxford University Press.

Hurlburt, R. T. 1979. Random sampling of cognitions and behavior. *Journal of Research in Personality* 13: 103–111.

Hurlburt, R. T. 1990. *Sampling Normal and Schizophrenic Inner Experience*. Plenum.

Hurlburt, R. T. 1993. *Sampling Inner Experience in Disturbed Affect*. Plenum.

Hurlburt, R. T. 1997. Randomly sampling thinking in the natural environment. *Journal of Consulting and Clinical Psychology* 65: 941–949.

Hurlburt, R. T. 2006. *Comprehending Behavioral Statistics*, fourth edition. Wadsworth.

Hurlburt, R. T., and Akhter, S. A. 2006. The Descriptive Experience Sampling method. *Phenomenology and the Cognitive Sciences* 5: 271–301.

Hurlburt, R. T., and Heavey, C. L. 2001. Telling what we know: Describing inner experience. *Trends in Cognitive Sciences* 5: 400–403.

Hurlburt, R. T., and Heavey, C. L. 2002. Interobserver reliability of Descriptive Experience Sampling. *Cognitive Therapy and Research* 26: 135–142.

Hurlburt, R. T., and Heavey, C. L. 2004. To beep or not to beep: Obtaining accurate reports about awareness. *Journal of Consciousness Studies* 11, no. 7–8: 113–128.

Hurlburt, R. T., and Heavey, C. L. 2006. *Exploring Inner Experience: The Descriptive Experience Sampling Method*. John Benjamins.

Hurlburt, R. T., Happé, F., and Frith, U. 1994. Sampling the form of inner experience in three adults with Asperger syndrome. *Psychological Medicine* 24: 385–395.

Hurlburt, R. T., Koch, M., and Heavey, C. L. 2002. Descriptive Experience Sampling demonstrates the connection of thinking to externally observable behavior. *Cognitive Therapy and Research* 26: 117–134.

Husserl, E. 1960. *Cartesian Meditations*. Martinus Nijhoff.

Intons-Peterson, M. J. 1983. Imagery paradigms: How vulnerable are they to experimenters' expectations? *Journal of Experimental Psychology: Human Perception and Performance* 9: 394–412.

Isen, A. M., and Levin, P. F. 1972. Effect of feeling good on helping: Cookies and kindness. *Journal of Personality and Social Psychology* 21: 384–388.

James, W. 1890/1981. *The Principles of Psychology*. Dover.

Jaynes, J. 1976. *The Origin of Consciousness in the Breakdown of the Bicameral Mind*. Houghton Mifflin.

Johnson, A., Johnson, O., and Baksh, M. 1986. The colors of emotions in Machiguenga. *American Anthropologist* 88: 674–681.

Johnson, M. K., Hashtroudi, S., and Lindsay, D. S. 1993. Source monitoring. *Psychological Bulletin* 114: 3–28.

Kahneman, D. 1999. Objective happiness. In *Well-Being: The Foundations of Hedonic Psychology*, ed. D. Kahneman, E. Diener, and N. Schwarz. Sage.

Kassin, S. M., Tubb, V. A., Hosch, H. M., and Memon, A. 2001. On the "general acceptance" of eyewitness testimony research. *American Psychologist* 56: 405–416.

Klatzky, R. L. 1975. *Human Memory*. Freeman.

Kosslyn, S. M. 1980. *Image and Mind*. Harvard University Press.

Kriegel, U. 2006. The same-order monitoring theory of consciousness. In *Self-Representational Approaches to Consciousness*, ed. U. Kriegel and K. Willford. MIT Press.

Kuhn, T. S. 1962/1970. *The Structure of Scientific Revolutions*, second edition. University of Chicago Press.

Lakatos, I. 1978. *Philosophical Papers*. Cambridge University Press.

Lambie, J. A., and Marcel, A. J. 2002. Consciousness and the variety of emotion experience: A theoretical framework. *Psychological Review* 109: 219–259.

Lamiell, J. T. 1981. Toward an idiothetic psychology of personality. *American Psychologist* 36: 276–289.

Lange, C. G. 1885/1922. *The Emotions*. Hafner.

Larson, R., and Csikszentmihalyi, M. 1983. The Experience Sampling Method. *New Directions for Methodology of Social and Behavioral Science* 15: 41–56.

Leippe, M. R. 1995. The case for expert testimony about eyewitness memory. *Psychology, Public Policy and Law* 1: 909–959.

Leippe, M. R., Manion, A. P., and Romanczyk, A. 1992. Eyewitness persuasion: How and how well do fact finders judge the accuracy of adults' and children's memory reports? *Journal of Personality and Social Psychology* 63: 181–197.

Lewis, C. I. 1946. *An Analysis of Knowledge and Valuation*. Open Court.

Lindsay, D. S. 1994. Memory source monitoring and eyewitness testimony. In *Adult Eyewitness Testimony*, ed. D. Ross, J. Read, and M. Toglia. Cambridge University Press.

Lindsay, R. C. L., Wells, G. L., and O'Connor, F. J. 1989. Mock-juror belief of accurate and inaccurate eyewitnesses: A replication and extension. *Law and Human Behavior* 13: 333–339.

Locke, J. 1690/1975. *An Essay Concerning Human Understanding*. Oxford University Press.

Loftus, E. F. 1979. *Eyewitness Testimony*. Harvard University Press.

Longino, H. E. 1990. *Science as Social Knowledge*. Princeton University Press.

Lycan, W. G. 1996. *Consciousness and Experience*. MIT Press.

McKelvie, S. J. 1995. The VVIQ as a psychometric test of individual differences in visual imagery vividness: A critical quantitative review and plea for direction. *Journal of Mental Imagery* 19: 1–106.

Mill, J. 1829/1967. *Analysis of the Phenomena of the Human Mind*, second edition. Augusts M. Kelley.

Mill, J. S. 1882/1961. *Auguste Comte and Positivism*. University of Michigan Press.

Miller, G. A. 1956. The magical number seven, plus or minus two: Some limits on our capacity for processing information. *Psychological Review* 63: 81–97.

Misiak, H., and Sexton, V. S. 1966. *History of Psychology: An Overview*. Grune and Stratton.

Monson, C. K., and Hurlburt, R. T. 1993. A comment to suspend the introspection controversy: Introspecting subjects did agree about imageless thought. In R. T. Hurlburt, *Sampling Inner Experience in Disturbed Affect*. Plenum.

Münsterberg, H. 1908/1927. *On the Witness Stand*. Clark Boardman.

Nagasako, E. M., Oaklander, A. L., and Dworkin, R. H. 2003. Congenital insensitivity to pain: An update. *Pain* 101: 213–219.

Nagel, T. 1974. What is it like to be a bat? *Philosophical Review* 63: 435–450.

Narby, D. J., Cutler, B. L., and Penrod, S. D. 1996. The effect of witness, target, and situational factors on eyewitness identifications. In *Psychological Issues in Eyewitness Identifications*, ed. S. Sporer, R. Malpass, and G. Koehnken. Erlbaum.

Natsoulas, T. 1988. Is any state of consciousness self-intimating? *Journal of Mind and Behavior* 9: 167–203.

Newcomb, T. M. 1943. *Personality and Social Change*. Dryden.

Nisbett, R. E., and Wilson, T. D. 1977. Telling more than we can know: Verbal reports on mental processes. *Psychological Review* 84: 231–259.

Noë, A. 2004. *Action in Perception*. MIT Press.

Orne, M. T. 1962. On the social psychology of the psychological experiment: With particular reference to demand characteristics and their implications. *American Psychologist* 17: 776–783.

Pearson, R. W., Ross, M. A., and Dawes, R. M. 1992. Personal recall and the limits of retrospective questions in surveys. In *Questions about Questions*, ed. J. Tanur. Russell Sage Foundation.

Pitt, D. 2004. The phenomenology of cognition, or what is it like to think that P? *Philosophy and Phenomenological Research* 69: 1–36.

Popper, K. 1963. *Conjectures and Refutations*. Routledge and Kegan Paul.

Price, H. H. 1941. The foundations of empirical knowledge. *Mind* 50: 280–293.

Prinz, J. J. 2004. *Gut Reactions*. Oxford University Press.

Redelmeier, D. A., and Kahneman, D. 1996. Patients' memories of painful medical treatments: Real-time and retrospective evaluations of two minimally invasive procedures. *Pain* 66: 3–8.

Robinson, W.S. 2005. Thoughts without distinctive non-imagistic phenomenology. *Philosophy and Phenomenological Research* 70: 534–561.

Rorty, R. 1970. Incorrigibility as the mark of the mental. *Journal of Philosophy* 67: 399–424.

Rosemberg, S., Marie, S. K. N., and Kliemann, S. 1994. Congenital insensitivity to pain with anhidrosis (hereditary sensory and autonomy neuropathy type IV). *Pediatric Neurology* 11: 50–56.

Rosenthal, D. 1986. Two concepts of consciousness. *Philosophical Studies* 94: 329–359.

Rosenthal, R. 1976. *Experimenter Effects in Behavioral Research*. Irvington.

Rosenthal, R., and Fode, K. L. 1963. The effect of experimenter bias on the performance of the albino rat. *Behavioral Science* 8: 183–189.

Rosenthal, R., and Jacobson, L. 1968/1992. *Pygmalion in the Classroom*. Irvington.

Ross, L., and Nisbett, R. E. 1991. *The Person and the Situation: Perspectives of Social Psychology*. Temple University Press.

Russell, B. 1945. *The History of Western Philosophy*. Simon and Schuster.

Schacter, D. L., Cooper, L. A., and Delaney, S. M. 1990. Implicit memory for unfamiliar objects depends on access to structural descriptions. *Journal of Experimental Psychology: General* 119: 5–24.

Schwitzgebel, E. 2002a. How well do we know our own conscious experience? The case of visual imagery. *Journal of Consciousness Studies* 9, no. 5–6: 35–53.

Schwitzgebel, E. 2002b. Why did we think we dreamed in black and white? *Studies in History and Philosophy of Science* 33: 649–660.

Schwitzgebel, E. 2003a. Do people still report dreaming in black and white? An attempt to replication a questionnaire from 1942. *Perceptual and Motor Skills* 96: 25–29.

Schwitzgebel, E. 2003b. How trustworthy are imagery reports? *Journal of Mental Imagery* 27: 238–241.

Schwitzgebel, E. 2004. Introspective training apprehensively defended: Reflections on Titchener's lab manual. *Journal of Consciousness Studies* 11, no. 7–8: 58–76.

Schwitzgebel, E. 2005. Difference tone training. *Psyche* 11, no. 6.

Schwitzgebel, E. 2006. Do things look flat? *Philosophy and Phenomenological Research* 72: 589–599.

Schwitzgebel, E. 2007a. Do you have constant tactile experience of your feet in your shoes? Or is experience limited to what's in attention? *Journal of Consciousness Studies* 14, no. 3: 5–35.

Schwitzgebel, E. 2007b. No unchallengeable epistemic authority, of any sort, regarding our own conscious experience—contra Dennett? *Phenomenology and the Cognitive Sciences* 6: 107–113.

Schwitzgebel, E. In preparation. The unreliability of naive introspection.

Schwitzgebel, E., and Gordon, M. S. 2000. How well do we know our own conscious experience? The case of human echolocation. *Philosophical Topics* 28: 235–246.

Schwitzgebel, E., Huang, C., and Zhou, Y. 2006. Do we dream in color? Cultural variations and skepticism. *Dreaming* 16: 36–42.

Searle, J. 1992. *The Rediscovery of the Mind*. MIT Press.

Shepard, R. N., and Metzler, J. 1971. Mental rotation of three-dimensional objects. *Science* 171: 701–703.

Sherif, M. 1937. An experimental approach to the study of attitudes. *Sociometry* 1: 90–98.

Shoemaker, S. 1963. *Self-Knowledge and Self-Identity*. Cornell University Press.

Shoemaker, S. 1994. Self-knowledge and inner sense. *Philosophy and Phenomenological Research* 54: 249–314.

Shun, K. 1997. *Mencius and Early Chinese Thought*. Stanford University Press.

Siewert, C. 1998. *The Significance of Consciousness*. Princeton University Press.

Siewert, C. 2004. Is experience transparent? *Philosophical Studies* 117: 15–41.

Siewert, C. 2006. Is the appearance of shape protean? *Psyche* 12, no. 3.

Siewert, C. 2007. In favor of (plain) phenomenology. *Phenomenology and the Cognitive Sciences* 6: 201–220.

Siewert, C. Forthcoming. Who's afraid of phenomenological disputes? *Southern Journal of Philosophy*.

Skinner, B. F. 1953. *Science and Human Behavior*. Macmillan.

Slee, J. A. 1995. Vividness is in the mind (but not necessarily in the mind's eye) of the cognizer. *Journal of Mental Imagery* 19: 190–193.

Sporer, S. L., Penrod, S., Read, D., and Cutler, B. 1995. Choosing, confidence, and accuracy: A meta-analysis of the confidence-accuracy relation in eyewitness identification studies. *Psychological Bulletin* 118: 315–327.

Stoljar, D. 2004. The argument from diaphanousness. In *New Essays in Philosophy of Language and Mind*, ed. M. Ezcurdia, R. Stainton, and C. Viger. University of Calgary Press.

Stone, A. A., and Shiffman, S. 1994. Ecological Momentary Assessment (EMA) in behavioral medicine. *Annals of Behavioral Medicine* 16: 199–202.

Titchener, E. B. 1899. *An Outline of Psychology*, revised edition. Macmillan.

Titchener, E. B. 1901–1905. *Experimental Psychology: A Manual of Laboratory Practice*. Macmillan.

Titchener, E. B. 1910/1915. *A Text-Book of Psychology*. Macmillan.

Titchener, E. B. 1912. The schema of introspection. *American Journal of Psychology* 23: 485–508.

Tye, M. 2003. Representationalism and the transparency of experience. In *Privileged Access*, ed. B. Gertler. Ashgate.

Van Gulick, R. 2004. Higher-order global states—an alternative higher-order view. In *Higher-Order Theories of Consciousness*, ed. R. Gennaro. John Benjamins.

Varela, F. J., Thompson, E., and Rosch, E. 1991. *The Embodied Mind*. MIT Press.

Vygotsky, L. S. 1962. *Thought and Language*. MIT Press.

Watson, D. 2000. *Mood and Temperament*. Guilford.

Watson, J. B. 1913. Psychology as the behaviorist views it. *Psychological Review* 20: 158–177.

Watson, J. B. 1925. *Behaviorism*. Norton.

Watt, H. J. 1905. Experimentelle Beiträge zu einer Theorie des Denkens. *Archiv für die gesamte Psychologie* 4: 289–436.

Weber, N., and Brewer, N. 2004. Confidence-accuracy calibration in absolute and relative face recognition judgments. *Journal of Experimental Psychology: Applied* 10: 156–172.

Wells, G. L., and Loftus, E. F. 2003. Eyewitness memory for people and events. In *Handbook of Psychology: Forensic Psychology*, volume 11, ed. A. Goldstein. Wiley.

Wells, G. L., and Murray, D. M. 1984. Eyewitness confidence. In *Eyewitness Testimony*, ed. G. Wells and E. Loftus. Cambridge University Press.

Wells, G. L., Lindsay, R. C. L., and Ferguson, T. J. 1979. Accuracy, confidence, and juror perceptions in eyewitness identification. *Journal of Applied Psychology* 64: 440–448.

Wilson, R. A. 2003. Intentionality and phenomenology. *Pacific Philosophical Quarterly* 84: 413–431.

Wilson, R. A. 2004. *Boundaries of the Mind*. Cambridge University Press.

Wilson, T. D. 2002. *Strangers to Ourselves: Discovering the Adaptive Unconscious*. Harvard University Press.

Wong, D. B. 1991. Is there a distinction between reason and emotion in Mencius? *Philosophy East and West* 41: 31–44.

Wundt, W. 1896/1897. *Outlines of Psychology*. Wilhelm Engelmann.

Index